Between Two Rivers:

Stories From the Red Hills to the Gulf

Edited by:
Susan Cerulean,
Janisse Ray,
and Laura Newton

Red Hills Writers Project
A Heart of the Earth Initiative

Published 2004 by Heart of the Earth and the Red Hills Writers Project.
Printed in the United States of America.
Book design by Lou Cross III.
Cover and interior illustrations by Nancy Meyer.
Interior maps by Lou Cross III and Nancy Meyer.
The text of this book is set in Sabon.
This book printed on acid-free, recycled paper.

First Edition

ISBN 0-9759339-1-4
ISBN 0-9759339-0-6 (pbk.)

Red Hills Writers Project is committed to preserving ancient forests and natural resources. We have elected to print this title on 50% postconsumer waste recycled paper. As a result, this book has saved:

34 trees (6-8" in diameter and 40' tall)
1,585 lbs of solid waste
14,375 gallons of water
3,113 lbs of greenhouse gases
5,781 kw hours of electricity

Red Hills Writers Project is a member of Green Press Initiative, a nonprofit program dedicated to supporting publishers in their efforts to reduce their use of fiber obtained from endangered forests. For more information, go to www.greenpressinitiative.org.

A human community . . . if it is to last long, must exert a sort of centripetal force, holding local soil and local memory in place.

—WENDELL BERRY

Between Two Rivers:
Stories from the Red Hills to the Gulf

❦ CONTENTS ❧

Between Two Rivers:

Stories From the Red Hills to the Gulf

Foreward

On behalf of my family, my clan, and my Nation, I am honored to share with you a story that I believe is important to keep alive for the future of all of our children. It is the story I have been taught of the First Nations, the people native to this land, the people whose own history tells a creation story of being from this place from the very first times; the people who say the spirit of this land is Red.

Many native people tell of a creation time when they emerged from the belly of the mother earth at a place they know as the center, the heart of their land, the heart of their people. It is not uncommon to find traditional communities who have oral and written histories that go back many thousand years in relationship with the same land. Such people do not see themselves as apart from the land, but rather as a part of the land, children born of the mother earth, grandchildren of the sun, siblings of the plants, birds, and animals that share the same place. Traditional Native People are taught a worldview that demands respect for the land in the same way that they respect their mothers, fathers, elders, and other kin. So believed the Apalachee people who lived here in the Red Hills long before European invasion, and the Creeks and Seminoles who arrived in the early 1700s.

When the Spanish first arrived here in 1528 looking for gold, they found flourishing Nations living in concentrated urban centers. They encountered a People who truly practiced "sustainable development." They found a People whose political and personal decisions were made with consideration of how their actions would impact the people and the land for seven generations.

When the Spanish marched into this region, they recorded traveling through seven miles of planted fields and orchards cleared for as far as you could see on either side of a wide avenue. Rows of fruit trees were interspersed with companion plantings of corn and beans, squash and grains, enough to feed tens of thousands of residents. The Native People managed the surrounding forests with controlled burning to facilitate the harvest of acorns and nuts and to enhance populations of quail, turkey, deer, and other game. They harvested fish, turtles, alligators, and mussels in abundance from clean surface waters. And they lived in close-knit, large communities with complex social and spiritual organizations, the evidence of which remains today in the ceremonial mound complexes we see at sacred gathering places across this landscape. This land was treated with respect, and so the air and water remained clean for thousands of years of continuous Native habitation. We live, walk, drive over these centers of indigenous secular and sacred learning and politics each day as we go to school and to work.

Current estimates suggest that within fifty years of contact with the Europeans, 95 percent of the indigenous population had been killed, either from introduced diseases or by direct assault. Large urban centers such as Anhaica (present-day Tallahassee) could no longer be maintained. Political and ceremonial centers were abandoned. Survival became the focus of everyday life. Consider what would happen to society today if we lost 95 percent of our spiritual leaders, artists, teachers, doctors, scientists, architects, and historians, and 100 percent of our military leaders, in such a short time span. Think of what would be lost. Such a loss of a balanced, earth-centered social organization and a rich, healthy, orderly way of life occurred here.

I suggest to you that there is much to be learned and gained from a real understanding of what remains of that earth-centered way of life. We cannot turn back the clock, but we can choose to move forward by making political and personal choices that put respect for the earth, clean air, and clean water, as our top priority. If our children's children are to be sustained on this land between the two rivers, then we must take steps to stop the heedless destruction and relearn how to live as a part of the land. We begin by learning the many splendors of this place and by loving it as our own kin, not just as a resource to be exploited. Thank you for listening to my story.

— Susan Anderson
Lamont, Florida

SUSAN ANDERSON *is a longtime social justice and environmental activist and member of a traditional ceremonial community of the Easter Band of the Cherokee.*

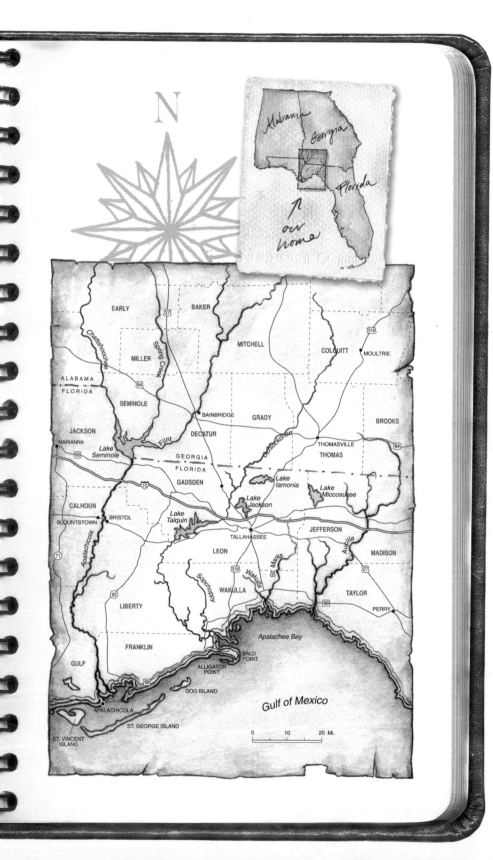

N

Alabama Georgia Florida

↑
our
home

EARLY   BAKER

MILLER   MITCHELL   COLQUITT   MOULTRIE

Chattahoochee

Spring Creek

ALABAMA
FLORIDA

SEMINOLE

BAINBRIDGE   GRADY   BROOKS

JACKSON

MARIANNA   DECATUR   THOMASVILLE

Lake
Seminole   Flint   THOMAS

GEORGIA
FLORIDA

GADSDEN   Lake
                          Iamonia   Lake
                                           Miccosukee

CALHOUN   Lake
                          Jackson

BRISTOL   Lake
BLOUNTSTOWN   Talquin

                 TALLAHASSEE   JEFFERSON

Apalachicola   LEON   MADISON

                          Sopchoppy   St. Marks

                                    Wakulla   Aucilla

LIBERTY   WAKULLA   TAYLOR

                                                      PERRY

FRANKLIN   Apalachee Bay

GULF   BALD
                                  POINT
                 ALLIGATOR
                 POINT

                 DOG ISLAND

APALACHICOLA   Gulf of Mexico

          ST. GEORGE ISLAND

ST. VINCENT
ISLAND

0   10   20 MI.

Introduction

Susan Cerulean, Janisse Ray, and Laura Newton

If you live in and love the Red Hills and Gulf Coast of north Florida and southwest Georgia, this collection of essays is for you. Here we describe the geophysical, biological, and social forces that created this place, with its tall pines, its wild coast, its multitude of springs, and its diverse peoples. Our intention is to bring to light and celebrate some of the defining stories of our region, and raise this question: how can humans live in this place sustainably, in balance with the natural world, for many generations to come?

The Red Hills and Gulf Coastal Lowlands bioregions exist apart from any government's boundaries; they are etched deep into the land. The winding watersheds of the Aucilla River to the east and Ochlockonee to the west embrace both bioregions; the headwaters of the two rivers originate in Georgia, near the small town of Boston. In this anthology, we have widened our scope west to the Apalachicola watershed so that we might include important stories.

The north-south boundary between the two bioregions is the Cody Scarp, an ancient shoreline where the land drops from 215 feet above sea level to less than one hundred feet. You can drive along portions of the Cody Scarp and

3

get a feel for its elevation by traveling Tram Road west of Tallahassee's capitol complex.

South of the scarp, the Gulf Coastal Lowlands gently descend toward the coast in sandy hills clothed with longleaf pines, turkey oaks, and wiregrass. Gum swamps, cypress-rimmed lakes, and seasonal ponds dot the pine flatwood forest. Much of the land is very porous; lime rock juts at or near the land surface, and there are many conduits to underground water aquifers including sinkholes, springs, and caverns. The southernmost boundary of the bioregion is the nearly pristine seagrass beds and salt marshes of Apalachee Bay.

To the north, the Red Hills reach into Georgia, including the plantation lands between Thomasville and Tallahassee, a significant portion of the native longleaf pine forests remaining in the United States, and lakes Iamonia, Jackson, and Miccosukee.

The unity of these two diverse bioregions is in the movement of their shared water. Every fragment of moisture that the sky hurls down on this landscape wends its way through one of many dozens of area creeks and rivers, or the great underlying lime rock aquifer, to the coast. Our bioregions rest atop one of the highest recharge areas of the Floridan aquifer, the underground drinking water supply for millions of Florida and Georgia residents.

If you choose to read *Between Two Rivers* from beginning to end, you will travel with us north from Apalachee Bay through the forests and springs of the Gulf Coastal Lowlands and then into the Red Hills as far north as Moultrie, Georgia. Interspersed among the longer essays are brief journal entries written by Susan Cerulean that move through the seasons of our calendar year. These snapshots are intended to stimulate each reader's own recollections of how weather and climate uniquely shape experience of this place.

Even if we treasure our homeland just as it is, monumental change is headed our way; some has already arrived. The same forces that have run roughshod over much of south Florida—large developments and unplanned sprawl—have set their sights on our clear rivers and mild hills. The true face of our landscape is slipping through memory, redesigned and renamed by corporate interests, and blurring into predictable strip malls and chain establishments. Between 1990 and 2000, Wakulla was among five Florida counties that rocketed in population by more than 60 percent. Southwest Georgia's growth rate was slower, but also steadily upward—12.1 percent. These rates of growth are projected to continue, even increase, and it's safe to say that nowhere in our area are we prepared with the infrastructure, vision, and protective policies to handle what's coming our way.

We're a highly mobile society: perhaps that's one of the reasons we have such a hard time protecting our places. We don't really understand the ecological constraints of the landscape, especially in Florida, where so many of us are transplants. For these reasons, we at Heart of the Earth, the sponsoring organization of the Red Hills Writers Project, have developed a pledge that everyone is invited to take: "I vow to investigate what it means to become native to this place, and to do so in accordance with the ecological realities of the landscape." We wish to begin together a practice of permanence, even knowing full well that none of us now living today are native to the area in the way of the Apalachee and Creek Indians and their predecessors, who thrived in this productive province between the two rivers for more than fourteen thousand years. We know that with our consumptive lifestyles we are living out the mentality of the European empires whose incursions into this region led to the nearly complete demise of the native peoples. But we wish to live differently, understanding that our own survival and the continuance of the lives of the wild creatures and places we love surely depends upon our learning to "reinhabit" our homes.

Our region will prosper only to the extent that it remains a good place to live, and we will only survive as a species if we can craft a framework of governance and social values that conform the economy to the limits of nature. We can create a sustainable economy here if we put our minds to it, by training our cash economy to respect its biological origins.

In these fast-paced times, many of us long for a slower world, one that moves at the pace of something growing—a live oak tree, perhaps. We long for community and connection, and we want stories that help us better understand where we live, what has happened here, and how we ourselves might fit in. Since the beginning, stories are how humans have specified our connections to our history, our place, and to each other. We offer our chorus of voices, hoping that it will help all of us who live here name and take care of the territory that is our home.

Bald
Point

In the Presence of Grace on Bald Point

DONNA DECKER

I'm walking on Bald Point with my bull terrier, Lilly Belle, just us on the long curved beach. Closer to the road, hammers pound and the shrill whine of a drill cuts through the early January afternoon. The sand is shadowed with midday beige tones. In a few hours, it will glow in shades of orange. Gulls glide over unseasonably warm ocean currents. Just last week, I escaped the landlocked snowy terrain of central Wisconsin. I am happy to be here.

I stare out into the Gulf, hungry for the sight of all that water; an occasional pelican dips for a fish. As I scan the waves, picking out the fishing birds, a large dark shape emerges, and floats, about a half-mile down the beach from where I stand. I want it to be the thrill of a dolphin or sea turtle and wonder if I am divining outlines that are not there. It could be a buoy or a fisher's large crab trap. To my eyes, it is moving.

Lilly Belle and I continue west along the shore. As we get closer, the Gulf lapping alongside us, I discern that the dark contour definitely moves. I can't make the lines connect and keep on walking in its direction, conscious of my dog running off to the side toward the sparse pines and low dunes.

Now I am close enough to know by its fluid movement that it is alive. My mind tries to make sense of the bulk. Could it be a monstrously huge Hounds-of-Baskerville mongrel of a dog? A horse that fell off a strange boat, like the shipwrecked Spanish ponies that made it to shore a couple of centuries ago? It's too tall and wide for a gator, which will, at times, swim in the Gulf from marshes or rivers on its way to fresh or brackish water. Maybe it's a beached whale, although I've never heard of them swimming into Apalachee Bay.

The construction sounds stop. Lilly Belle has come back to nose along the shore. The rhythm of the low-tide waves and the caw of the gulls accompany us as we walk toward the mystery. About an eighth of a mile away, I see it and pull Lilly Belle close to my side. I can't believe it. It is a black bear, wading slowly, laboriously, on two legs through shallow water toward land.

The construction workers, who have been building the colossal house that has been dubbed "The Fortress," move as a group to the beach. A half-dozen of them, sweaty in shorts, t-shirts, work boots, and bandanas, converge with us next to a low dune. We all stare quietly at the bear about thirty yards out in the water.

It's the first time I've seen a bear in the wild, one says. The rest of us nod, murmuring *yes, me too.*

A man in his thirties, barefoot, his pants rolled, joins us. He had been checking his new lot when he saw the bear. A woman who lives next to the beach, observing it closely for years, and her neighbor's twelve-year-old son also reach the group. She says she's been watching the bear swimming and fishing through the morning. She tells me I'd better hold tight to my dog. Lilly Belle is at my legs, twisting her body from side to side, her mouth wide open, panting, excited by the number of possible petting hands. I wrap her leash around my hand.

The woman and the boy have been looking for the bear's paw prints in the dune to see from which direction it came. They try to educate me on the print pattern, but I'm not getting it, and keep finding large dog tracks instead. *Looks like it came down here!* the boy shouts, showing us strange marks in the sand. The prints are distinct, rounder and stouter than a dog's, the imprints of the nails long, narrow, and curved; evidence that this *Ursa minor* did not emerge from the sky or the waves. The woman tells us that over the years here, she has seen a few black bears, and that they sometimes swim from Bald Point to Alligator Point, a distance of at least eight miles.

The boy has a camera, but the animal is too far out to get a clear photograph without a zoom. It doesn't matter. We all drink in the bear's image with our eyes.

DONNA DECKER

How long has it been trying to make it in? I ask. One of the workers says, *for a time now,* and we wonder if it may be in trouble. However, as we watch it get closer, its clumsy movements become quicker and its slow-motion progress becomes more fluid.

I clutch Lilly Belle as, suddenly, the large lumbering bear reaches the shoreline. As soon as it frees the water it becomes a different animal, drops fast on all fours and races for the dunes. Before I take another breath, it's over the hill of sand and gone in the spill of pines.

We stand under the bright winter sun as the last impression of the wild black bear disappears. Then slowly we begin to rustle, talking in small sounds, snatching quick looks into others' eyes.

Nodding, the construction workers start to leave, back up the beach to the Fortress. The boy promises to send photographs of the bear prints. Reluctant to go, I talk to the barefoot man about the gator that lived in the marsh near his lot, Lilly Belle dancing around my legs. Finally, when the sun is far to the west, I gather my dog and we return to the small, almost hidden parking lot. I brush the ubiquitous sand from her coat, stomp it from my shoes, and then drive home past the workers. They hoot and wave from their perches on scaffolds; I holler from the car window, beeping my horn.

Since that day, I've followed stingrays and been followed by dolphins at the shoreline; I've rescued and released gulls, pelicans, and a red-shouldered hawk. I've seen a sleek black otter on Alligator Point, moved gopher tortoises from one side of Alligator Drive to the other, and one morning watched as a juvenile gator pulled itself across the road. I've held my breath as a red fox drew close to my porch, watched white squirrels on my patio, found deer prints near the little earthen pool in the back. I've heard at Bald Point there are panthers, coyotes, and rattlesnakes, one diamondback that reaches eight feet across. I know there once were twelve thousand black bear in Florida and now there are about two thousand, their numbers decreasing largely due to real estate development and lack of contiguous open land; I know how small isolated black bear populations need a minimum of five hundred thousand acres for their long-term existence and how the Florida Fish and Wildlife Conservation Commission says: *Seeing a wild bear is a rare sight that eludes most Floridians. When bears are seen in the wild, it's usually from the back end as they run away.* And I know that large-scale residential and commercial development is pushing its way closer to this peninsula. Yet, I am still wide-eyed with possibility as I walk the blessed, often-deserted beaches of Bald Point, hoping for another Florida black bear to make its way through the waves, as a straggly group of humans watches in spontaneous community.

DONNA DECKER *is a child of islands, having grown up on the Kill van Kull River in Chelsea, Staten Island, when Staten Island was indeed as Emerson has called it,* God's Little Heaven. *She is a Professor of English at the University of Wisconsin–Stevens Point in the fall; in the spring and summer, she reads, writes, renovates housing complexes; communes with family, friends, and animals; and walks the Southeast equivalent of another of God's small heavens—the beaches of Alligator and Bald Points—with Lilly Belle.*

DONNA DECKER

IN THE PRESENCE OF GRACE ON BALD POINT

Sopchoppy River

The upper Sopchoppy runs high and fast,
searching a quick, no-nonsense path through the
forest. We're riding the flood, cruising at the lip of
a levee that usually separates woods and creek.
From this unusual vantage, we can see runoff
cutting wide swaths across the wet flatwoods,
sheeting into the Sopchoppy.

The sun is warm and the wind fingers high
in the pines but all our attention is on our
downstream path. There's often more than one
choice: we have to make split-second decisions,
sometimes wrong, always brushy. The thorned
leaves of hollies slap and scratch at our faces.
Time and again we duck low and hold our
paddles parallel with the river's course, else
they will act as levers, slamming us hard and
unexpectedly against the trees. Long branches
are held beneath the surface by the flood; they
beat their imprisonment against still-standing
trunks, eerily tapping like enormous underwater
woodpeckers.

Halfway down the river, the swampy flatwoods pull back and allow the river's rightful banks to swell above the race, a more familiar Sopchoppy. Emerald moss lacquers the banks here, coating their sandy swells with skin-tight green leotards. Sparkleberry blooms, and fragrant titi. The water is still so deep we see none of the fantastically contorted knees we know nudge against the remnant mother cypress trees in this section of the river.

All afternoon, we hear dogs bay on the high wind, and gunshots. It's still general gun season: the hunters own the uplands, but we feel safe on the river. When we finally drive out of the forest, its edges are studded with men in camouflage, warming by impromptu fires, waiting for the dog-driven deer.

Sopchoppy River

Doug Alderson

Juvenile Kemp's ridley

isset

cerulean
blue

cream

bright
melon
orange

Blue
Crab

Catching the Shrimp, Calling the Turtle

ANNE RUDLOE, PhD

As I paddled a kayak out from the shore at St. Joseph Bay on a warm summer morning, a bald eagle hung like a pinpoint in the blue forever overhead. As always with eagles, it was so high that I had to look hard to be sure it really was an eagle and not an osprey. Anchoring the kayak, I pulled a diving mask over my face and rolled into the water. Sunlight swept over the underwater meadow in waves, a mesh of golden fire created by surface ripples and wind, a few feet above. Four species of flowering grasses grew together there, creating food and shelter for hundreds of species of fish and invertebrates. Scallops, blue crabs, pink shrimp, clams, mullet, trout, and redfish are the best known, but they are only a small part of the fauna. Red sponges and red sea anemones accentuated the green and white seascape. Red starfish with white polka dots wrapped their arms around the bases of the plants like children hugging their mothers. Blue-eyed hermit crabs scrambled over the swaying green blades of grass like squirrels in trees, hanging on as passing waves rocked them back and forth. Inside empty shells, dwarf octopuses hid, waiting for darkness to hunt the hermits.

At the edge of the white sand bars that lay scattered throughout the grass bed, endless schools of transparent mysid shrimp, each no longer than a baby's fingernail, hovered. There must have been literally billions in the bay. Each shrimp faced into the current, darting back and forth to seize even smaller creatures that swept past, crustaceans too small for a human eye to see. The shrimp intermingled freely with huge schools of equally transparent, equally small baby fish.

I swam back to my anchored kayak, reached into the boat and grabbed a net designed to collect the smallest things visible to one's eye. Catching uncountable numbers in a few minutes, I poured them into a tray of water for a closer look. Most of the mysid shrimp turned out to be one species, and, miraculously enough, it was *Mysidopsis bahia*, the species I needed. This mysid species was used in water quality monitoring research and I was trying to set up a mysid farm at our aquarium to grow them in an aquaculture facility for other scientists. The right species was easy to recognize because these animals have a black Y-shaped mark between their eyes. Mixed in with the *bahias* were a few other mysid species. Some had huge black eyes and looked like tiny raccoons. Others had elongated, needle-shaped bodies. What did these rarer mysids do differently from their explosively abundant cousins?

Five or six other species of tiny shrimp were mixed into the catch as well. One was bright green with lemon-yellow eyes, while another species could change colors from green to brown to match its substrate. That one stayed on the grass, its needle thin body aligned with the blades, along with tiny baby seahorses and pipefish that lurked in the jungle, ambushing the shrimp where grass bed met open sand.

I picked out the shrimp I didn't need and let them go. The rest went into an ice chest full of seawater to take back to the lab for breeding stock. I climbed back into the kayak and headed back toward shore as a powerboat sped past. It could get to more distant places, places I couldn't reach in one afternoon with my slow pace and limited time. But the people in the powerboat missed the nuances: the way the wind was gusting and dying and gusting, the blazing sun in each drop of water as it blew off the paddle blades. Now two eagles soared overhead. They banked and turned, soaring higher and higher, white heads and tails flashing and disappearing and flashing again. After a few minutes the sky absorbed them and they were gone.

The next day I was on the water again, this time on a little turtle fishing boat as it raced past the green marsh into the Gulf of Mexico near Panacea. In the bright morning everything seemed created anew in this instant, like the very first morning of the world, still sparkling fresh from Creation. The newly risen sun turned the calm sea to glittering gold; snowy cumulus clouds floated

ANN RUDLOE, PHD

16

over our tiny heads, and there was glory to just being alive in such a blue and golden morning.

On this day, we were fishing for Kemp's ridley sea turtles. Unlike the previous day's almost incomprehensible abundance of tiny mysid shrimp, Kemp's ridleys are the rarest and most endangered of the seven species of sea turtles. Their only nesting beach in Mexico hosted some forty thousand nests a year in the late 1940s, but due to years of egg harvest and drowning of adults in fishing nets, the numbers have now plummeted to only a few thousand.

Kemp's ridleys range around the Gulf and Atlantic coasts, feasting on the abundance of blue crabs that live in the marshes, bays, and sea grass meadows. How the turtles get to these coasts from their hatching beach is one mystery, and how they return to breed after they mature is another. If we caught one of these small sea turtles, it would be tagged and released. If, one day, we captured a turtle with a tag in its flipper, it would tell us something about where these young turtles go, how fast they grow, how long they stay around, where they travel. This slow, hard work would provide a few more details of how this endangered species uses its world—details that might help conservationists preserve it from extinction.

This day's fishing site was next to a huge oyster bar off Piney Island, several miles down the coast. When we got there, the falling tide was racing around the end of the bar, and in the calm lee, small menhaden swirled in huge schools. They looked like moving patches of raindrops hitting the water, and as a school approached, we listened to the pattering sound of them breaking the surface. Hundreds of gulls, cormorants, terns, and pelicans wheeled and screamed, feeding on the concentrated fish. Other birds, already full, rested on the oyster bar, motionless in the morning sun. In deeper water a little farther offshore, jacks and sharks leaped in their own dance of life and death. As we set out three hundred yards of net, a porpoise played alongside, watching our every move. It looked as if we might be the best thing that had happened for the porpoise all morning.

Waves slapped the bow of our boat as we pulled it along the top of the turtle net. Fishing for turtles takes a lot of patience. On many other days of fishing for this project, we caught nothing at all. On this day, we sat with the net for twelve hours, checking it every thirty minutes to ensure that if a turtle got caught, it wouldn't drown before we reached it. Most of the time we sat and watched the sea or read. We didn't talk much. No conversation could go on for that many hours, so after a while we quit trying and just relaxed. I did a lot of meditation.

The frantic swarming of menhaden and birds lasted for about an hour until the falling tide forced the fish schools to move farther offshore and the birds scattered. The sun rose higher in the sky, and the sea and marsh were silent under the weight of the heat and the glare. Not only was there nothing happening, but it was inconceivable that there ever was or could have been.

The tide fell, until by noon the sea grass began to be exposed on the tide flats. Then the place came to life again, this time with mullet. The mirror surface of the grass-streaked shallows broke into splashes and ripples everywhere as mullet rolled and fed. Ten or twelve ospreys hovered and circled overhead. They dropped from the sky like arrows, sometimes seizing a mullet, sometimes pulling out of the dive at the last second.

When it was time to check the net, we pulled our skiff along the corkline by hand, lifting it up, looking for the flash of white in the murky water that meant a ray, a shark, or a turtle. The mesh was so big that anything smaller passed through, and if a shark or a ray got caught, we released it. Most of the time the net was empty, and I realized in an experiential way I never had before that this once common sea turtle really was close to extinction. The empty net was far more real than all the statistics in all the scientific studies.

As I sat there watching the water beside the net, I thought a lot about the disappearance of so many of earth's other species. Preventing extinction is one of the primary issues in ecology today. This green and blue planet, shining in the sunshine, is the only one we know is alive. Life is divided up into millions of different species, so many that after centuries of work we still don't have an accurate count. It has been ruthlessly pruned back in repeated mass extinctions in the past—the most severe, approximately 230 million years ago, is estimated to have resulted in the loss of 75 to 95 percent of all species on earth. Eventually, after millions of years, the survivors rediversify and new species fill the vacancies.

Today we find ourselves in the midst of another mass extinction. Songbirds are disappearing, due mostly to forest destruction both here and in the tropics. Frogs and salamanders are dying all over the world from disease and perhaps from increased ultraviolet light and the ozone hole. One-third of North America's freshwater fish species are biologically endangered or threatened, mostly owing to habitat destruction. While the causes of earlier

ANN RUDLOE, PhD

mass extinctions are the source of heated scientific debate, there's no doubt about what's causing this one—us.

Well, so what? Do we really need every last frog and bird that came with the bargain? What good are they anyway? Besides, we don't need to worry about it—the planet will take care of itself. It's just another mass extinction. While it's true that millions of years after we're gone, the planet will heal itself, that's not what the argument is about. The issue is really about us: what kind of world we want for ourselves and our grandchildren and their grandchildren. Will we leave them their full heritage of the living beauty of this planet?

Even if we assume that these myriads of other species must be judged only by their usefulness or lack of it to humans, do we know enough to decide what's worth keeping? The total number of species may be some 3 million. But some recent estimates put it closer to 30 million. Three or thirty? If we don't even know that, how can we possibly pretend to understand how the planet works, which species are essential and which aren't. Despite the efforts of some of humanity's best thinkers, we don't have a clue.

Tagging turtles, growing mysid shrimp—these are only a few of the many nuts and bolts efforts being made by people all over the world to preserve what's left. The work with the mysid shrimp might contribute to a less polluted ocean, one in which sea grasses, scallops, mysids, and sea turtles could someday thrive again everywhere as they did here in these north Florida coastal waters. And this work might also contribute to a world in which humans would again remember their interdependence with other species.

Stone Age hunters, when they stalked game, had a wealth of knowledge of the animals' habits, behavior, and movement patterns, knowledge that they used to track the game effectively. But they did more. A hunt was often preceded by a period of meditation and purification, and in the hunt they tried to let go of thinking, to merge themselves with the world, to let the animal know their need. Then the animal would come and compassionately allow it to be taken so that the people might continue to live. The hunter and the hunted were bound together in mutual relationship and respect that most people today have forgotten.

It was time to pull the net for the tenth time of the day. We had chosen the most likely tide and the spot that we knew from previous fishing was in the best turtle habitat. We had built a net that would fish efficiently, had talked to other fishermen about where they'd spotted turtles. But when the rational, analytical mind had done everything it could to ensure catching a turtle, when the long silent waiting began, we found ourselves settling into the ancient still meditation, asking the turtle to come and allow itself to be caught. And when it did, we gave thanks for the gift of the turtle, tagged it, and sent it on its way with respect.

ANNE RUDLOE, PHD, *lives in Panacea, Florida. She and her husband run the Gulf Specimen Marine Laboratory, an independent nonprofit environmental center and aquarium. She received her PhD from Florida State University, where she has taught courses on marine biology and environmental issues. Her writing has appeared in* National Geographic, Smithsonian, *and numerous scientific journals. She is the author of* Butterflies on a Sea Wind: Beginning Zen.

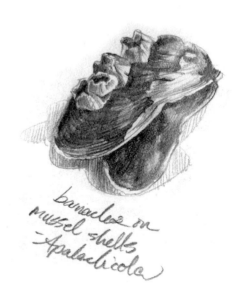

barnacles on
mussel shells,
—Apalachicola

CATCHING THE SHRIMP, CALLING THE TURTLE

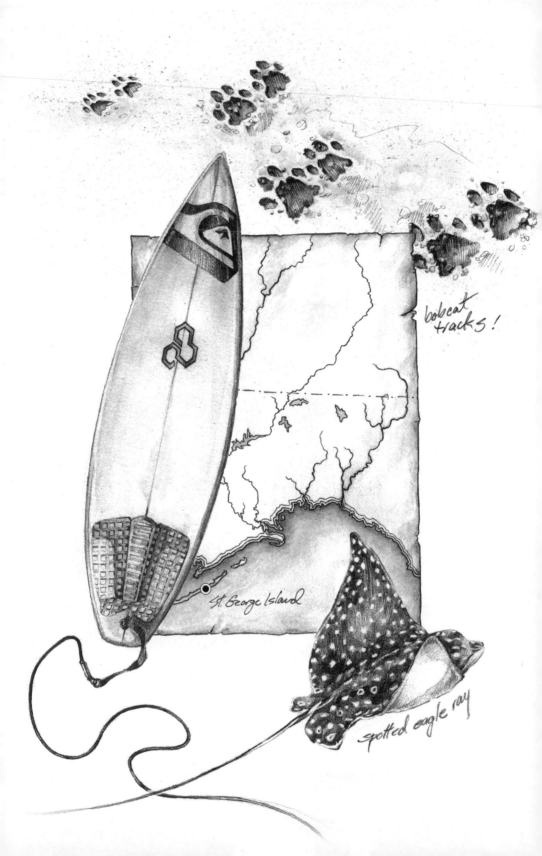

bobcat tracks!

St. George Island

spotted eagle ray

What I Teach Ariel:
Perspectives on Beaches

MICHAEL TRAMMELL

My daughter is sturdy, all muscle. She dances, rides horses, and skis on Colorado slopes. She can balance on a thimble. Wouldn't surfing be the next logical step for her?

So I wanted to think.

We floated in the sea off St. George Island, Florida, near the public beach at the end of Florida Route 300, my ten-year-old on one of my longboard surfboards. I did a slow, treading-water backstroke. We waited out a lull, hoping for another ridable wind swell to lump its way to shore.

"Can we go in now, Daddy?" she asked.

"No, not yet. You have to catch a wave first," I said. I was determined to make her share my love of surfing. "When you catch one, you'll want to keep riding them. One after another. It's like eating chocolate."

She sighed.

I stood up on the sand bar and stared into the Gulf of Mexico. The sting of salt burned my eyes and lips and tongue, but it was a burning that was familiar, comforting, a reminder of endless days surfing on Florida's east coast, from Boca Raton to Jensen Beach.

The dorsal fin of a bottle-nosed dolphin broke the surface fifteen yards from where we waited. The fin had a distinct one-inch notch right at the tip, as if it had been clipped by a boat propeller. The dolphin's skin looked as smooth as the surfboard's fiberglass.

"Ariel, look!" I said, pointing. The creature surfaced again, its entire head rolling out of the water, its eye blinking at us, giving us a curious glance.

"Cool!" she said and laughed. "We're surfing with Flipper."

Several shell seekers wandered out of a row of tall, narrow town houses nearby, pointed out to sea where we waited. These townhouses were a disappointment to me, but at least they weren't the towering condos I'd grown up with in south Florida. The dolphin cracked the surface again.

The last time we'd seen dolphins we'd been on the other side of a human-made "inlet" of sorts called Bob Sike's Cut, wading along Little St. George, an uninhabited chunk of land a stone's throw away from the larger St. George Island.

We'd crossed the cut on my twelve-foot longboard to explore, both of us paddling on the lengthy plank, our arms spinning in simultaneous motion as if we rode an ocean-going version of a bicycle built for two. Little St. George offered miles of trees pushed up against the border of the dunes, a sharp contrast from the houses springing up like toadstools on the bigger island. The coastline of Little St. George was completely deserted.

Ariel waded in the water and asked why no one built houses here. Before I answered, a large party of dolphins broke the surface, two strutting out of the water and tail dancing just to our right. We stood, the sea up to my waist and up to Ariel's neck, completely transfixed, in awe. The water sprayed up from the surface in chaotic arcs.

At the public beach at the end of Florida Route 300, I continued to teach Ariel to ride the longboard; the dolphin with the notch in its dorsal fin seemed content to stick around, curiously watching our next step. I kept glancing at the flag flapping above Finni's Bar and Grill. The breeze remained brisk. The wind swell wouldn't die out yet. I so wanted Ariel to ride her first wave.

A set approached, a rising lump of water that stood above the surface like a green wall. I slid across the sand bar, the waist-deep water dragging at my legs, grabbed the edge of the board, and whipped it around so that it and Ariel pointed toward shore.

"Hang on!" I shouted. "I'm going to give you a push just as the wave comes. Then you get ready to stand up." I was intense, all adrenaline.

"I'm scared, Daddy," she said.

Was I being too aggressive? Pushing her too hard? Trying to give her too much of a shove into a rough, topsy-turvy, male-dominated sport?

The lip of the wave was just behind us now. I had to make a decision.

"Hold on tight!" I yelled. I shoved the board forward. The wave carried her.

I stood on my toes on the sand bar, leaning forward, trying to keep her in sight.

She scooted up on her knees, her weight edging forward toward the nose of her board.

All in a heartbeat it went wrong: her hand slipped, she leaned one way, overcompensated with her hips and fell the other, hit the sea face-first with a splat.

I slapped the water with the palm of my hand.

"Damn!" I shouted. She'd almost had it that time.

She'd also been so close to standing and riding when we'd been goofing around on Little St. George a few months earlier. But that time, like this one, she quickly became bored and frustrated. She kept wanting to paddle back across Sike's Cut and return to the beach house her grandfather was renting.

Sike's Cut was dug around the middle of the last century and divided St. George Island into two separate spits of land. The big island has quickly been developed, reminding me very much of the Palm Beach, Martin, and St. Lucie county coastlines that I'd witnessed changing from beautiful quiet beaches into a megalopolis of never-ending development as I grew up in Boca Raton. Most of the large and beautiful dunes that William Lee Popham wrote about in his little booklet of poetry and prose advertising St. George near the turn of the century (circa 1918), "the natural sea wall from 18–30 feet high," have been leveled and developed. But on Little St. George, some signs of these "natural sea walls" remain. These small towers of bright-white sand protect the pines and vegetation that grow just beyond the dunes.

Later that day on Little St. George, we left the surfboard on the sand and trekked up the beach, away from Sike's Cut, and studied the dune line. Ariel asked if we could scale one of those "white hills," as she called them, so we headed up and found ourselves on a dune plateau. Ariel and I shuffled across the surface, our bare feet kicking up small clouds of the fine sand. I stopped and scanned the sea, saw the dorsal fins of five dolphins split the surface. Ariel called me over to where she stood and pointed at the ground. Animal tracks cut across the sand. One set, clearly a raccoon's, the other, the soft pads of a bobcat.

"I told you we were being watched," Ariel said. She'd been repeating that litany the entire time I'd tried to teach her to surf.

I pointed to the Gulf of Mexico.

"Look! Now we can watch the dolphins, but they can't watch us." The backs of the five dolphins suddenly sprang from the water.

Ariel laughed. She explored the dune plateau; I scanned the sea, studied the other dunes that lined the coastline like a range of small hills. I imagined this range as any number of landscapes: snow-covered hills; the veritable surface of the moon; a forest-bordered pale desert; an ivory ocean of frozen storm-churned groundswells.

The intermittent chirp of cicadas broke my concentration. The sun slid out from behind a cloud. The light was blinding. In the intense sunshine, the dune surfaces glowed bright white; our skins seemed translucent in the brightness. I imagined Ariel and me stretched together as one pale human canvas, both canvas and brush as we painted the dunes with our footprints. Our shadows were the brief sculptures of the sun. Ariel accidentally broke the long leaf of a palmetto frond growing near a dune and called me over. We both breathed in the earthy, green smell. Smiled.

Slowly paddling the surfboard back across Sike's Cut later that day, I told Ariel about secret surf spots that my friends and I had found as teens in Martin County. These spots were accessed by a crisscross of sugar-sand roads that tunneled under twisted scrub oaks. We'd had as much fun beneath the trees eating our peanut butter sandwiches and drinking warm bottles of tap water as we'd had surfing the quiet and glassy East Coast swells.

The dolphin with the notched dorsal fin popped above the surface again. The waves stayed stuck in a lull. We both watched the flag snapping above Finni's Bar and Grill.

"Is the wind dying, Daddy? Are the waves dying too?"

"No, we just have to be patient. Another good wave will come. You just wait and see."

MICHAEL TRAMMELL

Ariel turned her head back to the horizon, placed her hand over her eyes to scan the view and keep out the glare, and watched the Gulf for white caps.

The dolphin peeked its bottle nose out of the water about ten feet from us, and we both laughed. It eased the tension, the frustration I felt because she wasn't learning faster, and the guilt she felt because she sensed my disappointment.

How disappointed was I twenty-five years ago when my brother and I drove up to one of our secret spots near Jensen Beach and found the groundwork for condos instead? "KEEP OUT" signs had been plastered everywhere, ropes blocking the dirt roads to our private waves. My brother, three years younger than I, stepped out of the car onto a ground of gravel and sandspurs and spit through his teeth a low, venomous curse. I crawled up on the hood of my Toyota, careful to avoid the surfboards jutting from the roof, to survey the damage. Carcasses of scrub oaks lay twisted and mangled in the dirty sand, piled together in makeshift heaps. A dead armadillo, its body pierced by a metal rod, rotted on top of a pile of cinder blocks. Decapitated Spanish bayonet plants poked their browning spears into the ground. We were in shock. I stupidly had thrown a rock into a vacant bulldozer's windshield, wanting to release my bitterness into the spider web of shatter marks.

I'm glad my daughter has yet to see a beach construction scene anything like the one I witnessed at Jensen Beach. On this day she blissfully soaks in the sun as she lies on the board, waiting out the lull. We decide to take a break, pull the board to shore and stroll by the waterside. The waves seem to waste away, putter into the beach half-heartedly. We walk the shoreline for a few hundred yards. I let my toes scrape the sand; Ariel chases translucent crabs from the edge of water into tiny, deep holes. We watch a spotted stingray glide through the shallows near shore.

A bank of clouds spins on the horizon, a squall line, with a cumulonimbus as black as smoke. I describe to Ariel a day when a storm might hit, and we'd have real waves to surf, waves as tall as dunes crashing onto the white beach, stirring up the gray clouds of offshore sand. At high tide, white water would rip at the sea oats. The stingrays and crabs would disappear into the shallows. Fishermen's nets might wash up on the shore, like old chain link fences, ripped and carried for miles by hurricane winds and tides.

Developers had stretched a chain link fence across our 40th Street surf spot in Boca Raton when I was a teenager. They'd decided to run a metal barrier from Highway A1A through the coastal dune plants, across the beach, and down into the low-tide line of the Atlantic Ocean. This four-foot-high fence especially scarred the flora of the dunescape. The fence builders had knocked over a sea grape tree, uprooted several Spanish bayonets, ripped up a bay cedar, and completely destroyed and buried beautiful patches of beach creeper, necklace pod, cocoplum, salt grass, spider lily, and sea oats.

The locals who surfed 40th Street did not approve of the change. We especially thought it ridiculous that the fence dragged all the way into the water at high tide. Did the developers actually think they owned the ocean?

Two weeks after they erected the fence, ten of us—my brother and I were part of the crew—went down to 40th Street after midnight armed with shovels and heavy-duty wire cutters and ripped down the fence in a matter of hours and pulled the scraps deep into the sea.

A month later another fence went up, and three weeks after that we arrived in even greater numbers, again in cover of morning darkness, to tear down the metal barrier. We were determined to keep a foothold on our tract of ocean, beach, dune.

The developers gave up and never built another fence at 40th Street. The coastal landscape healed itself, and all the green and flowering dune plants returned.

"Should we do that here at St. George, Daddy?" Ariel asked me. "Should we tear things down as they're being built?"

I'd told her the story of the fence at 40th Street and now began to regret it.

"No, we were a bunch of reckless, no-brain kids," I said. "But that doesn't mean we shouldn't keep an eye on things; we should be ready to speak out if things get out of hand. And it also means we should enjoy what we've got and not take it for granted. What do you say we grab the board and hit the surf?"

Ariel paused and watched the water. This time two dolphins appeared.

"All right, Dad. One last try."

We dragged the longboard into the choppy water. Ariel practiced her paddling as I swam beside her. She asked for a bar of surf wax, one of her favorite parts of the surf paraphernalia, and began pressing the coconut-smelling wax onto the board's deck, her hands making circles of wax flesh up on the board, as if the board had thick, translucent, goose pimples.

"Now remember," I said, "I'm just going to give you a little push. And then you let the wave catch the board."

Ariel nodded her head.

I'd been telling her not to stand too quickly. She just needed to let the board catch the wave, belly-ride it as she gained speed and cruised out in front of the white water. *Then* she should try to rise up. Trying to stand from the get-go would be a recipe for disaster, a spillout on the top of the wave, a mouthful of salty soup.

And it happened. A three-foot face rose up, and I gave Ariel the perfect push. The longboard zipped toward shore as Ariel rode along on her chest, belly, and knees.

I shouted and hooted and yelled when she stood up and rode that wave, a sleepwalker gliding toward shore, her shoulders parallel with the beach, a Madonna soaring shoreward with the mermaids crying each to each as she aimed perpendicular to the white sand beach.

We both shouted for glee at the shoreline after I swam into the beach. Ariel suddenly pointed out to sea. I turned and saw our favorite dolphin, the one with the notched dorsal fin, crest from the surface about ten yards from where we stood in the shorebreak and slap its tail in the water.

MICHAEL TRAMMELL *teaches business communication and technical writing at Florida State University. His work has appeared in* New Letters, Pleiades, G.W. Review, Gulf Stream, *and other journals. He's currently an editor for the* APALACHEE REVIEW. *He goes surfing with his daughter every chance he gets.*

WHAT I TEACH ARIEL: PERSPECTIVES ON BEACHES

Sandhill Cranes Mid-February

It's the prospect of cranes that draws
me east to Madison County this
stormy Valentine's Day. I've heard
they roost in Hixtown
Swamp winter nights,
and I know they will
start their migration
to nesting
grounds in
Wisconsin any
day. I cross the
headwaters of
the Aucilla
River, a collection of streams, river swamps, and
open wetlands that drains our bioregion's eastern
flank. As I leave tiny Greenville on County Road
150, the land swells north toward Georgia in a
sweep of mounding green hills and misty gray
sky. The emerald winter rye fields are set with
pastel flowering trees: redbud, plum, peach, and

sandhills take flight

red maple. I can almost imagine myself in the English Cotswolds.

But the specific search image in my mind is not just spring, but sandhill crane. We rarely see them this far west in the Panhandle, but I often think of how they marked the end of spring when I lived in Gainesville, their rich bugling cry rolling above the city as they circled and circled, gaining the necessary altitude to fly to their far northern nesting grounds. I miss that wild call.

And here's the bird, standing with another of its kind at the edge of a muddy field. I'd forgotten its impressive height—five feet, minimum. Its body is shingled slate gray, with a visor of crimson atop its ever-alert head. The cranes stalk about, twitching worms and succulent roots from the black earth, vigorous. They are silent, feeding, so I don't get to hear their cry, but I'm satisfied to intersect with their lives, even briefly.

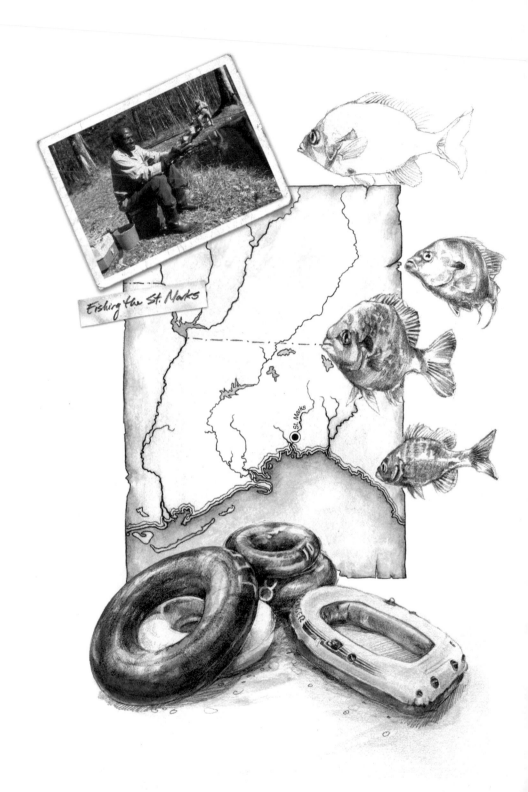

Fishing the St. Marks

Watery Thread through Time:
The St. Marks River

DOUG ALDERSON

Some people yearn to hear symphonies in their heads and compose great music. I yearn to hear a great river and listen to its stories.

I often paddle the upper St. Marks River east of Woodville, Florida, north of Natural Bridge State Park, late in the day. The river, divided into mirrors of shadow and light, lures me on. A heron or an anhinga, always prominent birds, keep moving ahead, reappearing at bend after bend before flying off as I approach. Fading sun rays illuminate centuries-old cypresses, weathered trees that have known the rap of ivory-billed woodpeckers and the fluttering wings of Carolina parakeets.

I often pause to watch water bugs etch their ever-changing designs on the river's surface. Every creature, eddy, and arching branch of the St. Marks is a masterful work of art, worthy of appreciation.

Once I paddle past moss-covered stumps of pilings from a long-forgotten bridge and pull my canoe or kayak over the first downed tree that blocks most boat traffic, there are few signs of people. That's when I really listen. A part of me begins to touch something very old.

I sense mastodon, saber-toothed cat, Paleo hunter and dugout traveler, and wonder about their stories. How did native people regard this flowing lifeblood of water, the hues of which change from rich brown to red, yellow, and occasionally a clear blue, depending on rainfall? What did they call the river before seventeenth-century Spaniards christened it St. Marks after one of their religious saints?

I yearn for a longer bridge over the abyss of time.

While barred owls give voice to the waning light, the presence of those vanished species and tribes seem as much a part of the river as the water itself.

Of course, the river speaks in myriad other ways, appealing to many senses—murmuring eddies, the popping of bream and bass, choruses of frogs and cicadas and goodnight songs of unseen birds. Even trees and plants seem to speak: the canopies of Florida maple, cypress, gum, holly, water oak, ironwood, American beech and fragrant wax myrtle. The sweet smell of lush willow takes me back to my earliest childhood days of fishing along waterfronts. It is a pure aroma, fresh and cleansing.

The prevalent sweetgum along the shore often reminds me of a Creek Indian story. A group of women who were laden with many emotional burdens gathered daily beneath a large sweetgum and talked of their problems. Each day, as they talked, their burdens seemed lighter, until one day they felt the entire weight had been lifted. Intuitively, they realized that the sweetgum tree, their daily companion, had absorbed much of their pain. Today, in the women's ribbon dance at the Creek ceremonials, some women carry a sweetgum branch if they are troubled and later burn it in a special fire.

Maybe it's the sweetgum, or the river, or all of it, but I feel lighter after I've paddled the St. Marks. Even if my burdens haven't been entirely lifted, still they don't seem as important.

On occasion, I've spotted otters swimming the St. Marks, as well as cottonmouths and banded water snakes. Once, while driving along Highway 27 near the St. Marks River Bridge, just below where a series of streams converge to create the river, I braked for a Florida black bear crossing the highway. I began to wonder what wild foods bears would eat along the river, where they might sleep, where they would mate and den. I yearned to communicate with bears.

How does the St. Marks River differ from other Florida streams? I like to think of rivers as possessing natural, unaltered DNA. All rivers are unique; there are no clones. Each has its own stories.

Sometimes, if I feel ambitious and there's time, I'll paddle from Natural Bridge to Horn Springs, about three miles upriver. Horn Springs is often clear and blue and deep. I used to party there as a teenager, before the sand access roads were closed, but I look at the springs through different eyes now. Someday, if the land around the spring becomes public property, and it might, I'd like to help stem erosion along the worn banks, and fill in the moonscape of holes left by disrespectful people searching for prehistoric Native American artifacts. Law enforcement officers, spread thin, play a cat-and-mouse game with the illegal artifact hunters, who often wear camouflage clothing, use portable police scanners, and dig at night while wearing headlamps.

If I don't have time to paddle the river, I'll often drive to Natural Bridge and stroll along this forested land bridge, admiring the glassy reflections of a river slowed to a near standstill as it swirls underground. On one spring afternoon, I met an aged man, Detroit Holton, fishing the dark waters. Detroit's wrinkled face bore a look of concentration and hopeful anticipation as he eyed his red and white bobber. "When you're retired," he said, "you ain't got nothing to do so you come down here instead of going to your job. I catch bass, a bream or two, a speckled perch or two, cats, mudfish."

His friend, Jimmy Martin, chimed in, "I keep a fishing pole in my car because I can't stand to go around water and see someone else fishing."

I stood with the men for a spell, watching bobbers, before I wished them luck and quietly left. As I walked away, I heard most of a story Jimmy shared with Detroit: "This guy told me he was fishing here by himself and three guys popped up out of the sink. About scared him half to death. Then he saw they was wearing scuba gear and they came up from down river. . . . " The two men erupted in laughter.

One year, I visited Natural Bridge on the first weekend in March. No fishermen lined the sink. Civil War reenactors had come from across the South to set up an 1860s-style encampment and to fire blanks at each other. Originally, it was here at Natural Bridge that General John Newton and more than five hundred black Union soldiers tried to cross Natural Bridge in hopes of occupying the Florida capital of Tallahassee. Nearly six hundred well-entrenched Confederates, mostly old men and young cadets, repeatedly drove them back. The Yankees, charging uphill, lost 148 of their number; the Confederates only three.

The impact of the battle never sunk in until I was alone at Natural Bridge one evening. Facing west, I stood on the land that splits the St. Marks River and suddenly felt emotions of young Union soldiers marching toward the hill on the western bank, marching toward cannon and well-entrenched Confederates pointing loaded muskets. I sensed their anxiety and fear, and also their determination. I marveled at the sensation until I felt the pain of their defeat, the cries of the wounded, the release of the dead. I quickly moved off the land bridge, sidestepping the ghosts, curious as to how painful echoes of the past could reverberate off such incredible beauty.

Below Natural Bridge, after the river rises for good at a place called "the basin," my friends David and Casey Gluckman built their wood home in 1980, setting it 350 feet back from the water. A winding boardwalk through an untouched floodplain forest gives their property a park-like atmosphere. If you're going to live on a river, they set a good example. I love to perch at the end of their boardwalk and gaze at the water.

David once told me about an age-old winter run of mullet he witnessed heading up the river. "I put my kayak in the water and mullet started exploding," he said. "The water was clear and I noticed that when I looked across the river, it was solid mullet from bank to bank, top to bottom. I paddled upriver and they erupted in front of me just continuously, and it was solid fish almost a mile upriver."

My own familiarity with the section of river below the Gluckman's house was firmly established by several annual moonlight canoe trips. They were our junkets for legislators in the 1970s and 1980s when I lobbied for environmental causes with the Gluckmans. The river in this section was perfect for such a trip. It was wide, relatively free of snags, and completely wild until it reached the Highway 98 bridge at Newport. We would provide the canoes, fried chicken, and obligatory wine and beer. The moonlit St. Marks River would provide the magic. The whole experience would cost about a hundred bucks, but the gains made for environmental causes were immeasurable. Lawmakers are human; they like to please their friends, and by trip's end, we were often counted among their friends. So was the river and all that it represented.

One Labor Day weekend, my cousin Tom and I decided to embark on a kayaking trip on this middle section of river. We dropped my truck off at the U.S. Highway 98 public landing at Newport and launched two kayaks at the Gluckman's house. We enjoyed a leisurely three-hour paddle.

Upon returning to the public landing, we were shocked to find more than a hundred revelers in advanced stages of inebriation. Large sunburned men watched us with amusement. We felt like a pair of deer with handsome racks, leisurely strolling through a hunt camp on Thanksgiving weekend.

Tom and I looked for my truck. To our chagrin, we found it nestled among trees far from our original parking spot. It was blocked in by pickups and a loud horseshoe game. The ground was littered with trash, mostly beer bottles, which angered me particularly, since I had fought unsuccessfully for a bottle bill in Florida.

A young man ran up to us. "Is that your truck?" he asked nervously. I nodded.

"We didn't hurt nothing," he blurted. "It was just in the way of the game." He nodded toward the wild-eyed men tossing horseshoes. By the excitement that each shot generated, I gathered that more than pride was on the line.

"How did you move the truck?" I asked, incredulous.

The man flashed a prideful smile. "About twenty of us just picked up the back end and rolled it by the front tires," he said. "It didn't hurt nothing."

I chuckled. Two bare-chested men began rolling on the ground in a drunken brawl. Their grunts were momentarily drowned out by screeching brakes and blaring horns from the bridge area as someone tried to pull out in front of oncoming traffic.

"You mind helping me get the truck out?" I asked, nonchalant.

"Yeah, no problem."

With the helpful man directing traffic and getting friends to move trucks, we managed to avoid thick mud, flying horseshoes, the brawlers, and a massive guy who swayed back-and-forth but stood his ground; he taunted us to run him over.

On our slow drive past throngs of people along the landing road, some high school-aged girls called to us, "Got any marijuana?" Being two clean-cut 40-somethings, Tom and I could have passed for FBI agents. Instead, we merely drove on, wanting to somehow recapture the tranquility of the St. Marks River.

On another occasion, this time on a weekday, I visited the Newport Bridge and met a man who was seeking crewmates to raft with him to the Texas coast. Friends had stimulated my curiosity, describing how the man sought to reenact the voyage of Spanish conquistadors who built makeshift rafts near the mouth of the St. Marks River to escape hostile Apalachee

Indians in 1528. The desperate Spaniards created a bellows out of deer hides and forged nails and tools out of weapons, spurs, and stirrups. They felled towering pines and shaped oars from junipers. They crafted sails from clothing, water bags from horse skin, and ropes and rigging from palmetto husks and horsehair. In the end, they had constructed five primitive sailing rafts for 242 men. Cabeza de Vaca, one of four survivors of the journey, wrote a journal of his ordeal, a journal that had evidently inspired the man beneath the bridge.

After parking at Ouzt's Oyster Bar on the west side of the river, I walked toward the bridge and approached a stocky, sunburned man sewing together a crude sail. He sat on a long raft made of pine logs. A pot of a black, tar-like substance smoldered on a smoky fire nearby. I don't remember the man's name, so I shall call him Cabo.

Cabo glanced up and brushed stringy brown hair from his sweat-stained face. I deduced that his dark eyes revealed Spanish heritage. I asked him about his project. Cabo sighed, slurped a Budweiser, checked on the smoldering substance of what I assumed to be pitch for waterproofing lashings and logs, and began his story.

Like Cabeza de Vaca, Cabo planned to sail to the Texas coast and then walk inland for several hundred miles to Mexico City, often through desert terrain. De Vaca, he said, had been a messiah. "He healed people," he asserted. "He made his way to Mexico City by healing the Indians he met. Many Indians started following him."

Cabo admitted two main problems with his plan. He had no sailing experience, and he needed a crew—not the nearly fifty men who squeezed onto de Vaca's raft. Three or four would suffice, enough to help launch and guide the boat and man the sails. "You interested?" he asked.

I glanced skeptically at the stick lean-to Cabo had built on the deck. Not exactly the Love Boat, I thought. I had been prone to crazy adventures in the past, but sailing a makeshift raft along the Gulf coast with no motor or running lights seemed an invitation to disaster. There was a reason why the would-be Spanish conquerors of 1528 lost four out of five rafts and 238 men. Any number of misfortunes could doom the journey, storms and large ships at night being among them. Plus, Cabo's raft looked heavy. The logs weren't seasoned. I feared it would sink soon after launching.

"My wife would kill me," I finally answered.

DOUG ALDERSON

38

A few weeks later, I visited the Newport Bridge again. Cabo was gone. So was his raft. I heard later that, unable to find a crew, he abandoned his efforts. The raft lies at the bottom of the St. Marks, the newest addition to the river's storehouse of historical memorabilia.

Below Highway 98, the St. Marks wends its way past oil refineries, seafood restaurants, bars, and a bed and breakfast in the town of St. Marks, and then it gets wild again—abruptly—merging with the spring-fed Wakulla River at the ruins of Fort San Marcos. For almost three hundred years, the fort was at the center of a tug-of-war between Native Americans, Europeans, pirates, and Americans vying for control of north Florida. Now it is a peaceful tree-covered spot, contrasting its long and often violent history.

Nearby, abandoned Confederate salt works along the coast, and a series of large impoundments have become havens for egrets, ducks, alligators, and other wildlife, at the 68,000-acre St. Marks National Wildlife Refuge. Nature's recuperative powers, always strong, seem to display extra vitality along the lower St. Marks River.

The refuge's unspoiled tidal marsh and a small section at Natural Bridge are currently the only public lands along the St. Marks. The rest is in private ownership. That situation concerns many river lovers. Riverfront property is prime real estate and the St. Marks could end up with rows of houses and docks like so many other Florida rivers.

Currently, the St. Marks River is on the priority list for purchase by the state of Florida.

The St. Joe Company, Florida's largest landowner, owns the entire upper river from Highway 27 to Natural Bridge. "You could walk all the way from Highway 27 to the town of St. Marks and never leave St. Joe land," said George Willson, corporate vice president for conservation lands for the St. Joe Company. They are offering to sell it to the state of Florida in two phases. A possible third phase would include their vast holdings below Natural Bridge.

Willson, formerly of The Nature Conservancy, describes the potential land sale as "awesome." The first and second phases involve 13,000 acres and sixteen to seventeen miles of river frontage. It includes virgin cypress trees, longleaf pine hills, old-growth bottomlands, flatwoods lakes, several karst features, and Horn Springs.

The purchases would help protect the river and ensure recreational access. Trails for canoeing, kayaking, bicycling, and hiking are future possibilities.

But water pollution is still a concern. A Tallahassee sewage spray field along a feeder creek poses threats of nutrient-rich discharges into the river. The St. Marks headwaters are immediately adjacent to Lake Lafayette, which receives large amounts of urban runoff. The lake feeds into the river during high water and there is the possibility of underground connections.

I often dream about the St. Marks. In one dream, I am floating down the river, the new leaves of spring casting bright green reflections on tannic waters. Birds speak to me, and fish, otters, and manatee. The river herself communicates—a whisper, an understanding. I begin to see those who have gone before: Apalachee, conquistadors, the Spanish fort, Civil War combatants, and abandoned river towns such as Port Leon and Magnolia. The St. Marks has absorbed them all, and each year new leaves sprout, the mullet run, manatees return, and colorful warblers fill the trees.

The river keeps on flowing.

DOUG ALDERSON *published his first freelance magazine article at age eighteen and he has been writing for publications since. Over the years, he has published articles and accompanying photographs in publications such as* American Forests, Sierra, Mother Earth News, Campus Life, America, St. Louis Post-Dispatch, Wild Outdoor World, Florida Naturalist, Florida Sportsman, Tallahassee Magazine, *and* Florida Wildlife. *He is former associate editor of* Florida Wildlife *magazine. In July of 2003, Doug received a first-place national writing award from the Association of Conservation Information for a three-part article on the Everglades system.*

WATERY THREAD THROUGH TIME: THE ST. MARKS RIVER

41

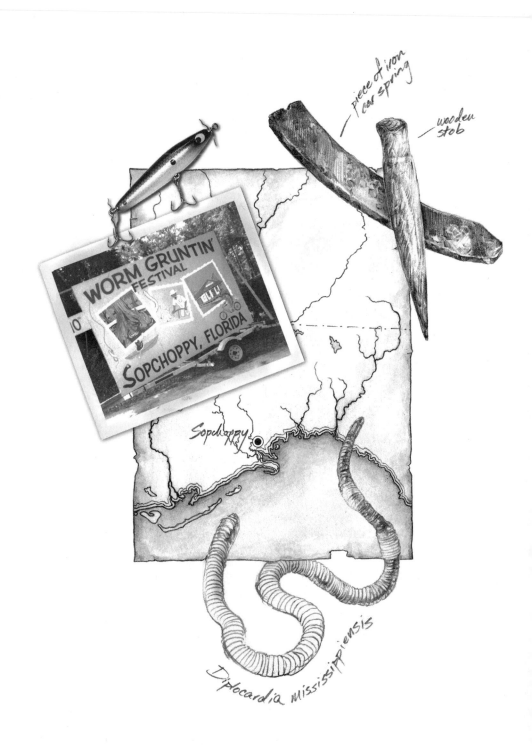

piece of iron
car spring

wooden
stob

WORM GRUNTIN'
FESTIVAL

SOPCHOPPY, FLORIDA

Sopchoppy

Diplocardia mississippiensis

Worm Grunter's Wisdom

SAUNDRA GERRELL KELLEY

Fred Lawhorn was waiting for me when I pulled into Natural Bridge State Park. The eighty-two-year-old Florida native, a retired worm grunter, had invited me to come down to his place on the St. Marks River for supper, an invitation I gladly accepted. I wanted to learn more about the history of worm grunting in southern Leon and Wakulla counties.

Greeting me with a warm hug and a twinkle of mischief in his eyes, Lawhorn told me to follow him, saying I would probably think we were going to the "middle of nowhere." By the time we reached his place on the river, I was a believer.

The road twisted and turned around huge live oaks, American holly, clumps of palmetto, ferns, cabbage palms, and cypress trees. We passed opaque sinkholes, their surfaces covered by bright green duckweed and sheltered by graceful willows and water tupelo. As we drove, the woods grew dark, long before the sun went down. I'll have to admit I wanted to stop at every turn, but I had worm grunting on my mind, as well as the very real possibility of getting lost without my guide. I followed the little green beacon flying ahead of me.

The winding, sandy track ended at Fred's doorstep. Sheltered by huge magnolia trees and sitting very near river's edge, the house blended into the forest and made me think of a mossy-green mushroom sprung from the earth after a hard rain. I found my senses fully engaged by the intense emerald green of the riverine environment. I knew that to be in this special place was an honor beyond words.

First, Fred showed me the river. Water splashing upstream announced a family of beavers building a dam, Fred told me. Tea-colored water, rich with tannin, pushed over their dam, rushing past us and on to the sea, creating a strange, pulsating rhythm that played underneath that of the breeze, birdsong, and our conversation.

As we walked near the river's edge, fighting battalions of mosquitoes and watching for water moccasins, a family of mallard ducks took flight, blending into the dense stand of trees and wild grape vines on the opposite shore as though they had never been visible at all. As they flew away, the loss was mine and I found myself walking more carefully and speaking more quietly.

The notion of 'making do' characterizes Lawhorn. Living and raising their children in Woodville, Florida, Lawhorn and his wife Bell built the little house on the river by hand with the intention of using it as a fishing camp. Constructed mostly from downed timber from the river and salvaged wood, the house measures exactly 22 by 24 feet. No trees were felled to make the winding road we followed to his house and the land has been little disturbed from the time he bought the property in 1950. The tall, courtly gentleman needed no university degrees to tell him how sacred was this land.

Time stood still while I was at the river. Fred's son and daughter, who live nearby, came down to prepare dinner while we talked about worm grunting. As we sat around the table eating home-cooked Southern fried chicken, Fred told me why he grunted for worms.

After returning from World War II, Lawhorn said he had a family to feed and the worms were there, in the ground, waiting to be harvested. Times were hard and bait was expensive, so he grunted worms to catch fish for his own family. According to Lawhorn, grasshoppers, crickets, flatheads (a wrinkled white and brown worm with a flat head found under the bark of dead pine trees), and July flies, from dog fennel plants, all make great fishing bait, but to this day, nothing holds up better in the water than the fat earthworm named *Diplocardia mississippiensis*. The extra worms Lawhorn grunted he sold to buy necessities.

Lawhorn and his wife raised four children on the proceeds earned from fishing, worm grunting, and cutting wood survey stakes. Fred worked at the local lumber mill cutting stakes, netting ten dollars a day when his children were young. After work he grunted for earthworms to earn another five to seven dollars to sell to bait shops in Woodville before heading home for dinner. Weekends, he hitchhiked into Tallahassee where he could make another forty dollars selling worms to bait stores, but often he earned nothing—his profits depended on fishermen too busy to grunt for their own bait. Inclement weather and no sales led to lean times for a man with a family to feed. Hard work and a frugal lifestyle took Lawhorn through lean times, allowing the family to continue living on the land they loved.

"I was born into worm gruntin'," he told me. As a small boy, he and his friends learned the fine art from local African-American families who fished on the river. From them, he learned to hammer stakes called stobs deep into the ground, leaving just a couple of inches of rough wood surface exposed. Then, using either a brickbat or a metal ax-head (or these days, a metal car-spring) to scrape over the stob, he made the wood "grunt." The rhythmic action on the stob caused the earth to vibrate, causing the earthworms to rise to the surface like holy-rollers at a tent revival.

There are a number of interesting theories about what makes the worms come to air. Some folks think the vibration is uncomfortable to them and the firm, light-colored worms escape to the surface only to be caught; perhaps, as Charles Darwin theorized, the worms interpret the vibration as a potential threat. Still others think the surfacing is a response to hard rain—I have seen worms do this. Nobody knows for sure what makes them pop out of the earth and the worms aren't talking.

Transporting the living cargo of worms was a challenge. Lawhorn filled five-gallon paint buckets with muck from the St. Marks River bottom, dirt from the pond bottoms on Old Plank Road and later, sawdust from the mill. In the absence of modern coolers, selling his product the same day he harvested it was crucial. Earthworms lived longer in cooler temperatures, but hot weather spelled death for his investment.

In the 1970s, popular television commentator Charles Kuralt focused the national spotlight on the venerable trade of worm grunting when he paid a visit to the Apalachicola National Forest. His informative broadcast changed the way people thought about the humble earthworm, and he is generally referred to by native grunters as "the one who started it all." Since then, grunting for worms has become a recognized industry in the forest and has even spawned a festival in the sleepy little town of Sopchoppy. The spring festival draws grunters young and old to the national forest to practice the primitive art of worm grunting.

Nowadays, a profit can be made in the worm market. A worm grunter with a fifteen-dollar monthly permit can make up to thirty dollars during peak season on a can of five hundred worms. To grunt that many earthworms takes about thirty minutes, making worm grunting sound like a sweet way to make some quick money.

When I asked Fred if he thought excessive worm grunting had contributed to the decline of the earthworm population, he grunted, sounding for all the world like a piece of metal grating across the top of a stob. "No, I don't think so, at least not along the St. Marks River."

"Worm grunting never has been the major industry around the St. Marks River that it is today in the Apalachicola National Forest," Lawhorn continued. "Locals grunted for the worms they needed for fishing and some extra to sell to feed their families. Now, with the festival bringing more attention to it, more and more people go to the Forest to grunt."

But Lawhorn admitted that there are fewer earthworms in the St. Marks area than in the past. He theorized that the St. Marks River earthworms, which are a slightly different color than the Apalachicola National Forest worms and may have interbred with invasive European earthworms, have declined in part from clearing for agriculture and the clear-cutting of forests.

When I consulted historian and author Pete Gerrell, a Woodville native, he told me that when the Apalachicola National Forest area was initially settled, before it became public land, it was heavily cutover. Farmers soon gave up and abandoned the land. The nutrient-poor sandy soil of the Apalachicola National Forest couldn't support farming. This left the native earthworms the opportunity to do their job of restoring the forest. That the Apalachicola National Forest has been able to restore itself to what it is today could be in large part because of little 'twelve heart,' the earthworm.

The function and importance of earthworms to the environment is very clear. According to ongoing research by Paul Hendrix, an ecology professor at the University of Georgia, their job on the planet is to aerate the soil, adding "fertile droppings" to the mix. Hendrix says the earthworm is probably a "major factor in maintaining a healthy soil and, thus, a healthy forest." He

SAUNDRA GERRELL KELLEY

adds that although research is continuing, he sees "no reason yet to be too concerned about short-term reductions of native worm populations that seem to follow baiting."

But changes in Lawhorn's native place, beyond the decline of worm populations, distress him. "Just a few years ago," he said, "I could sit in that chair by the water, pull my bait out of the cooling bucket, throw a line in there and have supper in a matter of minutes. It's just not that way anymore."

"When I was a boy," he continued, "fish and wildlife were plentiful. Thousands of geese and other birds overwintered here. They are not here now, and we didn't kill them all. Newcomers just don't know what they missed. It's changing fast and not for the better. You move a bunch of people in here with their pavement, sewage, and fertilizer and you can forget it."

"I've watched this place change a lot, partly because of fertilizer from farming, logging debris, oil from motorboats, garbage, sewage, and pollution from Tallahassee. Wasteful logging practices changed the ecology of this environment, and now it's about to happen again through massive development." Lawhorn referred to the St. Joe Development Company's plans to develop the "Great Northwest" on its extensive holdings in northwest Florida.

In contrast, the footprint that Fred Lawhorn has made on the land he loves is a small one. His spirit is of this place and his grief for its unnecessary losses is strong. His years living on the river have kept him attuned to the land; his identity with the river has made him who he is.

Some people are born to live on rivers, becoming a part of the ebb and flow of the water. These people know the look of it at dawn. They know it as the sun goes down and the moon silvers the water at night, and they know it when it changes. Fred Lawhorn is one of those people.

Lawhorn's worm-grunting tools occupy a place of honor on the front porch. When he showed them to me, it was with a touch of nostalgia for days gone by. Worm grunting is labor intensive, requiring kneeling, hammering and gathering, and at this point in Lawhorn's life, he prefers watching wild turkeys strut in the yard. "Life in nature makes life worth the living," he says.

Worm Grunter's Wisdom

SAUNDRA GERRELL KELLEY *is a fifth-generation North Floridian. Her love of Florida's environment is as deep as her roots and she has been writing about it for many years. From the series printed in the* Tallahassee Democrat *called* "Stories My Daddy Told Me," *to articles in various periodicals addressing environmental issues, Kelley's voice is always that of one deeply attached to the land.*

man wormgrunting c. 1970's

WORM GRUNTER'S WISDOM

Turkey Oaks   Late March

The coal-black trunk of the turkey oak is deeply furrowed, designed to hoard what rain falls on these droughty sandhills. Most of the year this tree guards itself well, but just now, supple young twigs spring from their woody fortress, gentle as skin. The twigs bear lemon-tinged leaves, softly lobed like the feet of small mammals, not yet grown into their lacquered summer fullness. Sprouting from the juncture of new growth and last year's wood are flower stalks limp with pollen. All these vulnerable tree parts are sought by a legion of caterpillars, hatched just in time to profit from the oak's undefended growth. The tree can only stand in the spring-cool air, pushing out baby leaves and flowers as fast as it can, and chance that all will be well.

How benevolent, then, are the songbirds returned all the way from South America, just

Friday morning Birdsong
turkey oak sapling
new dry grass ground
Birds!

in time to glean the hungry caterpillars one
by one from the turkey oak's fragile young
leaves. I watch a parula warbler lift one such
soft-bodied worm, pummel the wriggling
animal sharply against a twig, and then
gulp it whole. The bird picks the tree over;
some caterpillars are so small they require no
beating. Between mouthfuls, it explodes into a
shout of song, body all atremble. If the turkey
oak could sing, I'd hear its voice, as well.

Anne
&
Jack

Why We Sunk Our Money into a Swamp

ANNE AND JACK RUDLOE

Bushes slapped hard against the windows, and the clean whitewall tires of our uncle's shiny rental car splashed through puddles. We were on a sand road, deep in the pine forests of northern Florida, some twenty-five miles south of Tallahassee. Uncle Charles and Aunt Milly had just arrived from New York for a visit and we wanted them to see the property we had recently acquired. Finally, after lurching over a washed-out section of road and getting past the place where the big car was in danger of getting stuck, we arrived at the edge of Alligator Lake.

Sunlight flashed on the black water. Our relatives gazed at the twisted cypress roots and the spot where wild pigs had grubbed up the leaf litter. "Nine thousand dollars for this!" Uncle Charles finally stammered. "You're crazy. Why, it's a . . . a . . . swamp!" He said *swamp* with loathing, as if great scaly things with teeth and slime were going to reach up any minute and pull us all down into the abyss. "Why?" he asked incredulously. "You could have bought a waterfront lot or a business site, some investment land down here. But this!"

The answer was difficult to put into words. It was the classic case of selling Florida swamps to suckers, but unlike many consumers, we knew what we were doing. We had always wanted a swamp. Marine biologists by profession, we operate a small biological supply company in nearby Panacea, Florida, that provides live starfish, crabs, and sea horses for research and teaching in universities.

When the tide seeps out of the marshland and exposes the mud flats, we dig up clams and sea anemones, seal them in Styrofoam boxes and put them on jets to destinations all over the country. And to supplement that meager income we periodically venture into the office buildings of New York or Washington to scrounge up a book contract or freelance magazine assignment.

In order to exist on this pastoral coastline with its quiet bays, salt marshes, and unspoiled woodlands, we lead a frenetic existence; for us, the swamp would be a place to escape for a few hours and clean out our souls.

It had value beyond that. We had been involved in endless controversies over the years to slow down the conversion of our wilderness coast into condominiums and trailer parks. The swamp represented fourteen acres where the concrete, steel, and asphalt could not follow. We had bought a refuge from the carscape that was overwhelming much of the rest of the country. It cost us nine thousand dollars–not easy money to come by. But five years ago, we earned some extra money from an unexpected assignment: a contract to work on a federal fisheries management plan. We made more money than we ever had before, and we knew right away what to do with it.

Uncle Charles and Aunt Milly listened to all this over dinner, but it was clear that they thought we'd taken leave of our senses. The next morning, after waving goodbye to our still puzzled relatives, we loaded a canoe into the back of the pickup truck and drove back to the lake. From the landing we paddled out through the dark canopied cypress forest into the open expanse of lily pads, following the old fence line that marked the property boundary. In the morning mists the cypress and cabbage palms formed eerie shapes, as steam rose from the black water. It was a marvel. By buying fourteen acres, we'd essentially acquired a private wilderness lake. All the rest of the shoreline was federally owned, part of the adjacent St. Marks National Wildlife Refuge.

Sprawling across the Gulf coast south of Tallahassee, St. Marks is one of the nation's oldest wildlife refuges. It was pieced together during the 1930s when local hardscrabble dirt farmers, impoverished by years of fighting soil that was nothing more than sand, were finished off by the Great Depression. The worn-out, logged-over land was sold for taxes and the federal government acquired most of it. A few acres here and there had remained in private hands, inholdings surrounded by the refuge. Our swamp was one such piece.

Now, after some fifty years, the native pine forest and cypress swamps are recovering and the wisdom of those Depression land purchases is more apparent. The refuge represents one of the few surviving examples of the pine forest ecosystem that stretched for thousands of miles across the southeastern United States a century ago. The forests and swamps are alive with deer, wild turkey, and bear, and bald eagles nest in the coastal marshes that mark the seaward edge of St. Marks. Having one of those few private islands in the refuge was like having a last surviving piece of the American wilderness–to us, it seemed a miracle.

Suddenly, as we paddled our canoe through the lake water, the lily pads boiled up and we came face-to-face with the largest alligator we'd ever seen, every bit as big as our sixteen-foot craft. It surged ahead, throwing a wake. Across the lake, wood ducks rose and noisily winged their way off.

Veering away from our reptilian escort, we beached our canoe between two buttressed cypresses and slogged our way up onto a high ridge. There, massive water oaks stood draped with Spanish moss and towering slash pines spread their needled branches above the red swamp maples. We hiked up away from the water and wandered the leaf-littered forest floor. A deer flashed through the trees and we heard wild turkeys calling from the scrub oaks. This was what Florida was meant to be, not sprawling motels, hamburger stands, and row upon row of subdivisions. We gazed up at one enormous pine. Somehow it had managed to escape loggers fifty years ago when much of the virgin timber in northern Florida was cut. Now it stood as a veritable museum piece against the ever growing landscape of young, even-aged pines of tree farms. That tree alone, we thought, was worth the price of the property.

It was strange to think that we *owned* this. Of course, during summer, no one but the red bugs and mosquitoes really own it. Before, we could walk through this forgotten swampland only because no one bothered to stop us. Now we had guaranteed access and the knowledge that it would not suddenly be bulldozed. That meant something. Even in the St. Marks refuge, foresters were cutting large tracts of commercial timber.

Soon after buying the land, we set out to inventory our new holdings. University botanists came down to run transects through the woods, making detailed vegetation maps and pointing out a giant red maple that was probably a state record. A visiting expert on mushrooms from Tennessee was drafted to give us a list of the species of lichens, fungi, and mushrooms on the site.

But most of what we had, we could see ourselves. The shallows swarmed with millions of tadpoles in the spring. A line cast into the deep holes of Alligator Lake produced bream, crappie, and, now and then, a largemouth bass lurking among the lily pads. The woods were full of squirrels chattering and jumping from tree to tree. If you divided the fetterbush, the magnolia trees, and the soft green spongy bogs of sphagnum moss and their red sundews into the purchase price, we got each one for a fraction of a penny. And that wasn't even counting the five-foot-long diamondback rattlesnake that gave us such a start. There were scaly gray fence lizards with blue bellies that darted on the scrub oaks, blending in perfectly. Delicate lichens and bracken fungi–it seemed amazing that other people felt compelled to scrape such land down to bare black dirt, fill it in, and build on it. "Look, tree," we said, slapping the trunk of a majestic cypress, "think how lucky you are that you belong to us." The tree said nothing to our absurdity.

In cooler months, we set about the business of "improving" our property. The swamp was perfect unto itself, and "improving," like "ownership," is a human-made term. But we could make it more accessible, cutting trails with snippers and machetes to find the prettiest spots. We made our 14 acres seem more like 50 by snaking paths around the palmettos and down to the fern patch. We put up survey flags on trees to mark the trail, and hoped someday we'd build a boardwalk and a small unobtrusive dock out into the lake. Occasionally, biology students from a local school came over and helped work on the trail. In return we took them out into the lake on field trips. Using dip nets, they caught crayfish and aquatic insects and clear glass shrimp that flipped and jackknifed in the webbing.

Over the last five years the swamp has proved its worth. We will never actually build there. We know the swamp really isn't ours. All the property deeds and records in the courthouse are meaningless to the lily pads and cypress trees, the sunlight filtering through massive oaks, the resurrection ferns gleaming with water droplets after a rain. We can alter the land, change it, even destroy it entirely. Or we can do our best to protect it during our lifetime–but we will never own it. No one will.

ANNE AND JACK RUDLOE

ANNE RUDLOE, PHD, *lives in Panacea, Florida. She and her husband run the Gulf Specimen Marine Laboratory, an independent nonprofit environmental center and aquarium. She received her PhD from Florida State University, where she has taught courses on marine biology and environmental issues. Her writing has appeared in* National Geographic, Smithsonian, *and numerous scientific journals. She is the author of* Butterflies on a Sea Wind: Beginning Zen.

JACK RUDLOE *was born in New York City in 1943 and moved to the remote Florida panhandle when he was fourteen, where he learned to hunt, fish, and roam the swamps. He has published six nonfiction books,* Sea Brings Forth, Erotic Ocean, Living Dock, Time of the Turtle, Wilderness Coast, Search for the Great Turtle Mother, *and a novel,* Potluck. *With his wife Anne, he has published numerous articles in popular magazines, including* National Geographic, Smithsonian, *and* Sports Illustrated. *Over the years, Jack Rudloe has appeared before civic clubs, schools, universities, and government agencies, often incorporating both slides and creatures into his lectures.*

WHY WE SUNK OUR MONEY INTO A SWAMP

Camellia blooms

C.S.A.
61–65

Southwood
land

2/18/04

The Golf Course and the Blackwater Slough

DIANE ROBERTS

I fell into the slough one time. I was four or five, fishing with a cane pole and wigglers. I don't remember if I caught anything that day. I do remember sliding down the bank very slowly. I could see the gray mud and the red clay and the green moss. I could see the black water of the slough. And the water was alive, moving every which way, spirals and zigzags, tails and eyes.

Of course, it didn't happen slowly, it happened fast. I fell in. There were moccasins in the water. My father, even faster, hauled me out by my hair.

The slough lolls along out of Mack Lake in the deep swamps of Wakulla County, not far from the Ochlockonee River. The slough belongs to the moccasins and the bream and the alligators and the tupelo and the cypress. Someone of my blood has been fishing in this slough since the mid-1830s, Browards, Tuckers, Vauses, Revells, Robertses. Before that, Seminoles hunted along it: bear, deer, wildcat. Before that, the remnants of the Apalachee, descendants of the people who had lived in Florida for ten thousand years, counted this as part of their territory: the ones not killed by Toledo blades or smallpox. In 1528, Panfilo de Narvaez, Alvar Nunez Cabeza de Vaca and a posse of on-the-make Spaniards wandered lost and hungry in our swamp. They found no gold, no emeralds. They had to eat their horses. Even then, only four survived to tell their Florida story—four out of four hundred.

When Hernando de Soto came to Florida in 1539, he brought his own groceries, long-legged range pigs from the hot western province of

Estremadura. Some of them escaped and ran wild in the swamp, over the years interbreeding with domestic porkers. I've watched their descendants swim across the slough, eyes hard as flint. They held their snouts daintily out of the water like sorority girls at a pool party, trying to keep their hair dry. My grandfather called them "conquistador hogs."

Our land—half earth, half water—is one of the secret places of Florida, a hidden vessel of Florida's secret history. It's mostly a secret history because Florida isn't even supposed to have a history: not like Virginia or New Hampshire or France or China. Most people see Florida as a *tabula rasa* and come here to inscribe their fantasies on it. In Florida, life is supposed to be a beach. The beach has no past, only a constant, happy present and the promise of an even sunnier future. Yet despite the best efforts of Henry Flagler, Walt Disney, the U.S. Army Corps of Engineers, U.S. Sugar, Jeb Bush, the St. Joe Company, and everybody else who thinks the place is much improved by draining, dredging, paving, and building, filling up what they see as empty spaces, Florida has a long, long history.

Florida is as old as Stonehenge, as old as Sumer, as old as Rome, as old as the Sphinx, as old as Shakespeare. When the first mud-hut village at Jericho was built, Floridians were using stone tools and ceremonially burying their dead. When Athenians were making exquisite red and black pottery, Floridians were making exquisite incised Deptford pottery. When God-fired masons were raising the stones of the cathedral at Chartres, Floridians were raising the holy mounds on the north shore of Lake Jackson, the biggest almost as tall as a spire. When Catherine the Great was bending all the Russias to her will, William Bartram the naturalist was wandering the territory from the St. Johns to the Suwannee, calling Florida "a glorious apartment in the boundless palace of the Sovereign Creator, inexpressibly beautiful and pleasing." The year that Napoleon Bonaparte was sent into exile on the island of Elba, my great-great-great-grandmother, Jane Broward, was born at Broward's Neck in Spanish east Florida. It was 1814. She was already the third generation of her family to live in Florida.

Do you know where you are? Do you know what lies under your feet as you stand on Florida ground?

Once upon a time swamp was the metaphor for Florida: dismissive, but descriptive. That was back when people understood that Florida was part of the South and could be counted on to have inbred people who might or might not have shoes or electricity or indoor plumbing or the alphabet, plus the added attractions of weird pink birds, palm trees, and toothy amphibians. Slick natives and slick Yankees tried to sell Florida swampland to unslick ones. They said: you can drain it, truck in a little sand, put up a few umbrellas in pretty colors and—*Voila!*—you have Miami Beach. Paradise.

Nowadays the metaphor for Florida is the golf course. We need those satiny rolling acres set off by perfect shrubs and trees, framed like a watercolor landscape, attracting men with money like a dumpster attracts raccoons. We don't just drain the swamp now; we pull the water away to a picturesque "lake," bringing in the right kind of soil, dumping millions of gallons of other water on the grass so that the grass thinks this is England or Scotland; it's infusing that greenness with herbicides, with stuff to keep moles and nematodes at bay, and fertilizers to make it fat and happy. Now developers sell Florida real estate as Edenic dreams. They say: it's eighteen holes, designed by a pro out of Augusta, gated, "homes" (never mere houses) 200K (and up) so as to keep the riff-raff out, a pool and a bike track.

Or SouthWood. SouthWood is the St. Joe Company's model village. It sprang up like a mushroom outside Tallahassee, just off the Camino Real, the Spanish colonial highway we now call the Old St. Augustine Road. The ruins of Verdura, grandest of all the Red Hills plantation houses, lie nearby, five great columns rising out of grapevines. Judge David Macomb raised cotton on a lake here. He called his place "Ben Venue on Loch Acray," a name he got out of Sir Walter Scott, and he once fought a duel over politics with Prince Achille Murat. The prince (a crack shot) didn't kill the judge, just, as he said, "scared the lice out of the judge's shirt." Southwood itself belonged to the Virginian planter George Ward. Later it became part of DuPont grandee Ed Ball's St. Joe empire. Now, with its middle "w" inexplicably capitalized (probably something to do with a focus group), it has been transformed into a so-called "sustainable community," with a cute little shopping street and cute little shops and cute cottagey houses in the "New Urbanist" style that looks like the set for a movie about some front-porchy small-town America full of well-scrubbed middle-class "folks," a place where it never rains till after sundown.

You should see the golf course at SouthWood: green as a rain frog and smooth as a supermodel's thigh. In "Sunshine State," John Sayles's film about blithe destruction, a Yankee retiree armed with a smart mouth and a nine iron delights in Florida as Paradise Sold. Hotels, malls, suburbs, and golf courses have, he says, "civilized" us. Especially golf courses, the ultimate triumph of Middle-class Man over Wilderness. The Yankee retiree calls them "nature on a leash." Before, he says, Florida was just an afterthought hanging off the bottom of America, a backwater often under water, populated by white people who ate catfish.

SouthWood has been planned to within an inch of its survey lines. There's nothing random, nothing eccentric, except the weeds that will, no matter what you do, shove their heads up in the best-regulated rose bed, and the sumac and poison ivy that will, no matter how many chemicals you deploy, creep back like Freud's return of the repressed.

But that's small stuff. SouthWood in macro represents order. This is the way St. Joe means to redraw the map of north Florida—in pastels. The company has one million acres. One million acres of beaches and wetlands and hardwood hammocks and forest and swamps. Those acres may be home to bears and hawks and conquistador hogs; there may be the sites of Apalachee villages or Franciscan missions. But that land needs to turn a profit. So St. Joe will treat its million acres as a mere emptiness, maybe with a pesky infestation of rednecks here and there, crying out for resorts and marinas and condos and houses and roads. St. Joe says they cherish the "quaint" little towns of Carrabelle and Panacea and St. Marks and Port St. Joe, with their oyster shacks and Piggly Wigglys and old gabled houses with bottle-brush plants and lantana in the front yard. But they don't. Those places, those things, belong to the past. There's no money in the past. The money is in the future, in galloping growth, in "re-branding" the place we call the Panhandle as "Florida's Great Northwest" as if to evoke some semi-tropical Seattle. The money is in that new airport—bigger than the international airport in Tampa—that St. Joe wants to build near Panama City on four thousand acres of wetlands and woods, right next to Pine Log State Forest. The money is in the "Gulf Coast Parkway" that St. Joe wants to build across the emerald heart of West Florida, a multi-lane monster connecting U.S. Highway 98 to U.S. Highway 231, bypassing the "quaint" little towns. It won't do for the owner of a $450,000 faux Cape Cod at WindMark to get stuck behind some Cracker's raggedy old pickup.

Peter Rummell, the chairman of St. Joe, used to head Disney's wonderful world of real estate. He calls what he does "regional place-making." He says, "My goal is to create some interesting towns, some interesting places."

And here's us thinking that the places of north Florida were already made; here's us thinking they're pretty interesting, too.

I am one of those catfish-eating white people. I belong to what Gloria Jahoda famously called "the Other Florida," Old Florida, un-Republican Florida, little Florida. The Florida without the golf courses, nature without the leash.

In 1834, Jane Broward married a boy from a neighboring plantation. His name was Rufus Tucker. Instead of expanding the already-expansive Broward and Tucker properties in the St. Johns country, they packed up the wedding presents—a few silver spoons, an old French soup tureen, a couple of slaves—and rode west down the Camino Real. They stopped on the near side of the Ochlockonee. They settled in lower Leon County, what later became Wakulla County. It was 1835, just in time for the Second Seminole War.

Four of Jane Broward and Rufus Tucker's sons joined Florida regiments during the Civil War. Two died in Virginia. Two were part of the Baby Corps, cadets from the West Florida Seminary who fought at the Battle of Natural Bridge. They survived. Their descendants became lighthouse keepers, oystermen, firewatchers, farmers, railway workers, poets, politicians, judges, bus drivers, growers of crazily-ruffled camellias, builders of elegant bridges, and lawyers—lots of lawyers. Almost all of us stayed in Florida, almost all between the Apalachicola and the Aucilla Rivers, near our swamp, near our slough, and handy for our burying ground where the kinfolk lie, some under granite angels carved with hymns, some under a square of oyster shells, white as salt in the sun.

I guess you could call my ancestors developers. They shoved the original inhabitants off the land, cleared it, planted cotton, logged the piney woods, built houses. My great-uncle Malcolm Roberts said that his great-great-grandfather Rufus was "the first white man to cut a tree in Leon County" (a slight exaggeration). But white men have been cutting trees here ever since, to make shopping centers and roads and subdivisions named after whatever was destroyed or driven out to put them there. I guess you could call me a hypocrite. I have benefited from my people's exploitation of the land. And now I want it to stop. Unless you will cherish this place for its oldness and

THE GOLF COURSE AND THE BLACKWATER SLOUGH

wildness and quiet, I want you to stay away. I embrace my hypocrisy: I say not in my back yard. Not in yours, either. If you want a grocery store and a gas station every ten feet, you can get that in Orlando.

And not with my money. Or yours. Developers, especially St. Joe, aren't paying for the lucrative havoc they wreak all by themselves. You are expected to pay for eighty percent of that Panama City airport. And you've put at least $2 million (by now it's probably double that) into the "Gulf Coast Parkway." Peter Rummell and St. Joe give tens of thousands of dollars to the Republican Party of Florida. Governor Jeb Bush isn't very interested in swamps or sloughs or old houses or old books or old trees. Miami is his model of Florida life. Like I said, the past isn't where the cash is. And the people that live in Leon, Franklin, Wakulla, Liberty, Bay, Washington, and Calhoun counties—"Florida's Great Northwest"—well, we aren't such a great source of revenue, either. There aren't many of us, to start with. And most of us are Democrats.

So we'll be cured of our two-lane, "y'all"-saying ways by an influx of rich people from Atlanta, Charlotte, Nashville, Cincinnati, Dallas. St. Joe and the governor—all the developers—they tell us that this is going to be good for us, good for our economy, good for jobs. They say they will "maximize economic opportunity." Maybe so, if waitressing at a chichi WaterColor resort restaurant or scrubbing the beautifully-tiled floors of a WaterMark mansion or groundskeeping at the golf course counts as maximizing economic opportunity. But even if paving over the whole place from St. Marks to Perdido Key would make the over-extended owners of the Piggly Wigglys and the out-of-work shrimpers and the debt-laden peanut farmers all as rich as old Ed Ball himself, would that really compensate for the loss of our history? Our heritage? The beauty of this Other Florida?

It's difficult to manufacture memory. Most people in Florida now come from somewhere else. They never knew that Wal-Mart there as a meadow or that "gated community" there as an oaky hill. And if they knew that Publix there as a pasture, well, it's a pity, but having corn flakes, Bud Lite, Alpo, and sushi only five minutes down the road sure is convenient.

Being born in Florida, coming from a family that's been here since before Florida became American, confers no special status on me or anyone else. It does give us the responsibility of memory. Mine is the last generation that can remember the Conjure Woman—an old lady with a bag of hexes, cures, and charms—on Tallahassee's south side or a mule cart riding down the Old

Bainbridge Road. Mine is the last generation to live without light pollution: on winter evenings the Milky Way arched over our field like a silver rainbow and the Corona Borealis looked like diamonds tangled in the bare limbs of the pecan trees. Mine is the last generation to know the sacramental quiet of Orchard Pond Road, unpaved, carnelian-red: Governor Richard Keith Call, who owned Orchard Pond Plantation in the 1850s, would recognize it.

But more and more the subdivisions and the superstores encroach on it and the night sky is no longer lapis blue but dirty orange. Mine is the last generation to walk on the sand of a deserted and undeveloped beach like the ones the Apalachee knew or that Cabeza de Vaca described in the story of his Florida shipwreck. My Florida is disappearing fast.

Except for the slough. It's still the slough, nut-brown shallows changing to black in the middle, branches interlaced overhead so thick the sun has to shove its way in, hog tracks on the far bank, leading to Mack Island, deer tracks on the near bank, bee hives near the tupelos, hollies, huckleberries, and magnolia trees up on the bluff. The family swamp off the Smith Creek Road is still surrounded by the Apalachicola National Forest and so feels safe—for now. And the moccasins still lounge on the lower limbs and spiral through the dark water.

DIANE ROBERTS *is an eighth-generation Floridian, born and raised in Tallahassee. A commentator for National Public Radio, political columnist for the* St. Petersburg Times, *and occasional contributor to the* New York Times, *the* Times of London, *the British Broadcasting Corporation, and* The New Republic, *she divides her time between Tuscaloosa, where she is Professor of English at the University of Alabama, and Tallahassee, where she lives in a pecan grove. Her third book,* Dream State, A Personal History of Florida, *will be out from Simon and Schuster in October 2004.*

mmmmm mulberries warm in the sun...

enormous
bright green
leaves

Mulberries

Late April

We shook down a purple rain of mulberries this morning from our favorite tree near the creek. My son David climbed high into the canopy, displacing robins and cedar waxwings from the bounty we sought. He took a while to make his way; the mulberry guards its fruit well. It's not an easy tree to ascend. Meanwhile, the rest of us positioned an odd patchwork of tarps and sheets on the grass below. At our signal, David rattled the heavy limbs and the dark sweet berries let go, falling with a rattle and a splat. We ran to claim them one by one, improbably huge and ripe. In the end, our T-shirts, tongues and fingers were inked violet: a sticky, messy, blessed business.

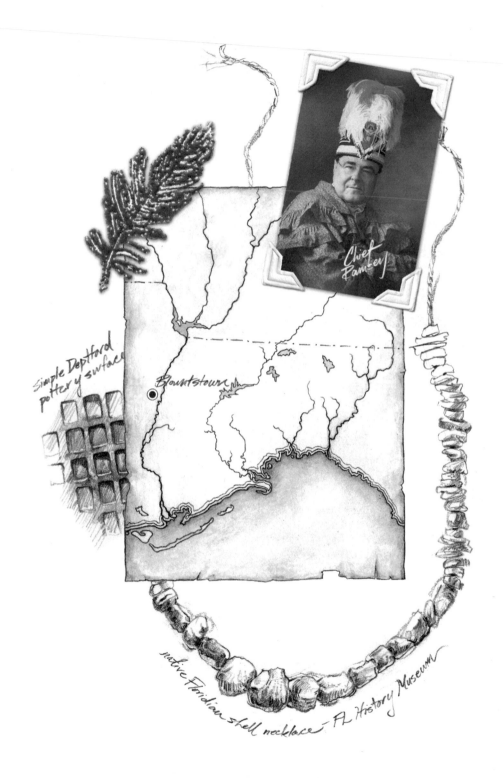

Simple Deptford
pottery surface

Blountstown

Chief
Ramsey

native Floridian shell necklace — FL History Museum

Healing River

FAITH EIDSE

I took my ache to the river, driving west toward the glinting Apalachicola to see Creek Chief Andrew Ramsey on a Friday in November 2002. The water flowing beneath the Bristol-Blountstown Bridge was vast, flat, and reflective, giving back oak and tupelo, maple and black willow. It was a picture larger than my grief, its southern direction sure and constant. It flowed present to future, without doubt or misgiving. Along its margins a blue heron flew, neck tucked, and I understood its caution, as well as its need to fly.

The light was blinding as I pulled into the clean circle drive in Blountstown that had once been the center of a Creek-Muscogee village and absorbed the modern red brick house with white shutters. A huge man emerged, as though he'd anticipated me. Tall, barrel-chested, and dark haired, Chief Ramsey moved deliberately in the morning light, extending an engulfing hand.

It occurred to me as I warmed to Chief Ramsey's kind eyes that there was no one left in the entire river basin more qualified to welcome me to this land than this large Native American. He ushered me into his modern bungalow and I followed, eager to learn what he had endured to welcome me so unconditionally.

I'd just broken a contract to direct the creative writing program at a small college near Pittsburgh. I'd chosen to stay with my family in the Florida Panhandle. The Pennsylvania campus was a green island in a coal-dusted, garage-front town, a mine shaft piercing its gut. My family had blanched at

69

the town's squalor and descended into silence. For six weeks my husband and I pulled in opposite directions until finally, the day the moving trucks were to arrive in Florida, I relented and sent the fax that ended my academic career. In a moment I'd snuffed my expectations. The degrees, awards, and service I'd accumulated could mean nothing without my two growing boys, age eleven and fifteen, and my husband of twenty years by my side.

Anger at my failure to anticipate such an outcome, sorrow at the loss of a dream so close, and depression at letting down mentors and prospective colleagues gripped me. Determined not to sink into a pit, I'd applied for a public information job at a state agency. I was pleased that the job involved interviewing longtime residents of the Apalachicola River and Bay. Perhaps these deeply rooted people could draw me closer to this place.

The day I entered Chief Ramsey's house I'd already spent a year tramping the river valley, talking to the last steamboat pilot of the Apalachicola-Chattahoochee-Flint rivers, the last sharecropper in Jackson County, the first black mayor of Apalachicola, who'd sobbed to recall poll taxes and blacks excluded from polling places.

During travels through the Apalachicola National Forest, I'd been studied by a juvenile bear, standing on its hind legs, feeding on gold leaves at dusk. He'd crossed State Route 65 in front of my rolling cage, gazing at me with onyx eyes, closing the distance between us. I'd been hailed by yellow trumpet pitcher plants full of rainwater, spiders, and frogs. I'd gazed down 300-foot bluffs into a riverbed carved 25 million years before when bear dogs roamed the land. I'd been baptized by thundershowers on the Garden of Eden trail, greeted by star anise and the nearly extinct Florida torreya. Apalachicola tributaries had washed my feet and cooled my body; bay oysters had nourished me. Fishermen and shrimpers had taught me about the Apalachicola's salty gestation. "We came from the water," they said, unified with nature.

I yearned for these people, these pines, these gopher tortoises and pileated woodpeckers to cure my whipsawed heart. They had spent an entire lifetime in one ecosystem; they'd remained despite the advent of paved roads and gasoline engines. Could I, a perennial outsider, absorb their deep identity with this place? Would their geographic permanence translate into peace for my wounded heart?

I took my ache to the river and Creek Chief Ramsey answered. Muscogee chief in one culture, doctor of education in another, he could teach me what it meant to be native. Heir of the Blountstown Piggly Wiggly, he'd also carried on the business his great grandfather had started as "Honest John Ramsey's Rolling Store," the name chosen from thin air.

Descended from the two-hundred-year unbroken line of Tuskiehajo Cochrane, a member of John Blount's clan, Ramsey's people are acknowledged on a bilingual, Muscogee-English, historic marker at the Blountstown courthouse. They avoided Indian removal and death in 1838, hiding near a remote, outlying pond. Florida's March of Tears had been so violently opposed by Creeks and Seminoles that ten thousand died resisting it. Some committed suicide rather than leave the lands that had received their ancestors, or the river that had become their life source and highway.

This attachment to place had been everywhere evident during my year on the river. I had entered a cottage at Prospect Bluff built by a woman whose husband had lost his leg to timbering, a job that had sustained him and his family through the Depression and their childbearing years. I studied the decades of rootedness that covered every surface. The kitchen counters were stacked with tube radios and transistors, the walls hung with primitive wood paintings and studio portraits.

The woman who'd built the cottage, slightly crippled by stroke, was stalwart, determined that the tape recorder capture her husband's story, perhaps sensing he would be gone within the year. "Gatorman," he joked, though his leg and entrails had been smashed by a tree, not a prehistoric reptile. LaVere and Thelma Walker had rallied after his injury, creating and selling conical catfish traps—Walker baskets. One is on display at the Gorrie State Museum in Apalachicola, their contribution already acknowledged by history.

These people had dug in their heels and endured freakish mishap, byzantine social services, no disability payments. They had not loaded the car with their six children and driven for higher ground, cooler breezes, an easier fortune elsewhere. They had remained steadfast through each trial, each tragedy, each setback, loyal to the pine forest and the river that nourished them.

I, on the other hand, had not claimed a sacred land. I had not wrestled against fate to stay rooted and identified with one sheltering tree or a single perennial river. Instead I had wandered. Born and raised the daughter of a

Canadian linguist, in an African village, a place I loved but could not claim, I had moved often. I grew only tentative tendrils, sinking no roots, wary of more loss.

In another sense, I had come full circle. A legacy had been handed down and tradition was being fulfilled as I compiled oral histories. It was a project just like my linguist father's, who'd raised us wandering along the Congo, the Red, and the Hudson rivers. Would this Apalachicola basin, these people, sustain and release me for stronger attachments? Gradually I lulled to the sound of their voices, such a contrast to my staccato life. Their stories calmed the urge to keep launching myself out.

Chief Ramsey's people were "boggots," a Muscogee word meaning the last people and their last refuge. As soldiers were rounding them up to be shipped to Oklahoma, Chief Ramsey's people had taken refuge on Bogg's Pond in central Jackson County, west of the Apalachicola River. To survive, they dug mud from its depths and threw it up on the sand flats to grow corn and okra. Only when Jackson County was opened to timbering a generation later did they emerge to reclaim their homes in central Blountstown.

Portraits hung in the formal entrance: the chief wearing quilted points (Miccosukee) and rounded edges (Muskogee) ceremonial dress. He led me past them, into the family room where three more portraits gazed down upon us, three sons, all conceived, I learned, after his wife, Wisa (Sassafras), was told she could not bear children.

One day while visiting Ramsey's grandmother and great grandmother, Wisa was overcome by menstrual cramps. "Ander," his great grandmother, Cedar Woman, said, "Go get me some cedar bark." Ramsey pulled on his jacket and hiked into the cold river valley. His petite grandmother used to carry him piggyback into these river sloughs, wading deeper and deeper until, gazing down, all he could see was the top of her head and her nose above water. That's how they had survived for decades, the grandmother teaching the boy her Muscogee language and taking him to her fishing holes. It was his job to gather wood and kindling and start a fire on shore as she cleaned fish. He'd dip water from the river for her coffee, he said, something he would no longer do for fear of contaminants. He'd bring the water to a boil and plunge in a muslin cloth containing ground beans.

In recent years he'd begun carrying her piggyback to her favorite fishing holes, the cycles turning, renewing themselves on this river, in this place, through each generation. And yet the promise of children had eluded him and Wisa.

Ramsey returned to the warm house where Cedar Woman had already boiled the water. Wisa gazed at him with dark eyes, and smiled through her pain, her thick black hair shining in the lamplight. She took the mug Cedar Woman offered her, stiffening a moment with cramp, and breathed in the resinous aroma. Then she sipped the steaming tea and drank more deeply. Finally the cramps subsided.

Wisa said, "Thank you, Granny, that's the most wonderful drink I ever took." Cedar Woman said, "I don't know if you're going to think it's so wonderful. You're going to be pregnant in 4 to 6 weeks." Wisa laughed and said, "Granny, the doctor said I can't have any children."

Within four weeks the couple had conceived their first child, a son. Two more boys followed, and the children were raised as members of two cultures. Native and white cultures offered separate and contrasting promise. One provided western education and monetary gain, the other offered hearth and devotion to the land. It was complicated growing up as cultural nomads, shuttling between shoes-on classrooms and barefoot fishing in the river.
And yet the boys could not risk getting stuck in either place. At school they had to make frequent eye contact and speak up in order to pass. Among Muscogees they were expected to avert their eyes, shun speech, and walk softly. They were not free to act Muscogee among Euro-Americans; in public their Muscogee culture was despised. At home it was valued and preserved. The boys were groomed to be community leaders and successor chiefs. One son could not reconcile the pressure of always feeling like an outsider. "We had our son to commit suicide," his father said. "The biggest tragedy of the modern day Indian is suicide."

Her husband, Wisa said, was the target of animosity during a springtime Tallahassee parade. He was representing the Creek's long history in Florida, riding alongside an Andrew Jackson figurehead. Perhaps the Andrew Jackson protestors who called him down did not know that Andrew Ramsey was a real chief. Wisa's eyes flashed at the recollection; Ramsey said sadly, "It was the only time I was called a name."

Wisa called us to the table. I had not intended to invite myself to lunch and yet they insisted, firmly. Wisa, recuperating from surgery to ease arthritic knees, approached the table carefully, carrying boiled potatoes, chicken, and okra. She glowed with the success of her new knee caps, but sat down heavily, with a sigh, to rest.

"In the Indian religion we do not hold grudges," Ramsey said. He had long ago forgiven the men who invaded his ancestral village. "You know someone was raised an Indian if they don't hold a grudge. You go to the quicken post and you beat it and you throw it into the sacred fire. It's like the Christian religion; you forgive seventy times seventy times seventy. It's just endless."

Ramsey added that the settler grave across the river at Sycamore Cemetery marked, "The Last Indian Massacre," was probably "my people coming south. That was a time when we were being expelled from our homes," he said. The bottomlands the Creeks had cleared for planting were increasingly coveted as settlers moved south and west. In some cases Creek chiefs negotiated sales right from under their own clansmen but, usually, there was no negotiation.

A treaty signed at the Duval House in Tallahassee left Chiefs Blount and Cochrane (Ramsey's great-great grandfather) only the houses and lands they lived on in Blountstown. They had given up many acres for a promise of peace. But no sooner did they abandon their guns in friendship than their homes were raided by settlers, their slaves and children kidnapped, and their livestock stolen. Fleeing to Indian Territory, or hiding out, looked better than staying on a river highway where whites forgot their promises and Seminoles attacked them as enemies.

Chief Ramsey gazed through a lens full of suffering and bloodshed. But he paused to sing a prayer in Muscogee before eating, "Our creator who lives above all things but you're everywhere all the time, our creator you made the earth and everything in it. We thank you for this food. . . . "

"I am disciplined in the Creek and the Christian religions," he said, passing the chicken. An earthen mound at the center of the ceremonial grounds is layered in ordered levels. At its center, he said, is his grandmother's Bible. "Ours is the only mound with a Bible in it." His dark eyes softened as he thought of her. He had lost, and received, so much.

His sons are Bird Clan, like their mother, he explained. He is Wind Clan; the society is matrilineal. To marry someone from your own clan would be incest, but if you find someone from a different clan—he nudged his wife playfully, eliciting a dark-eyed giggle—"You get busy."

FAITH EIDSE

Ramsey got up from the table and led me behind the house to his bird yard. His wife is from the Aucilla River, he said. Her people gave up their ways to survive. Chickens, ducks, and a large black swan roam among large chicken wire enclosures, splashing fountains and bright impatiens. "I don't like cages," Ramsey said, "I grew up with the forest being everyone's, the river being everyone's." I nodded, knowing that none of us will likely be so free, or belong to a place so completely, again.

Ramsey shook my hand and then lingered under the oaks of his two-hundred-year-old homeplace as I backed out. I too would have to accept my situation and find my permanence and happiness as he had. I drove past the Amish furniture store going out of business, past the closed Five and Dime, and started across the bridge for home. Beat the quickening post and throw it into the flame, the chief had said.

The Apalachicola was a broad dark ribbon flowing between steep banks, sand bars, and vast forests. I had begun storing images of it like a doting parent or a besotted lover. I was ready to thank my family for holding me here. What was left of my resentment was like a tiny pebble, all that was left of the huge ache I'd started with that year. If Creek Chief Ramsey could do it, I could too. I could forgive seventy times seventy times seventy. I took my ache to the river, clutched it to me, and then arced it far into the water. It merged and was gone. The river swallowed it whole.

FAITH EIDSE *grew up in Congo/Zaire, Canada, and the United States, daughter of a Mennonite linguist and tropical medicine nurse. While obtaining her PhD at Florida State University, she won a Kingsbury fellowship and was nominated for the Bellwether prize for a first socially critical novel. She co-edited* Unrooted Childhoods: Memoirs of Growing Up Global *(Nicholas Brealey Publishing, London) and has appeared in several other volumes:* Swaying: Essays on Intercultural Love *and* Growing Up Elsewhere *(both Iowa Press titles). She has reported for the* Virginia Gazette *(Williamsburg) and* The Carillon *(Canada), was editor of* The Sunday Independent *(Acton, MA), and has been a* Tallahassee Democrat *community columnist and contributing writer.*

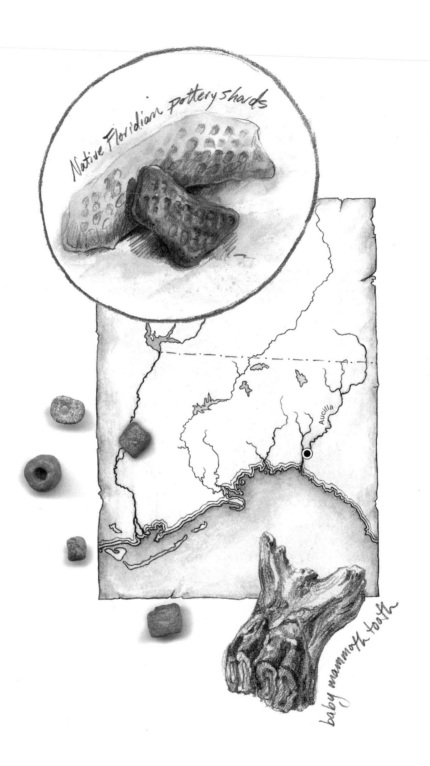

Native Floridian pottery shards

Aucilla

baby mammoth tooth

Aucilla River Time Machine

S. David Webb

My state of mind during the evening campfire was not what I had expected. This was the third day of our first field season on the Aucilla River Prehistory Project. So far, we had smoothly rotated three crews of scuba divers to the bottom of the river, troweling two-by-three meter rectangular test pits and taking samples and pictures at ten centimeter intervals or at natural breaks in the sediments. Our new divers were gaining confidence, and although tangible scientific results were meager, our prospects for success were perfectly sound. Yet I felt bewildered rather than exhilarated. What was this deep foreboding I felt?

I chatted briefly with my crew, and then, mumbling that I was the oldest, headed off to bed. Some hours later, a murky image emerged in my sleeping mind as if it crept up from the bottom mud we had excavated that afternoon. It was a human form framed against dark woods, a long-haired silhouette that seemed to wave; I sensed that he or she was not unfriendly. I startled awake. Had this vision come from somewhere deep within my unconscious? Or was this truly a pathway into the past?

All in a rush I realized the nature of my earlier foreboding: it concerned the invasion of the past. In a generic sense, this is the ethical quandary that confronts every archaeologist. But it was arising now in my own body, more organically than I had known in academic settings, wholly unbidden and wholly unexpected. In the torturous hours before I rose to the welcome morning smells of coffee and bacon, I reached two resolutions. First, I must continue to guide my crew on our march into the past, practicing our archaeological investigations with the greatest integrity. Secondly, I determined to work in every way possible to foster my personal connection with the past.

As the end of the first month approached, our team demonstrated on a daily basis that excavations can be conducted as meticulously in dark river water as on land. There were differences, of course: we invested far greater amounts of time and equipment to recover our samples and our data. Proper visibility alone required that one of the two divers in each team position a thousand-watt light to illuminate the work area and to minimize back-scatter in our silty tea medium. Our absolute commitment to safety, even before science, dictated that half our crew was engaged in support functions such as safety divers and equipment monitors. All of these inefficiencies, however essential, caused me concern about the substance of our scientific discoveries. The darkness of our workplace seemed a metaphor for the obscurity of our enterprise. If the primary objectives were safely and productively fielding a team of underwater archaeologists, we were successful beyond our highest hopes. But I had to admit to myself that any real illumination of the lifeways of the first Floridians had thus far eluded us.

Just a few days before the end of our field season, Buddy Page, our lead diver and a former U.S. Navy Seal, proposed to lead us to a deep hole upriver near the middle of Aucilla's Half-Mile Rise, informally known as "Booger Hole." It took an entire day to redeploy our equipment one mile by road and another three hundred yards by river to the location of the mysterious new site. Still another long day using airlift dredges was required to blow downstream the masses of decayed vegetation that filled the hole.

On the third day at "Booger Hole," we marked out a crude test pit and began excavating within the deepest part of the river. Immediately we began to spot numerous large bones. Sunlight filtering through the dark river water, rich in tannic and humic acids, suffused the ancient bones in mysterious tones of red and orange. Suspensions of silt swirled like windy veils in the shifting bottom currents. We carefully trowelled and brushed away the dark river silt in which the bones were buried, and mapped and photographed them.

S. David Webb

On the second dive of the fourth day, I gently lifted one of the large bones into my extended arms. Turning my mask from side to side, I realized that I held the radius of a mammoth, the lighter of the two bones that made up the animal's forelimb. I easily recognized the bowed shape that allowed it to rotate around the heavier ulna. As I turned it to view the convex anterior face, aided by the magnifying effect of the water, I was surprised to see that the outer cortex was worn almost through, partly exposing the marrow cavity. And then as I examined the bone from left to right, pondering its origin, I realized that it was broken, and lacked the distal third of its length.

At that moment a curtain of silt obscured my view. As I stared intently, waiting for the water to clear, a vision of a woman emerged from the darkness. She picked up an intact mammoth radius bone and began scraping a hide. She yelled strange sounds to a child seated nearby. Then she gave a hard thrust to the radius and I saw it snap. The longer piece fell to the ground; she stared at the distal end remaining in her hand. Even as I squinted in the back-scattered light to take in more of this scene, the woman and child faded into the darkness of the river sediments, and I was left astonished, cradling that same bone in my hands.

Among those yeomen divers who had stayed beyond the end of the first season and closed up camp, all doubts about our capabilities were answered. The earlier concerns we had about our methods were completely eclipsed by our keen excitement over the unique discoveries that were now falling into our hands in the depths of this quiet blackwater river. Still, we had no idea at that time that the Aucilla River eventually would be recognized and honored as a unique treasure trove of stratified prehistoric records, yielding lithics, wood, bones, teeth, hair, and even hormones.

For granting agencies to send us back for another diving season we would need to show that our underwater excavations and data recovery methods were concise, and that we had begun to recover key evidence of early human lifeways. We were certain we had accomplished both. But there were two further criteria that we would also need to meet, and these were not yet assured. First, we needed carbon dates from the Paleo-Indian time period, about twelve thousand years ago, based on organic material directly associated with our samples. Secondly, the carbon dates must be stacked in the correct sequence, with more modern dates from strata above and more ancient dates from those below. We had spent every bit of funding we had to get through the inaugural season, but we begged from our well-wishers enough money to send off six samples, three to Tucson and three to Miami, for carbon dates.

The sophisticated tests revealed that samples on which we'd recovered dates were indeed old enough and in correct stratigraphic order. We were thrilled three months later to receive full support from the National Geographic Society, enabling us to begin our first full season in "Booger Hole," now known by its formal name as the Page/Ladson Site. For the next ten years, our crews excavated many meters of ancient sediments, fine silts, and organic muds, rich in flora, fauna, and prehistoric cultures. These layers stepped up and down through time, like the pages of a book, ultimately revealing evidence of ten millennia, beginning about eighteen thousand years ago. We dubbed the main excavation, cut into the north bank of the river, "the stairway into the past."

Some seasons during the ensuing decade of field work, we got a jump on the summer rains, and then we could explore with relatively clear visibility. Pairs of divers slowly perused the bottom, linked by their chains of bubbles to surface support teams following above in boats. In this way we discovered new Paleo-Indian sites up and down the Aucilla. Over and over, our work confirmed that ancient sites containing diagnostic specimens of Ice Age peoples and extinct animals were regularly associated with deep holes in the river bottom. Originally, these had been quiet sinkhole ponds scattered through the relatively dry coastal lowlands, about one hundred miles from the coast. Nothing like the present river system ran into the Gulf back then. Later we determined that these had been watering holes and, thus, focal points for all manner of life. They had slowly filled with fine-grained sediments, a few millimeters per century. By the time the water table had finally risen enough to inaugurate a flowing Aucilla, driven by the rising sea level at the end of the last Ice Age, the Paleo-Indian peoples had long since disappeared.

The arrival of new peoples in the New World, including coastal Florida, coincided with the time of rapidly changing climate and steeply rising water tables. Of course these changes happened imperceptibly, and even from generation to generation. Most likely, a few of the oldest and most observant people noted the steady trends in environmental signals and were able to suggest the means to adapt.

At one of the new sites, some miles downriver from Page/Ladson, we

S. David Webb

discovered a number of finely worked pieces of mastodon ivory. A few complete ivory implements measured more than a foot in length, and one broken piece was even longer. Excited by these finds, we extended our season well into the summer, even though summer rains had begun to darken the water and stiffen the current. In order to prevent divers from drifting downriver, we deployed ropes from the dive boat to the work site. Toward the end of such an afternoon dive, I found myself trying to maintain a stable position in the water and keep my fins out of the excavation site. I arched my back, raising my masked visage upward toward the adjacent bank. At that moment I glimpsed a man seated with his legs crossed, with both hands clenching a gleaming white cylinder. I could see that it was an elegantly smoothed shaft of fresh ivory. Very deftly, with a dark chert graver, he inscribed a series of short lines, first up to the right, turning sharply, and then left and down, forming a zigzag pattern. Almost as soon as he finished, he began again, repeating the motion, adding seven more continuous strokes. The whole pattern resembled a stroke of lightning. I watched the man contemplate his work with intense reverence and then pass it to his left to a much younger man, perhaps an apprentice. Then, a shift of the current twisted my view back to my work site.

I began to realize that my glimpses of ancient people were associated only with deep holes where the river had accumulated a standing sequence of ancient sediments. And in most such instances, the phenomenon that I like to call my "Time Machine" seemed to be triggered by my intense interest in a specimen that would then connect me with a scene from the past.

One day, during one of our last seasons at Page/Ladson, I completed a morning dive and had taken a shift working the floating screen deck. I basked in the warm afternoon sun, enjoying the cool spray from the four-inch dredge as it spewed a slurry of sediments and their ancient contents over my screen. I picked through these materials, bagging promising fragments and sweeping the rest into the dark effluvial trace downstream. Even though divers on the bottom spotted most of our key finds, still the "screenmeister" above got a second look and could occasionally pick up an item of great significance that had slipped past, quickly vacuumed by the airlift. It was also possible for an experienced eye, working the materials that came topside, to gain a more general perspective than could the primary excavators working many feet below. On this particular afternoon I realized that another of my senses operated better at the river's surface—my sense of smell. The prevailing sediment I had recorded on the screen was peat, an aged and gently altered mass of plant matter. I had salvaged a number of kinds of seeds, including several that looked like watermelon seeds. But there was something more—an odd aroma that nagged at my consciousness each time a large bolus of peat burst onto the upstream end of my screen.

That evening I reviewed my thoughts from the balmy afternoon at the interface of sun and river. First I recalled that smell, somehow more like "hospital" than decayed vegetation. I recalled that the bulk of the peat had a yellowish tinge, like dried hay. Nobody on the bottom could have sensed either the hue or the scent. I asked two experienced student divers what they thought of the peaty environment we had excavated, but they were more intrigued with what we were finding within the peat, in particular a light- and dark-gray-striped piece of chert. It had evidently been flaked three times, and probably served as a tool, perhaps a crude knife.

Sometime in the early morning hours I half-woke, aroused by the return of that scent from the afternoon. I floundered in a strange yellow fog, as if I myself had been hurled upward out of the dredge pipe onto the screen. A profound sensitivity overtook my olfactory lobes, the most primitive part of the brain, and hung there demanding an answer. And then it came to me: the yellow hue and the hormonal aroma were as much animal as vegetable. The mass of peat had come from the stomach of a large herbivore. It had flowed onto my screen, pure and voluminous for more than an hour, from the depths of the past into the warm light of the summer sun. The pond where the Paleo-Indian lived had also become the death scene of a herd of mastodons. We had uncovered evidence that the great beasts had gorged on gourds and browsed on at least a dozen kinds of trees. But later, when they went to wash it all down with a drink, many of them had been ambushed. The piece of chert was a skinning knife, lost on the same occasion. I felt deeply privileged to share this scenario with my dive buddies over breakfast.

Fifteen years and nearly thirty seasons of delving into the depths of the Aucilla River have passed. And I still wonder what it all means. Last fall I drove with two students and a colleague together to a vast conference in Chicago to give papers on our Aucilla River work. As we passed through the glacial moraines of northern Indiana, we wondered whether our discoveries from the south would be understood among our academic peers. My advice to

S. David Webb

each of us was to present the evidence clearly and limit our interpretations to the most evident and logical inferences. Cloak yourself respectably in the garb of a scientist.

But as I catnapped in the back seat, I felt deeply discomforted by the echo of my own advice. Why hold back? These results were hard won and solidly based in science, some three thousand hours of volunteer and student labor. So I roused myself from the back and amended my advice. Yes, the unadorned data would do very well for the first half of our presentations. But then we must fully present our final interpretations, which could be based on whatever thought processes we had developed. We were the ones who had uncovered and studied these most ancient artifacts. Would I claim my visions as observations? Probably not. Were they gifts to us from the past? Perhaps. In any event, we would present our results with the force of these exceptionally key insights that drove well-supported hypotheses.

I still wonder about my "Time Machine" experiences, those deep fluxes of ideas that bind all these bits of evidence together. How did we gain these insights into ancient peoples' lives? Were those epiphanies that arose in the night and in the dark abyss legitimate? Do those lifelike visions of the past really count? When the deep well of the unconscious brain pours out scenes from the past, how do we separate research from exploration?

In the long run science is a cumulative process. It is subject to replication and reinforcement from sister disciplines. And so I remain proud of our team's findings, including the more fully embroidered presentations we have offered. Those of us who were fortunate enough to have witnessed these critical prehistorical vignettes are committed to conveying these remarkable glimpses of the first Floridians seen at the richest and most detailed time capsule in the eastern Gulf of Mexico.

Postscript: This story is based on my recollections of actual episodes in archaeological and paleontological research in the Aucilla River. Jim Dunbar and I initiated the Aucilla River Prehistory Project in 1984. Our team completed its last field excavations in 1999. Many scholars continue to produce publications on the materials collected during those seasons. The field data and archival material are maintained at our two institutions, the Florida Museum of Natural History at the University of Florida in Gainesville, and at the Bureau of Archaeological Research in Tallahassee.

S. David Webb, PhD, *is Distinguished Research Curator of Fossil Vertebrates at the Florida Museum of Natural History, University of Florida, Gainesville, Florida. He is also Distinguished Research Professor of Zoology and Geology. He received his undergraduate degree at Cornell University and his graduate degrees at the University of California at Berkeley. He has published over two hundred scientific papers and monographs as well as three books. One of these books,* Pleistocene Mammals of Florida, *published in 1974, did much to encourage underwater paleontology in Florida. Besides Berkeley and Gainesville, Dr. Webb has taught and lectured at Yale University, University of Michigan, and University of Chicago. He has received fellowships from the National Science Foundation and the Guggenheim Foundation.*

With James S. Dunbar of the Bureau of Archaeological Research in Tallahassee, Dr. Webb initiated the Aucilla River Prehistory Project in 1984. The most succinct summary of that project's results appears as a two-page restored view of the First Floridians in National Geographic's *December 2000 issue in the article, "Peopling of the Americas."*

S. David Webb

84

left behind by previous residents

AUCILLA RIVER TIME MACHINE

Yellow-breasted Chat

We headed out to Tall Timbers Research Station to look for yellow-breasted chats with our friend, ornithologist Todd Engstrom. The trip was a birthday present for my bird-loving nephew, Garrett, who, with my son David, hoped to add this secretive warbler to his life list of birds. As we moved slowly through the old pines, easing toward the brushy habitat preferred by chats, birdsong poured down from the sky. Todd quizzed us, tuning up our ears—the voices of birds coupled with a practiced ear are generally the best tools for identifying them in the field.

"Parula warbler," we named. "Pine warbler, great crested flycatcher, red-bellied woodpecker. Northern bobwhite."

"What about that one?" Todd asked, gesturing in the direction of a two-phrased call.

"Yellow-throated vireo," said my nephew Garrett, quickly, before I could shuffle a match between song and name.

"Good," nodded Todd.

We climbed out of the truck, and where Todd stood became the center, his arms the connections between human knowing and the hidden birds sounding in the airy woods all around. He stood at the heart of all that a lifetime of paying close attention in the woods had brought him, the knowledge of each avian voice, without hesitation.

"Indigo bunting." Right arm toward the west, paired notes, long phrasing. "Blue grosbeak."

A slurred pee-e-wee: "Eastern pewee."

"Ground dove." Different from the common mourning dove, a single, distinct coo.

Each song I have learned before. Some I hear only once or twice a year, others daily. The neurons linking memory and name fire fast or slowly, depending on intimacy, mine, with each bird's call.

"Yellow-breasted chat!" Todd signaled. There it was, and the boys were happy, plunging off into the brush to see the bird, for that is how they love to keep their lists.

"Orchard oriole," says Todd, arm directed high, east. I do not even pick out the notes from the rest, at all.

"Where, where?" I ask, and Todd is quiet and we wait.

"There," he says again, chopping his extended arm more precisely in the direction of the bird's singing.

I'm frustrated at how barely the oriole's song registers in my brain. I am eager to memorize its notes, but how can I, when I hear it so infrequently? The danger is this: if I cannot hear the bird, or don't see it, in a sense, it doesn't exist. How can I advocate for the protection of its habitat, the things it requires to live, if I don't even know when I'm in its presence? The bird must sing. We must hear it call and be able to name the animal and what it needs. Then it is time for our voices. Our responding. Our protection of their lives.

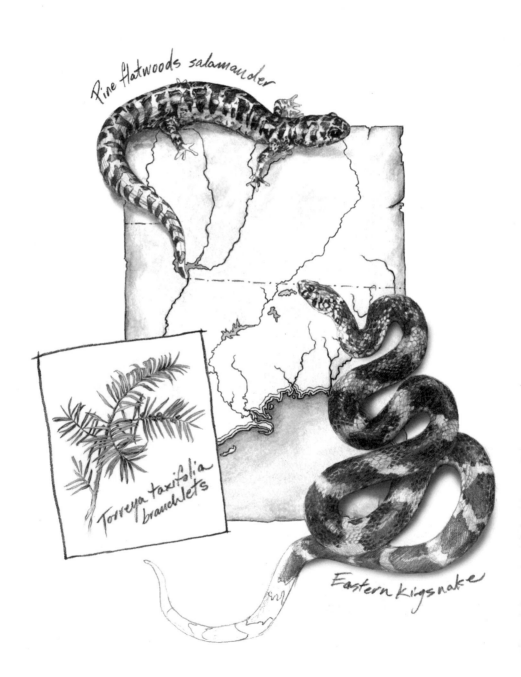

Pine flatwoods salamander

Torreya taxifolia
branchlets

Eastern kigsnake

Ghosts of the Red Hills

D. BRUCE MEANS, PhD

I got my first glimpse of Tallahassee in August of 1961 while approaching the Capitol from Apalachee Parkway. The skyline then was the silver dome of the 1947 Capitol building peeking through live oaks. Apalachee Parkway was a two-lane road. I was nineteen, married, and looking forward to my first undergraduate classes at Florida State University (FSU).

We made a right turn and drove our powder-blue 1957 Chevrolet through the heart of town, past McCrory's dime store with its creaky wooden floors, the State Theatre half a block down College Avenue, and the Floridian Hotel on the corner of Call and Monroe streets. Beyond Lake Ella we were out in the country. There were no malls then, nor Capital Circle, nor Interstate 10, nor convenience stores, nor alcoholic beverages for sale. Tallahassee's population was about 48,000. Now it's 159,000.

Agriculture was the mainstay of the Leon County economy in 1961. One could drive anywhere north of town in the Red Hills and encounter cornfields, watermelons, and tobacco. Two-story, red tobacco barns dotted the countryside from Chattahoochee to Monticello. South of Tallahassee we swam in Blue Sink, when its waters were sky blue instead of pea-green with contamination from Tallahassee's stormwater runoff through Lake Munson. The highlight of the week was a drive-in movie followed by a milkshake and hamburger at the Corral on South Monroe Street where carhops dressed in cowboy clothes suspended our food on half-raised car windows. Once a month we might splurge and have fried chicken at Tucker's Four Points Restaurant. A formal dinner could be had at the ritzy Talquin Inn way out Tennessee Street just before you reached the Seaboard Railroad underpass.

While helping BBC Television film a wild-caught Virginia opossum in the Apalachicola National Forest off Springhill Road, I was grousing about human overpopulation and the alarming extinctions that are taking place globally as a consequence. The show's host, David Attenborough, looked up and startled me with a challenge: "Name five species that man has caused to go extinct in the past twenty years!" I struggled to think of some, but was mentally blocked by what seemed an out-of-character challenge by one of the world's greatest champions of nature. While I was stammering, "Uh, uh, uh," Attenborough interrupted, "I ask that because we must be careful not to cry wolf. If we can't give the public examples, although hundreds of species of rainforest insects may be going extinct each year, our cries of alarm may go unbelieved."

Attenborough's challenge frustrated me. Like so many people living in north Florida who haven't had my experiences and insights, he was unaware of my painful burden of knowledge about local environmental problems and the decline of things I have loved and witnessed passing. I can't quickly recite a litany of species that have gone extinct in the past twenty years, but we really have lost a lot of the quality of original nature that once so richly endowed the Tallahassee area. Too many species and ecosystems such as those I have studied over four decades have disappeared, declined, or become severely degraded locally.

Holding Dick Ohmes's left wrist in my right hand and pinching my nose with my left, I sank into the eerie, black waters of Sloth Hole under the Aucilla River. It was late November 1970, and the water was cold. This was my first plunge underwater using scuba and I was apprehensive. Very quickly daylight faded as we dropped into the inky, tannic waters. I didn't have time to be frightened, however, because I was preoccupied with blowing air into my eustachian tubes to equalize the increasingly painful pressure on my eardrums. I got a chill as we passed into colder water under a thermocline and everything went pitch-black. The silence was so noticeable you could almost hear it,

D. Bruce Means, PhD

except for the rhythmical intake of pressurized air in and out of my lungs that sounded like the breathing of Darth Vader. I had a sensation of falling, as indeed I was. Soon, my outstretched arms and legs, bent slightly at the knees, passed into a fluffy ooze and my body came to a soft rest.

Dr. Ohmes had prepared me for what was to happen next, but it was more dramatic than I anticipated. He took my right hand and placed it on a wire-screen bucket that was attached to a forty-foot-long inch-diameter rope tied to an inner tube floating above us. This was to be our lifeline to the surface, and the bucket was there to carry our treasures to the boat. I reached out with my left hand and gingerly pressed it into the soft ooze. My fingers touched something like hard cobbles under the cold slime. It didn't feel like rotting wood. It was bones and teeth. In the blackness and the silence, I forgot all my trepidation about the newness of scuba diving. I swung my hand in a wide arc. Everywhere I felt bones . . . long bones of legs, some short fragments half broken, skinny bones, fat bones, vertebrae, a few big bones, and lots of little chunks of all dimensions. I scraped up a handful and let the bones drop into the bucket.

Back on the surface we carefully picked through five gallons of black, shiny bones. Many were of deer. Lots were of turtles. Alligator scutes and teeth were common. Then I found a horse tooth, but it had not been in the mouth of a horse introduced by the Spaniards. It was an ancestral horse, one whose descendents had migrated across Asia to Europe then became extinct in the North American homeland. Then a beautiful polished tooth from an animal today living in Central America, the tapir. Then a scute from a giant ground sloth.

On my first day scuba diving with Ohmes, we found the jaw of a small cat that later was named as a species new to science, and bones of the mastodon, peccary, ground sloth, and dire wolf. I had been invited to dive with Dick because of my love of Pleistocene fossils, which we found in abundance. Dick had his own reason for diving. He was keen on human artifacts. In our time together he recovered a few pieces of ivory foreshafts made by human hands from fresh ivory of a mastodon or mammoth. One day after Dick had picked from our bucket's spoils an especially perfect fluted Clovis point, I fondled it closely and felt its exquisite manufacture from local chert, a flintlike rock that is abundant along the Aucilla River. On one of my later dives with Dick, I pushed my hand into the soft bottom sediments back up under a large, dead tree that had fallen into the water and felt a strange bone—flat, with one edge smooth and the other jagged. When I surfaced with it I was thrilled to find the lower jaw of a giant Florida lion in my hand; the jagged edge was the carnassial, or meat-shearing molars. In the pitch-blackness at the bottom of the river, I was constantly thinking about what all these bones and human artifacts meant.

At this very place, more than ten thousand years ago, at the edge of what then may have been a large watering hole, animals played out their roles as predator and prey, much as similar giant mammals do today in the savannahs of Africa. All around me where I probed the bottom sediments, humans had feasted on giant mammals they killed there. Because bones deteriorate much faster in air than in water, one can't find such evidence on the surface of the ground that Florida was a paradise for more than forty-five extinct mammals. Ten thousand years ago may seem like a long time, but lying on the bone bed of Sloth Hole and feeling all those intact remains transported my thoughts right back into their time frame. Being able to touch and feel those bones in their natural resting place brought the extinct animals alive for me. Tapirs, horses, llamas, capybaras, and peccaries still roam the globe, although not in Florida for at least ten millennia. Mammoths, mastodons, ground sloths, glyptodonts, saber-toothed tigers, dire wolves, giant tortoises, and giant beavers are gone forever, and yet, I know they have been here.

In a deep ravine that cut into the escarpment running along the Apalachicola River, I stood looking down at a thirty-foot-long dead tree, straight as an arrow, with no bark but lots of stiff lateral branches. The main stem was streaked with parallel, inch-deep furrows running down its long axis. Its spongy outer wood was gray, but with my pocketknife, I scraped down to undecomposed wood with an unusually bright yellow color. The wood had a peculiar, offensive smell, reminiscent of iodine.

"That's the skeleton of a torreya tree," said my companion and renowned botanist, Bob Godfrey, between puffs on his pipe, "and this sucker over here," he said, pointing to a thirty-inch high shoot with dark green, flat, prickly leaves, "is about all that's left of the species."

Dr. Bob, as he was affectionately known by his admirers, told me that in 1962—only eight years earlier—he had reported in *Science* magazine, "On the original sites there remain but a scattering of skeleton trunks, a few of which

D. BRUCE MEANS, PHD

have abortive sprouts at their bases . . . it seems clear that the relict Florida torreya, known to professional botanists throughout the world, and locally of significant general interest, is even now all but extinct in its natural habitat." I never got to see an adult torreya tree in the wild. The suckers and the rotting dead trees are now, in 2003, all but gone. Soon you won't be able to see even these evidences that a small area about twenty miles long by one mile wide in north Florida was the sole home of this endemic conifer.

The world's largest woodpecker, the ivory-billed, hasn't been gone long from our area, according to a fascinating passage from the diary of Harry Beadel of Tall Timbers Plantation in northern Leon County. One pleasant day in late March 1894, Harry and brother Gerald made a long, thirteen-hour surrey ride down Meridian Road from the north shore of Lake Iamonia to Wakulla Springs, and back. Harry was building his egg collection, a hobby of naturalists of his day. His diary recounts, "Least Bitterns and Little Green Herons would jump from the bushes with queer squawks and hurry off among the cypresses as though possessed. Gallinules and coots darted out at every corner. Black Vultures dotted the gnarled cypress limbs . . . an Alligator flopped off a log . . . heard an Ivory Bill Woodpecker." The ivorybill was common enough to rate only a passing comment.

Beadel's friend, Herb Stoddard, was the consummate ornithologist. His studies of the bobwhite quail and the WCTV television tower bird kills are classics, but what he didn't publish shows that he had great depth of character, too. In the spring of 1952, Stoddard—whose bird-identifying skills were unimpeachable—saw two female ivorybills together in southern Thomas County, Georgia, not too far north of the Leon County, Florida, line. Stoddard kept the observation secret to protect the birds; his sighting was probably the very last of the species in this region.

My love of salamanders often takes me out on winter nights during the passage of winter frontal systems. In advance of the cold front is always a cold rain, the stimulus that triggers breeding migrations in four species of large, chubby salamanders about which we know very little, even their geographic distributions in north Florida. The reason we know so little about them is because they are secretive burrowers for most of the year, and when they choose to be above ground when we might see them, it is always at night in a cold rain in midwinter–the very times we choose to be snuggled warmly inside our homes and beds. I began driving a circuit in the Red Hills looking for the tiger salamander in the winter of 1966. I drove the small, two-lane paved roads out of Tallahassee, going up Centerville Road to Bradfordville/Roberts/Crump Road and back to Tallahassee down Miccosukee Road.

After about three such winters and about twenty night road cruises, I discovered that the best and most reliable population, where I saw the most of these giant, eight-inch amphibians, was inside the Tallahassee city limits at the intersection of Centerville Road and Doomar Drive. Every cold December and January rain, I could always find these yellow-blotched, black animals—tiger salamanders—moving into Goose Pond on the west side of Centerville Road. It was not uncommon to see four or five individuals during only a few back-and-forth passes in the four-block-long area between what is now the Centerville post office and Woodgate Way. In those days, the late 1960s and 1970s, there were no homes or businesses along Centerville Road. All I remember is mixed pines and hardwoods on either side of the road and live oaks overhanging it.

Now Centerville Road is heavily trafficked and the woodlands along the road at its intersection with Doomar Drive are all built up with homes and lawns, no longer the habitat of tiger salamanders. The pond has been deepened and the small, woodland stream leading into it has been channelized and its margins clear-cut. Where tiger salamanders once burrowed in soft red clay soil under pines, I now pay regular visits to the sprawling Capital Health Care complex to get my body and eyes fixed when they are in trouble. If there were any tiger salamanders left, the Blairstone Road extension, which terminates at this intersection, is the final death knell of these rare animals. Neither I nor others whom I have told about this once-special place have seen a tiger salamander crossing Centerville Road at Doomar Drive for at least twenty years. Nor do we expect to ever again.

In those days I was also curious about a strange amphibian called the flatwoods salamander. Finding none after a few winters on those same cold December and January nights when I road cruised for tiger salamanders, I started cruising earlier in the season and made a publishable discovery. The flatwoods salamander migrates during the passage of cold fronts in October and November, two months earlier than the tiger salamander. On a lonely 2.5-mile stretch of Florida Route 12 in 1970 in Liberty County I was dazzled by

D. BRUCE MEANS, PHD

nightly migrations of two to three hundred adults. Most were moving east to west from longleaf pine forest into a large wet flatwoods of carnivorous plants and scattered cypress ponds in which they sought to breed and lay their eggs.

I studied this migration on many nights from 1970 to1972, recording which direction each salamander was moving, exactly where on the road it crossed, its sex, and other information. Just as I finished this project, the wet flat was bedded and planted to slash pines. Twenty years later a colleague, John Palis, and I returned to learn more about this five-inch-long black salamander with a mesh of fine silvery lines crisscrossing its back. We road-cruised the same stretch of highway in the same kinds of rains for about the same number of times from 1990 to 1992. Whereas in the early 1970s I had recorded an average of eight animals per hour, John and I found two specimens in three years! Today, the flatwoods salamander is a federally threatened species whose best populations are still located in the vicinity of my road cruises. The magnificent migrations I witnessed in the 1970s are now regarded as the largest breeding migrations known in this species. This natural phenomenon is not likely to be seen again.

The Southern dusky salamander, a muck dweller, is one of my favorite animals. It likes deep, black, wet, decomposing organic matter under logs and wet leaf litter at the edge of water. It was one of the subjects of my first graduate degree. I found it abundantly in floodplain swamps of the Ochlockonee, Wakulla, and Apalachicola rivers. In any blackwater river swamp it was common, and it lived at the swampy margins around lakes such as Iamonia and large ponds south of Tallahassee. Curiously, the salamander lived in very different habitats farther west in the Florida panhandle. Ravines called steepheads in certain small drainage basins on Eglin Air Force Base and along the Econfina River north of Panama City contained hundreds of Southern dusky salamanders.

The first sign that something was amiss with the Southern dusky was when a friend who collected them for the pet trade asked me, "What's happened to the Southern dusky salamander in the Ochlockonee River swamps?" That was way back in the mid-1970s. Then in 1998 biologist Ken Dodd published a paper reporting the strange disappearance of the Southern dusky salamander from Devil's Millhopper, a large sinkhole near Gainesville, Florida. Realizing that I had not seen the Southern dusky for a number of years, although I had not been specifically looking for it, I determined to check some of my old sites and see if the species was still abundant in them. In twenty-one steepheads in which I had collected 391 specimens of this species in the early 1970s, I found none in the late 1990s. The Southern dusky was also absent from an additional thirty-seven steepheads I had never visited and in which it was previously endemic, so whatever caused the decline probably was not me. Declines in populations of the Southern dusky salamander are also noted in North Carolina, South Carolina, Georgia, and Louisiana. I know of only two localities in the Florida panhandle where I can find the species, as of this writing. When the cause is eventually identified, it will probably have something to do with humans.

Over a six-year period, from 1976 to 1982, I marked and released twenty-four adult eastern kingsnakes on a 1,100-acre study area on Tall Timbers Research Station in northern Leon County. I or other biologists and technicians incidentally encountered these snakes while doing field research that did not directly involve them. In a recent study specifically designed to trap large snakes, biologist Seth Stapleton was unable to capture a single eastern kingsnake during a two-year period involving thousands of trap hours using large drift fence arrays on Tall Timbers, Pebble Hill Plantation, and the Wade Tract, an old-growth longleaf forest. Quail biologist Bill Palmer told me that he and other field biologists at Tall Timbers have not seen an eastern kingsnake there for at least six to eight years.

I witnessed the decline and last days of the Eastern indigo snake in the eastern panhandle. In the early 1960s I recovered a couple of roadkills on the Blountstown Highway in the vicinity of Fort Braden School. About 1968 a big black beauty was brought in to me from just west of Wacissa. The last one I personally witnessed was with a wetlands ecology class in 1985. We were standing halfway down the slope in the main steephead of Big Sweetwater Creek when a student hollered, "Look, an indigo snake!" It was so unusual that anybody would know what an indigo snake was, plus the fact that I knew there was an old tire partially buried in the sand where he was pointing, that I said, "Nope. It's just an old tire." Was I surprised to learn that it was, indeed, an indigo snake. I've not seen, nor heard of, another since.

Back in the 1960s and 1970s I used to see the Southern hognose snake on Tram Road in Leon and Jefferson counties and throughout the Munson Sandhills of the Apalachicola National Forest. The last ones I am aware of in

D. BRUCE MEANS, PhD

Leon and Wakulla counties I saw in 1989 and 1990 on the Leon Sinks Trail of the Apalachicola National Forest. Since then, I have operated a drift fence around a study pond off U. S. Highway 319 for nine years and haven't taken a single one. Rebecca Meegan spent six months on a small grant searching for the species in the Munson Sandhills using the techniques of road-cruising and drift-fencing. Her take? Zero. Local snake enthusiasts and pet store owners tell me they haven't seen one in years. A major research paper published in 2000 documents the decline of the Southern hognose snake all over its range. And now the Eastern hognose snake seems also to be declining.

Following heavy rains in the winter of 1996, my son Ryan and I dipnetted and seined 245 ponds just a few miles south of Tallahassee. We compared the use by frogs and salamanders of 160 ponds on the west side of Woodville Highway, which were surrounded by native longleaf pine/wiregrass savanna on the Apalachicola National Forest, with 85 ponds on the east side of Woodville Highway, which were surrounded by fifteen-year-old sand pine plantations owned by a private paper company. Five species, the striped newt, common newt, gopher frog, mole salamander, and dwarf salamander, were strongly underrepresented in ponds in the sand pine plantations. This finding, and old records there for the gopher frog and striped newt, indicated that these species formerly were more common in ponds of the pine plantations and have declined severely on that half of the study area.

The natural upland ecological conditions surrounding all these ponds is the longleaf pine-wiregrass community. Apparently the lack of sunlight in densely planted sand pine plantations prevents the native groundcover from growing. Salamanders and frogs are adapted to eating the insects of the longleaf pine/wiregrass groundcover and probably need certain qualities of the groundcover for hiding places in which to live. A forest devoid of a green, living groundcover and covered with a dense layer of partially decomposed pine needles is not the kind of habitat to which these five species are adapted, nor is it a community to which they can adapt. There simply is no food there, nor the right kinds of food, nor the many different qualities of living space they require, about which we know next to nothing for most of these species even in their native longleaf pine forest.

Back around 1968, when I was a graduate student in the FSU biological science department, I listened to Professor Andy Clewell arguing in a seminar that the Tallahassee Red Hills probably never had a longleaf pine-wiregrass forest because he had not found a sprig of wiregrass in the northern part of the county. Bob Godfrey, one of my committee members, told me that no one really knew how wiregrass colonized bare soil. Old-fields with wiregrass along the edge just grew up with weeds and you could see the wiregrass line there years later with no encroachment into the old-field. Then, with studies and observations, over the ensuing years we came to learn that wiregrass needs to be burned in the early growing season, April to July, to be stimulated to flower and set seed. Autumn, winter, or late summer fires don't trigger flowering in many of our native grasses, but fire at just the right season does.

If you eliminate plants by agriculture, they can't reseed a site if remnant plants nearby are not producing seed. In adjacent Georgia Red Hills counties, wiregrass comes right down to the state line. Geography professor Bill Brueckheimer cleared up the mystery by telling me that intensive slave-based agriculture destroyed the original longleaf pine-wiregrass forest in the counties around Tallahassee because it was the principal state hub of political activity, beginning precipitously when Tallahassee was chosen as capital in 1824. A land rush developed in the Tallahassee Red Hills but not in adjacent Georgia Red Hills counties, which were five hundred miles from Georgia's main political hub. So, only about 175 years ago, the rolling red hills of northern Leon County were, indeed, a sea of longleaf pines and wiregrass, but the evidence of it is long gone.

Looking out of my downtown dining room window, I see camphor trees and crepe myrtles, English sparrows and starlings, stray cats and–if I search the brick walls of my carport at night–a couple of Mediterranean geckos. These alien species and Japanese azaleas, Chinese tallow, greenhouse frogs, mimosa trees, and lawn grasses, lovely as some are, have replaced the red-cockaded and ivory-billed woodpeckers, indigo and king snakes, tiger salamanders and gopher frogs, longleaf pines and wiregrass that used to occupy my homesite. Because I have a lifetime's familiarity with all these wonderful gifts of nature, and am a firsthand witness of their passing, I can see into the future . . . and it scares me. Naturalist Archie Carr once said, "the most destructive enemy of the natural world will turn out to be the capacity of humans not just to change nature and environment but to be persuaded to like the changes, no matter how dismal they are." I hate to say it, but I'm

D. BRUCE MEANS, PHD

98

more pessimistic than that. I believe there is a limit to the amount of asphalt and concrete, lawns and golf courses, water and air pollution, strip malls, subdivisions, and just plain people that the world–and north Florida–can tolerate, ecologically. I worry that we, the people, are unwittingly sowing the seeds that will make us ghosts of the past, too, because we are not appreciative beneficiaries of the rich largesse that nature has bequeathed us. I don't even want to guess what the Tallahassee area will be like in another forty years; or how much more of the natural world will pass away, never to be recovered. By then I'll be just another ghost, too.

There is a way out of this dilemma. It means drastic overhaul of our thinking and actions. It means abandoning growth economy, volunteering to have two or fewer children, spreading financial wealth more equitably among everybody, and talking with each other about the details of making a better world and then following through with actions. It should be obvious to almost everybody what the quality of life will be if we keep the status quo. I believe we also have the brains to realize that it's theoretically possible to create a perfect world. So what's keeping us from getting on with it?

D. BRUCE MEANS, PhD, *is executive director of Coastal Plains Institute (since 1984) and Adjunct Professor, Florida State University Department of Biological Science. He served as director of Tall Timbers Research Station from 1978 to 1984. A field ecologist with more than forty years' experience in the southeastern United States, he has done research on fire ecology, the longleaf pine ecosystem, tropical biology, biogeography, pond ecology, and rare and endangered species. His long-term study of the Eastern diamondback rattlesnake is well known. He has published more than 235 scientific research papers, contract reports, and popular articles and has co-authored a book,* Priceless Florida: Natural Ecosystems and Native Species, *about the ecology of Florida. He co-produced and starred in two National Geographic Explorer documentaries, was featured in three episodes of the "Snake Wrangler" series on the National Geographic channel, and appeared in a National Geographic Explorer film featuring an expedition through the remote rainforests of Guyana to mysterious Mt. Roraima. For further information, check out his website, www.brucemeans.com.*

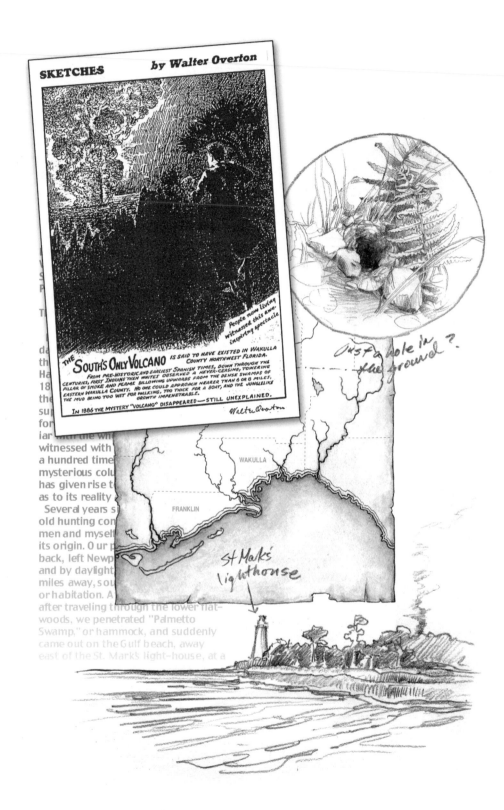

SKETCHES　　　*by Walter Overton*

People now living witnessed this awe-inspiring spectacle

THE SOUTH'S ONLY VOLCANO IS SAID TO HAVE EXISTED IN WAKULLA COUNTY NORTHWEST FLORIDA.
FROM PRE-HISTORIC AND EARLIEST SPANISH TIMES, DOWN THROUGH THE CENTURIES, FIRST INDIANS THEN WHITES OBSERVED A NEVER-CEASING, TOWERING PILLAR OF SMOKE AND FLAME BILLOWING UPWARDS FROM THE DENSE SWAMPS OF EASTERN WAKULLA COUNTY. NO ONE COULD APPROACH NEARER THAN 6 OR 8 MILES, THE MUD BEING TOO WET FOR WALKING, TOO THICK FOR A BOAT, AND THE JUNGLELIKE GROWTH IMPENETRABLE.

IN 1886 THE MYSTERY "VOLCANO" DISAPPEARED— STILL UNEXPLAINED.

Walter Overton

Just a hole in the ground?

WAKULLA

FRANKLIN

St Marks lighthouse

da
th
Ha
18
the
sup
for
iar with the wh
witnessed with
a hundred time
mysterious colu
has given rise t
as to its reality
Several years s
old hunting con
men and myself
its origin. O ur p
back, left Newp
and by daylight
miles away, sou
or habitation. A
after traveling through the lower flatwoods, we penetrated "Palmetto
Swamp," or hammock, and suddenly
came out on the Gulf beach, away
east of the St. Mark's light-house, at a

The Quest for Florida's Lost Volcano

KATHLEEN LAUFENBERG

Just before the new millennium, Tallahassee talk-radio personality Sonny Branch—a Southern-fried version of Rush Limbaugh—publicly declared that after four years of research and swamp search, he'd discovered the site of Florida's Lost Volcano.

Quite an accomplishment that, considering daredevils and adventurers have been searching for this mythical place, said to be buried deep in the Aucilla and Wacissa swamps of Wakulla County, for perhaps two hundred years.

But that's part of the beauty of living here. We still have our myths, our old stories of place, where the seeds of knowing are buried. Our wild land connects us to something larger, and more lasting, than ourselves. It provides safekeeping not only to our fellow creatures but also to our collective imagination.

We still have plenty of colorful characters here, too, as Sonny so vividly exemplifies. In the winter of 1997, while working as a reporter for the Tallahassee Democrat, I took him up on his offer to prove his volcano claim. And so began my quest to find the legendary, geologically impossible, volcano.

Our expedition party included myself, a photographer, Branch and a friend, two state geologists, and a wildlife officer. What follows is the tale of our search, a quest that has been undertaken since 1830, or perhaps much earlier, by more than a few hapless explorers.

Sonny Branch flips down the tailgate of his Blazer and quickly organizes his wares: maps, photos, letters, a black rock, and stacks and stacks of articles copied from books, magazines, and newspapers. Some articles bear Branch's garbled scribblings in the margins. Others are numbered like a treasure map. But all are on his favorite topic: Florida's Lost Volcano.

"Now y'all see here," he tells a restless group of would-be volcano explorers gathered outside of Ouzts' Oyster Bar in Newport. "I'm not about to take you out there to the spot until you hear what it's taken me four long years to learn."

Then Branch, a former talk-radio host and used-car salesman, goes to work.

"This all got started four years ago when a lady called me after the earthquake in California," Branch says of a call to his radio show. "She wanted to know if we ever had anything like that happen here."

Branch offered his homespun version of the mythical Wakulla Volcano. Although geologists say a volcano isn't geologically possible here, local folklore has it differently.

Beginning about 1830, the legend goes, Tallahasseeans regularly climbed onto rooftops–and, later, atop the old Capitol–to watch smoke belch from a mysterious volcano hidden deep in the Wacissa swamp. Most accounts say the smoke disappeared in 1886, following a South Carolina earthquake.

Moments after he told the volcano tale, Branch says, his telephone panel lit up.

"It began as a joke, and then it became a quest," he explains. "I've turned into an amateur archaeologist and a private detective because of this."

Branch promised his listeners he would solve the mystery. He's led countless volunteers on several different expeditions in search of what he calls "The Big Belch," and given two seminars on the topic at the Leon County Library.

And on this sunny morning in late winter, as black swallowtails zigzag through the air, he is determined to convince the world–or at least two skeptical state geologists, a wildlife officer, and a news team–that he has fulfilled that vow.

"You got to have a little Colombo in you, a little vision, a little

KATHLEEN LAUFENBERG

imagination," he cautions his listeners, "or you won't find nothing."

Then Branch folds up his volcano show, plops into his four-wheel-drive sports truck and rumbles onto U.S. Highway 98. Trailing behind are a green Florida Game and Fresh Water Fish vehicle and two geologists in an Isuzu bearing the license plate "Rock Dox." Let the expedition begin. But first, some lava lore. For the fifty-six-year-old Branch is not the first brave heart to strike out in search of the Wakulla Volcano.

One previous adventurer reportedly died in the mosquito- and snake-infested swamplands trying to find it. Others endured exhaustion and barely made it back. And at least one explorer fell out of a high tree he'd climbed, trying to eyeball the source of the smoke. Who first ventured into the Aucilla and Wacissa swamps to find the smoke's source, however, is unclear.

"No one knows when this supposed volcano first attracted notice," wrote Wilfred Neill in a June 1963 edition of *Florida Wildlife*. "According to Indian legend, it had always been there."

But during the 1830s, people reportedly began talking about the smoke almost as much as they did the weather. Some speculated it came from American Indian campfires. Others said it rose from a settlement of runaway slaves. Still others claimed it was outlaw moonshiners, nurturing the granddaddy of all stills. (According to one account, you could leave a quarter and an empty jug in an accessible area of the swamp, then return the next day to find your money gone and your jug brimming with whiskey.)

But it took the honed skills of a journalist to transform the mysterious column of smoke into a lava-belching volcano. The dubious distinction belongs to Barton Jones, who, while penning a piece for *Lippincott's* magazine in 1882, dubbed the smoke the "Wakulla Volcano." A legend was born. Soon men—manly men, of course, afraid of neither snakebite nor malaria—began eagerly lining up to find it. One of the first daredevils to venture into the swamps was yet another reporter. In the 1870s, according to several accounts, the *New York Herald Tribune* reportedly sent a news correspondent to investigate the smoke.

"He formed an expedition and hired several guides," wrote Neill. "The group fought saw grass, briar vines, mud, water, mosquitoes and cottonmouth moccasins . . . (but) the swamp finally became impenetrable and the party turned back. The newspaper correspondent inexplicably sickened and died before high land could be reached."

Next came explorers C. L. Norton and J. H. Staley, who set out in 1891. According to Neill, they also ended up turning back, with Norton later reporting that he "nearly lost his life in the attempt." Later that year, Staley guided two more men into the swamp. But the swamp defeated them, too.

But during the next century, at different times, two pairs of men did traverse the depths of the Wacissa swamp and reported finding earthly curiosities there. One pair:

A. L. Porter, a Wakulla County judge, and James Kirkland, a forester. The other:

William Wyatt, a Tallahassee office-supply businessman, and Fred Wimpee, a Jacksonville businessman.

Porter and Kirkland reported stumbling upon a crater while deer hunting in the 1920s. The two were in Jefferson County's Gum Swamp, near the Pinhook River, when Porter climbed a rocky knoll and discovered the strange crater. Later, in a September 1956 letter to the *Tallahassee Democrat,* he described the crater as "the size of a dishpan" with a bottom too black and too deep to fathom. Neither man ever attempted to return, though, because "a dense growth of jack pines, wire grass and other vegetation has covered the entire area and it would be difficult for Jim and me to find our crater again," Porter wrote.

Wyatt and Wimpee, on the other hand, deliberately set out to find the volcano in about 1932. Before going, they conferred with W. T. Cash, the state librarian, and professors Raymond Bellamy and Leland Lewis, then department heads of sociology and chemistry at Florida State University.

"They were real interested in the mystery of the volcano," Wyatt told the *Democrat* in 1964. "But if they had known the danger we faced they would not have encouraged us to go."

The men followed directions left by a Chicago newsman, who had reportedly gotten close to the smoke but turned back in exhaustion.

"Were we crazy!" Wyatt said. "We started out in a Model T Ford with a machete, a hand-ax, a flashlight, and a small bag of sandwiches."

After driving as far as they could, they hiked to an abandoned sawmill roughly thirty miles southeast of Tallahassee. Then they hacked their way through the swamp. Wyatt said they soon came upon rocks as big as houses, strewn over a four-mile area.

"The boulders were so big we would chop through undergrowth and come face to face with what appeared to be a solid stone wall," Wyatt told a *Democrat* reporter. "Some queer work of nature had gone on there. Right by great sinks, there were piles of rock that appeared to have been blown out of the ground. There was something eerie about the place because there were no trees as in the surrounding land, yet it had never been logged because there were no stumps."

Exhausted, the two young men collapsed on top of the boulders. In the morning, they fought their way out again.

Compared with those conducted by past explorers, the Branch expedition is a cakewalk. Roads now allow access to swamps earlier adventurers had to hack their way into. And that's good luck for the portly Branch, who is fond of describing himself as the "Round Man." Branch–who has the letter S tattooed on his arm, a memento of his Army days when a fellow recruit drunkenly offered to tattoo "Sonny" there, but stopped when a likewise liquefied Branch yowled that it hurt too much–leads his entourage along Highway 98, through Wakulla County into Jefferson County. About four miles inside the Jefferson County line, Branch (now a non-drinker) turns northeast onto an unmarked road used by hunters, toward swampland known as Hell's Half Acre.

After five bumpy miles, the explorers pile out. A red-tailed hawk swirls overhead. An owl hoots from its hideaway. And the swamp's green arms entwine everywhere around the land, making it nearly impenetrable.

"This is it," Branch announces, sweeping his hand to indicate perhaps a football-field-sized area of swamp.

But, at least from the road, there is no crater to be seen. No giant boulders. Nothing that dramatically sets this piece of swamp apart from any other within a ten-mile radius. For a moment, the explorers are silent. Then:

"This is it?" asks photographer Mark Wallheiser, incredulous. "I'm supposed to take a picture of this?"

"I hit the history books, I hit the library, I hit the newspaper files," Branch says firmly, "and everything points to this spot.

"The Wakulla Volcano is in Jefferson County, not Wakulla, and it's not a volcano," he continues, pulling down the rim of his National Rifle Association ball cap. "My theory is that it was a peat-bog fire that started in one place and burnt different types of vegetation."

THE QUEST FOR FLORIDA'S LOST VOLCANO

Branch has no evidence that the smoke came from a smoldering peat fire—but it's a theory others have entertained. And it could explain why historical accounts of the smoke column describe it as changing colors: Sometimes it appeared to be inky black, other times gray and still other times almost white.

"If you had a serious drought and the water table dropped, you could have something like that (peat fire)," says state geologist Tom Scott, who wears his long hair pulled back in a ponytail and a small gold hoop in his left ear.

Geologist Harley Means, who has been slogging around in the bordering swamp, now returns, holding a handful of swamp muck aloft. "It's organic and rich," he says, "and, yes, it would burn if it was dry enough."

"I wish it was a volcano," says Branch. "But if I'd found a volcano, I wouldn't have called the *Democrat*. I would have called David Letterman."

There are no big boulders to see because the big boulders were blasted apart years ago to make way for Highway 98, Branch contends. And the Gum Swamp and Pinhook River, used by the Porter expedition as landmarks, are nearby.

"All we have to go on is what the old people said and common sense," Branch says. "I am 99.9 percent sure I have found where the smoke came from. How else can you explain someone doing this for four years?"

Geologists Scott and Means shake their heads and shrug. They are not convinced. And they look a trifle downcast that they will not be asked to tromp through the swamp and look at rocks. But they try to be polite and not pummel Branch's theory.

"For years we've been fielding questions about the Wakulla Volcano and telling people that, geologically, it's not possible," says Scott, who wears an arresting picture of a hungry T-Rex on his t-shirt. "I'd like to think that this would put to rest the myth of the volcano, but I'm afraid that five years from now, it will come back up again."

Rather than tell people the site of the smoke has finally been discovered, Scott says he'll leave that to Branch. (And Branch invites anyone with a volcano question to call him on his "groupie, death-threat, and stalker line: 850-893-6241.")

Veteran Wildlife Officer Robert Daniels—on the trek, he says, only to ensure no city folk get lost in the swamp or step on a water moccasin—allows that he's not convinced by Branch's story either. But he strives for neutrality.

KATHLEEN LAUFENBERG

"There's a lot of strange things out in that swamp no man has ever seen," he says amiably.

Though surrounded by doubting Thomases, the Round Man remains confident. He maintains that a plaque should be erected on this spot someday, to memorialize the site of the smoke. With his name prominently included, of course, as the man who solved the mystery. But for now, he's on to his next excellent north Florida adventure.

"You ever heard of Billy Bowlegs?" he asks, a twinkle in his eye. "He was an ex-slave who was a pirate. He buried some gold in a chest somewhere in Franklin County. "That's my next project: I'm going to find Billy Bowlegs's treasure."

KATHLEEN LAUFENBERG *is a features writer at the* Tallahassee Democrat *and a volunteer fiction editor for the* Apalachee Review. *Her stories have appeared in the* Atlanta Journal-Constitution, Baltimore Sun, Miami Herald, *and other publications. She shares her home in the sandy pinewoods of north Florida with her songwriter husband and two marvelous mutts.*

Alligator Point

It was raining hard in Medart when we drove through from Tallahassee, but here at Alligator Point the cumulus are corralled back from the coast. On a slack tide, under a new moon, we walk toward the close of the day. Mullet turn and flip in the shallow mud flats—they leave pink curlicued wakes on the dark blue water. Our sweating bodies attract a double dose of bugs, no-see-ums and mosquitoes both. The air is hot and heavy, no wind. I keep saying when we get past the trees and the houses, it'll be breezier and we will stop itching, and surprisingly soon it is so.

Halfway to the Point, full dark drops. The first of the stars punch into view. When we kick at the sand, we are surprised by a scattering of small greenish flecks: they are so quick to illumine and then extinguish that we don't have time to study any single one. I squat and swirl my hands in the water. I seem to be enlivening a soup of the lit things: what can they be? "Single-cell algae," says my husband.

The water is muddy with light. I think it odd that it doesn't take more effort to stir these thousands of starry specks with my fingers; they are so thick it seems they should slow the movement of my hands.

We walk on; at the Point itself, we stand between two straining bodies of water, the harbor and the Gulf. Little wavelets break and trail the same phosphorescence we saw in the sand. We lie on our backs, watching Scorpio rise, until the sky is starshot, so full of lights, we can barely distinguish the summer constellations.

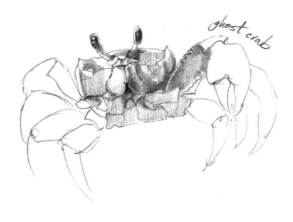

ghost crab

bright rust

banana
yellow

milky yellow
light shines
through

O Beautiful Scar:
Canal Built by Slaves

JANISSE RAY

In the karst limestone of underground north Florida, where rivers rise through high-magnitude springs then vanish again, swirling waters dissolve the soft rock to create a mostly hidden world of caverns, pools and passages. Across this land of mysterious, haunting waters a gash called the Slave Canal has been laid.

Twenty-one people have come to navigate the Slave Canal on a sweet August day. Irwin Friedman is our guide. "The Slave Canal is the wildest and most remote stream in Florida," he tells us, once he herds all twenty-one of us into a lopsided circle, "And this is a beautiful day to paddle." He says "beautiful" as if it contains the word "beauty," and as if he believes it.

Irwin I have known a year for every person present. By trade he is a teacher, an education visionary, not a river guide. But he knows the Slave Canal better than anyone and knows how to find it. He is a thin, heavily bearded man who has no money and cares not that he doesn't, except that he'd like to buy land and start the school of his dreams—out in the country sunshine, surrounded by fruit trees, with lepes of children learning local genius as they study algebra and Newton's laws.

"The trip will be quick," Irwin says, "because the water is high from all the thunderstorms this summer. It should take a couple of hours. Don't miss the entrance to the canal. If you miss it, the river diffuses into a huge, confusing swamp. We'll come find you. Just relax and enjoy the night you spend in wilderness."

We have about ten children with us, mostly teenagers who aren't wired yet for leisurely paddles. Tim, painter and wild adventurer, offers to take the lead and mark the opening, to ensure no one shoots past.

"No one gets ahead of Tim, then," Irwin says.

Although he orients the group seriously and makes sure everyone has a life preserver, of us all, children included, Irwin will have the most fun. I've been on enough rivers with him to know that he will manage to turn his boat over a few times, get into wrestling matches in the sandy shallows, and holler with delight when he finds some salamander or frog. He'll be more otter than teacher.

"Get ready for spiders," I hear one of the children say to another. The last time I was here, a year ago, was with Irwin's summer campers. One of the boys had a spell of terror about halfway through the Slave Canal, where it becomes very obvious just how many spiders are going about their spider business. Ripping through an unseen web, the boy had finally broken—*it's on me, on me,* he had shouted, almost capsizing his boat trying to escape. A flood of terror overtook him and he began to wail and cry. *Get it off, get it off!*

"Spiders?" the other child now shrugs. "Big deal."

Raven, my husband, and I are last in the water. Raven hauls in his boat a fat watermelon we have grown. Ahead of us is a happy sight, a flotilla of colorful boats, our friends and their friends.

We are on the Wacissa River, a couple of miles above the entrance to the Slave Canal. The Wacissa emerges through a series of clearwater springs eight or so miles north; the three-mile-long Slave Canal links it to the tidal Aucilla, a blackwater river that begins in Boston, Georgia, passes through Snead's Smokehouse Lake then disappears, rising again from underground past Nutall Rise, our takeout. The first thing we do is paddle to the far side of the river, to identify clumps of white flowers in trees. They are not flowers at all, but streaks of guano from a bird roost.

Soon the Wacissa narrows, although we can still see sky. We look for alligator eyes peering out of the hydrilla. A pair of prothonotary warblers, the swamp canaries, fly daredevilishly in front of us. (My little yellow boat is named for them.) Water edges are thick with aquatic plants—water hyacinth, still blooming, and pickerel weed. Occasionally we see a clump of cardinal flowers, popular with hummingbirds and butterflies.

If, instead of a human nature, I could have a wild one, I would choose a blackwater stream. Today I would.

Irwin was restocking bananas in the old food co-op, where it used to be on Gaines Street, the first time I met him. It was 1982 and I was newly arrived to Tallahassee as a university junior. I had begun to eat healthily, foods like brown rice and organic peanut butter, and, not owning a vehicle, had walked to the co-op from the BPW Scholarship House where I lived, near the football stadium.

The man with the dark beard kept looking at me. He smiled. I said hello, continued shopping. Mostly I was looking and sometimes placing small items in my basket. Reared in a poor, traditional, and very rural southern Georgia family, I had never tried avocado, nor kiwi, nor artichoke. I'd never heard of quinoa or mochi. It was all so new.

"Excuse me," the man finally said, "Are you a runner?"

"I do run," I said. "How did you know?"

"I was looking at your legs."

I stared at him. He looked earnest enough. "I mean, I was looking at the muscle down your leg. You can tell runners." Then he asked me if I would like to run together sometime. He knew a beautiful trail among sinkholes in Wakulla County.

Even then, he said beauty-full.

That moment began my lifelong friendship with Irwin, and an introduction to a region of the country that fills me with awe and fascination, and later, pure love. Irwin ate mostly raw food, and he packed picnics in cardboard boxes, blood oranges and bread dates and tahini, and picked me up in a succession of greasy, junky Datsun trucks to show me the land onto which I had arrived. Little by little I learned it. North Florida was so different from my place of origin, in south Georgia, only four hours away: Sinkholes. Spring-fed rivers. The Gulf. Red hills. Tidal creeks. Steepheads. Appalachian remnant ravines.

In those days, twenty years ago, the Slave Canal was a kind of secret.

O Beautiful Scar: Canal Built by Slaves

Only those who really loved the wild had been on it. The entrance was hidden among vine-draped cypress and river birch deep in the swamps of Jefferson County.

August is the time of year when spiders build elaborate webs across waterways, where they crouch with infinite patience and wait for fliers-by. They crawl along the branches of beech, they leap from thin air, they hang by threads. There are crab spiders and banana spiders and zipper spiders and so many others I do not have the names for nor the patience to identify. In the morning sunlight the webs of the golden orb weavers are spun of gold filigree, not the usual white cobs. The river is bright with all the gold.

If spiders have owned Slave Canal, today the butterflies take over. Rainy weather this year has multiplied them. Tiger swallowtails as big as my hand flit through the upper reaches of trees, and land on bright spots of swamp lilies and pickerel weed. There are others. Some of them fly into the beautiful golden nets of the spiders and lay trapped until they die, leaving their life stories written in the obituaries of loose wings.

Matthew Smith, my friend Susan's nephew from Jackson, Mississippi, a preeminent naturalist at twenty-one, knows the butterflies by name: Palamedes swallowtail, Carolina satyr, pipevine swallowtail, Gulf fritillary, checkered skipper.

Now the banks are close, the cypress and tupelo and red maple growing right up to water's edge, leaning over each other to touch the other side, as if the trees know their canopy is supposed to be unbroken. Scientifically, they reach for unclaimed sunlight; I think they want to heal.

I should keep paddling with Matthew, so I can learn what he knows. Or catch up with Susan, so we can continue our lifelong conversation. But I stay back, watching the bluets dance along the tips of the duck potato, and counting apple snail eggs clinging to pickerel weed.

Irwin is Jewish. His last name is Friedman, a name that frustrates him in its patriarchy. Once he tried to spell it with an *i* instead of an *a* in the "man." His mother was saved from the Holocaust in Poland. She was the oldest of five siblings. Her parents realized what was happening and sent her to an aunt in Palestine. The others never arrived and she never heard from or saw them again. After the war was over, she tried desperately to find them. Irwin remembers, when he was ten, watching the Eichmann trials on television. His mother, he said, was in front of the television hysterically crying and looking through piles of bodies for her family. So Irwin never had a grandmother, or a grandfather, or aunts and uncles, and that loss is a big hole he has lived with.

In the early 1800s Jefferson County plantation owner John Gamble and others schemed an idea to dig a three-mile canal through the unnavigable swamp that separated the Wacissa and Aucilla rivers. This water route would save Gamble and other cotton farmers, who desired to get their crops to the Gulf of Mexico, eighteen miles of difficult road travel. Gamble and his cohorts were filled with the "canal fever" that had beset the country following the successful completion of New York's Erie Canal in 1825.

In 1831, the Territorial legislature pronounced the Wacissa and Aucilla Navigation Company a corporation. The corporate body included such aristocracy as James Gadsden, Achille Murat, William B. Nuttall, and John G. and Robert Gamble. They were permitted to "clean out" and make the said rivers "sufficiently navigable for boats drawing not more than eighteen inches water." Apparently not much happened for twenty years.

On December 19, 1850, Florida's General Assembly passed at its fifth session the same resolution, giving the navigation company (which now included more stockholders) approval to make the Wacissa and Aucilla rivers sufficiently navigable for "steam or flat-bottom boats." Upon completion, the company would be able to charge tolls on all boats that might pass through the canal. If the work was not completed by January 1, 1855, the corporation would be dissolved.

Gamble it was: on the table were the lives of real people. Work began, using slave labor. Although the canal was completed in 1856, it never served its purpose well—in some places it was only a foot deep, prohibiting boat travel.

We will never know how many slaves lived, how many died. Surely some were lost in the digging, but this history went unrecorded or has never been found. If anyone knows the exact number of casualties, I do not know that person. Someone once told me the number was in the hundreds, but that figure would not have been economically feasible, nor historically possible. Joe Knetsch, historian with the Division of State Lands, told me that Florida's largest plantations had not many over one hundred slaves. The 1860 census listed seventy Florida plantations with over one hundred slaves.

O BEAUTIFUL SCAR: CANAL BUILT BY SLAVES

Yet, the work was grueling. Building the canal was a kind of holocaust in the land between the rivers.

My first trip through the Slave Canal, many years ago, I could feel the dark sorrow of the laborers. I could see them bent with shovels and picks in the black mud, thick with roots, or picking up rocks as if they lifted their own heavy hearts, carrying them across to land. I could see the men bending in the dimness of the bottomland hardwoods, at the edge of the water, with boulders of limestone in their arms. I could see them wrestling with the trees and shrubs, with the thick, deep roots. The rocks lining the canal banks were piled like the torsos of men. I could hear old spirituals being sung, and small moans.

When I paddled the tannic waters, the lonely dead softly called my name. I heard whispers in the black water. The sadness of the Slave Canal settled on me, and clung to me until the current dropped me at last into the Aucilla.

Irwin rowed with him the memory of his lost people. In my boat I rowed the bottomless tragedy of the racism of my own, one I had felt every day since I had become cognitive to the color of skin. To die for a thing you do not believe in must be a terrible death. Can it be worse than living enchained?

We say about the Slave Canal that we go in and come out, as if it had a door hinged at either end, curtained with vines—Virginia creeper and wild grape. A passage. Rite of passage. Built by a corporation of aristocracy who wanted their right of passage. The river of sticks. Where Michael rowed his boat ashore, hallelujah.

The canal is a scar through the deeply beautiful, cabbage-palm hammock, a wound gouged deep that healed but whose story will never be forgotten. A gash of river water. A laceration drawn in the 1850s on the map of the world. Unforgivable mark of history.

Yet, such beauty. I saw cottonmouths wrapped in the branches of fallen trees, hovering above water. I saw necklaces of cooters sunning on angled logs. I saw the flag of whitetail deer flapping off through the woods. I saw alligator. Royal fern.

Sometimes I think there is so much love between people that the human form, composed of corpuscles and atoms, cannot contain it and it overflows onto the land, which becomes a vessel for the superfluity of affection. The land gleans from us, and is nourished by and identified through us, as we are nourished and identified through it.

JANISSE RAY

But it cannot be love that fills the Slave Canal. The emotion spilled over has to be sorrow. None of the animals tend this sorrow, even though their own ancestors likely observed it—the barred owl, watching us paddle by as its grandmother many times removed watched the African-American men working waist-deep in water and mud.

In the years that followed my first voyage on the canal, when I was raising my son alone, when I was occupied with the paying of bills, with poetry, with doing my job well, caught up in the affairs of daily life, cooking and cleaning and caretaking, with looking for the husband I would not find for ten years, I would long to paddle the Slave Canal.

So many days and so many nights in my urban existence I dreamed of breathing air vaporized by sweet bay magnolia and river birch, paying attention to details on wing-backs, listening to the cardinals chatting, my eyes blinded with all the palmetto-sweetgum-duckweed green, the water running, running, washing out my worried mind. When the banality of my life threatened to overcome me, I toyed with the idea of escaping to the Slave Canal. It was wild with wild—accessible, immersible wild. I yearned to be there. I always thought of it as the place that would welcome me back into myself. I thought of it as the place that would save me, no matter what.

All those years, Irwin was my friend in the truest sense of the word. When I needed help—when I ran a traffic light accidentally and plowed into the side of a stranger's life—when I locked myself out of my own front door—when Silas was sick and I needed to run to the store—Irwin was the person I called. He became a godfather to my son, and later, when Silas was old enough for kindergarten, a teacher. At his school, Full Flower Education Center on Mahan Drive, Irwin tried to remake the world, a child at a time, to be a more loving, more generous, more benign place.

As often as I could, I traveled the canal. I've gone in and come out of it maybe a dozen times. Never alone. Even now, after all these years, all these passages, I don't trust myself to find the opening, not to end up in the formidable swamp that the river becomes, not to get lost. Maybe I don't trust the dead out there, who are always calling. I don't trust the door to open at the end and let me out.

Other than insects, or the occasional cardinal calling from the trees, I

O BEAUTIFUL SCAR: CANAL BUILT BY SLAVES

am surprised by an absence of wildlife on the Slave Canal this lovely August day. This is unusual. Surely the fauna has scattered because twenty people are ahead of me on the river. Even the adults get happy and rowdy where a new tree has tumbled in the water, and we must inch our way across it, or bend low in our boats to squeeze under, or where the current insists that we navigate carefully or end up nose-first in flotsam and weed. My favorite part of the trip, as usual, is passing through the wild rice. The bright-green grasses wave tall, scratching and whispering against the sides of our vessels as we pass through the clear swift water.

Rainfall determines how long the trip takes. High water is fast. Drouth is the worst time to paddle here; you're dragging, portaging, heaving over downed trees. There is a man I've never met who has made it his mission to keep the Slave Canal clear of trees, I'm told. A friend met him once, halfway down the stream, in his boat a chainsaw.

At lunch everyone (except Raven) decides to save the watermelon until the end.

Occasionally I think about the new clear-cut at Goose Pasture that I saw this morning for the first time. I can't turn a blind eye to a clear-cut. It's another kind of holocaust. But above the newly bedded rows, where sapling slash pine have been replanted, five birds were floating. They were kites—three swallow-tailed and two Mississippi. The kites appeared to be hunting the dragonflies, which were thick in the air, swooping and flashing their graceful, scissored tails.

At the end of the day our bird list isn't long: kites, yellow-billed cuckoo, Acadian flycatcher, white-eyed vireo, blue-gray gnatcatcher, pileated woodpecker. Matthew has identified them by song. I tally them in my head.

A visceral thing happens, on blackwater rivers. You literally absorb them. I am a wet sponge.

Mostly I ride the Slave Canal in reverie, completely in the present. I try to memorize how the cabbage palms rise in the floodplain, how the poison ivy looks when its vines get thick and hairy, snaking up the trees, how sharp the blades of wild rice feel as I glide through the kayak-wide channel, how happy Irwin looks shooting over a barely submersed log, how red-shouldered hawks sound in the distance. I study the walls of mossy limestone rocks piled up along the banks. I examine a new tree that has tumbled into the water.

I let my eyes fill with the innocence of green. I hear the right to speak in

JANISSE RAY

tupelo leaves, and dignity in water dripping off my paddle. I see freedom in the sandy-bottom water. I hear love in dragonflies as they clack and buzz. I listen to the children whooping ahead. I feel on my bare arms the forgiveness of the yellow sun.

JANISSE RAY *is the author of* Ecology of a Cracker Childhood *and* Wild Card Quilt: Taking a Chance on Home. *She is a political activist.*

O BEAUTIFUL SCAR: CANAL BUILT BY SLAVES

Sopchoppy

Dr. Crook's Trade-Mark and Label

DR. CROOK'S

Wine OF Tar

Apalachicola Nat'l Forest circa 1915

Gold in the Pines

GAIL FISHMAN

My great-grandfather, B.C. Williams, made his living running turpentine stills in Alabama and Florida. He was born in Baxley, Georgia, where he married Maria Prescott. They moved to Alabama before 1900, and then on to Florida. Pellagra claimed him in 1913; he was only forty-two years old. Before then B.C. ran turpentine operations at Sopchoppy, Florida, near Blountstown, and had recently moved his family to Tallahassee from Wauchula. He left "a wife and nine children to mourn his loss." It took lots of digging through census records to find out that his first name was Benjamin and we still debate what "C" stands for. One photograph of my great-grandmother exists, but no one knows what B.C. looked like.

I envision a compact man, eyes almost hidden in a perpetual squint, rough hands jutting from frayed cuffs of a coarse-woven shirt walking through the piney woods. He stops now and then to thump the trunk of a longleaf pine and listen to the red-cockaded woodpeckers and nuthatches fussing in the treetops. Thigh-high bunch grasses dip their heavy seed heads in a light

121

breeze and attest to the land's richness. He gazes across the landscape, noting numerous gopher tortoise burrows. When he spies one of the slow-moving reptiles, he turns it over and ties a red bandana to a nearby turkey oak. He'll pick up the animal when he leaves; his wife makes a tasty turtle gumbo that will go well with hot cornbread and cool buttermilk.

Mounting a long-legged bay gelding, B.C. turns to view the pines and smiles with satisfaction. The owner is asking a steep price for the lease but the stand is virgin; none of these trees has ever been chipped. The chip, or streak, is a narrow portion of sapwood that is cut from the tree trunk to stimulate a flow of crude gum (this is not the watery sap that eats the paint off the hood when a car is parked under a pine tree). The chipper makes the first streak low on the tree just above the collection box or cup. He cuts streaks higher each year, leaving a succession of chevron shaped scars, often called catfaces, down the trunk. Larger trees can be chipped higher than a man's head and on two or three sides. But wounding the tree in such a manner eventually weakens it.

B.C. judges that fire swept across these woods two or three years ago. Fire is a conundrum he often ponders. While it can kill and destroy, fire seems to bring exuberant life to the longleaf forest. Many times he has walked over a pineland the day after a fire when all appeared black and dead only to return in a few weeks to find explosions of green shoots on almost every plant.

The saddle creaks as he turns the horse for home, one saddlebag considerably fatter with the hapless turtle. Angles of light fall through the forest. October is giving way to November. There will be plenty of work for B.C.'s gang during the off-season, November through March. This is the time to repair tools and rake the duff, accumulated needles, leaves, and branches, from the trees to create a firebreak. Overhead, as he makes his plans during the ride home, birds chatter and ebony crows *caaaaw* at the piercing cry of a red-tailed hawk. Heavy bodied vultures cruise on thermals. Ahead, a large indigo snake glides across the path but the horse pays it no mind. Its hooves make a *ca-lumping* sound on the sandy road, which has been overlaid with a deep blanket of pine needles in heavily traveled sections to prevent wagon wheels from sinking.

I'd like to imagine that my great-grandfather studied and respected the piney woods and that some measure of gum resin—the raw material from which turpentine is distilled—seeped into his body and runs through my veins still. I wish I'd listened to my grandmother's stories of growing up in

GAIL FISHMAN

turpentine camps but by the time I was of an age to appreciate them we had moved five hundred miles away.

Longleaf pines go by a host of common names: American pitch pine, Amerikaanse pitchpine, broom pine, brown pine, fat pine, yellow pine, figured-tree, hard pine, heart pine, hill pine, langbarrig tall, long-leaf pitch, southern pine, longstraw pine, Madera pino, pino tea, red pine, Rosemary pine, soderns gul-all, southern hard pine, Gulf Coast pitch pine, longleaved pitch pine, sump-all, sumpf kiefer, tea pine, and turpentine pine. Florida, Georgia, and North Carolina all claim the tree by name—Florida yellow pine, Georgia heart pine, North Carolina pitch pine, and other combinations.

Pinus palustris by scientific terms, longleafs are sturdy, long-lived, majestic trees. Though not fireproof, their thick bark forms a protective wall. Typically found in deep, dry, sandy soils, longleaf pines grow well in richer wetter soils though they are not quite as marsh-loving as the epithet *palustris* implies.

When Columbus set sail for the edge of the world, Sweden was the primary source of tar and pitch. As word of the new continent floated to Europe, England, France, Spain, and other countries sent ships across the ocean. The demand for naval stores increased; Sweden raised the price for their products.

Five centuries ago longleaf was the dominant pine on more than 90 million acres along the southeastern coastal plain from southern Virginia to east Texas and deep into Florida's peninsula. Depending on soils, elevation, climate, and other factors, longleafs associated with slash and loblolly pines, scrubby oaks, palmettos, and a variety of small shrubs and grasses. To the explorers, America's vast forests promised endless fleets and supplies of pitch, tar, rosin, and turpentine. Translated into political terms this meant that whoever controlled those forests and ruled the seas would become the most powerful country in the world.

Millions of acres had been cleared for farms, fields, and towns by the end of the 1800s. When B.C. moved his family to Florida, the state harbored the best longleaf stands remaining. Longleaf and slash pines produced the most gum, and longleaf were preferred overall. In the twenty-first century, about 3 million acres of longleaf forest remain in scattered patches; about ninety thousand acres are old growth. South Georgia and north Florida contain most of the surviving old growth longleaf woodlands.

Cotton is the cash crop most associated with the South but the pines that needed no cultivation brought millions of dollars to the economy. Pines may be classified as softwoods by the timber industry but the lumber of a mature longleaf is, as has been said, "hard enough to break a termite's tooth." Timber sustained the South as the perfect construction material, and as part of a lesser-known business—naval stores.

All of the materials used in shipbuilding and keeping vessels afloat were collectively called naval stores. Wooden ships sprouted two, three, or more masts. Their ribs and spars were hewn from oak, birch, pine, and other timber. Their heavy canvas sails were woven from cotton and the ropes that controlled the sails were braided from hemp and other materials. Sun, salt, wind, heat, and cold took a toll on the ship; repair was a constant job. Sailors sewed rips in the sails and pounded pitch mixed with oakum—shreds of worn out hemp rigging—into cracks and crevices to prevent leaks.

Georgia and Florida led the naval stores industry in production until the 1940s. In 1909, 39,311 wage earners worked in the naval stores industry throughout the Southeast. Almost all of those workers lived in a separate world known as the turpentine camp. For African Americans, the camp was another kind of servitude.

The work was potentially dangerous and definitely long, hot, dirty, and hard. The laborers were almost all men, but a few women worked in the woods. Workers rose about 4:00 a.m. Some fed the animals and hitched teams to the wagons while others bought lunch or tobacco at the commissary. Lunch, carried in a gallon bucket with a handle, usually consisted of cornbread, cane syrup, bacon, and a syrup-sweetened water called "squeezle." Sometimes lunch was a mixture of cured meat, onions, and cornbread called "dooby." Lucky men had a baking powder biscuit, or raccoon or possum meat. Workers might ride in the wagons but more often than not they walked, beginning their day just as the sun came up.

Prior to 1900 a box to collect the crude gum resin was cut into the base of a tree. The box had to be smooth; an experienced worker could cut seventy-five to one hundred boxes a day. Each man worked a "crop" of about ten thousand faces; mounted "woodsriders" supervised the men working on four to ten crops. During the first year the trees could be dipped six to eight times and decreased each year thereafter. Boxed trees could be worked about four years. Around 1903 the Herty Cup was introduced. A metal cup—clay cups were also used—was fastened to the tree and metal gutters directed the gum into the cup. The cup could be moved up as the chippers cut their streaks higher, and trees could be worked five years or longer.

A worker called the "Dipper" scooped the crude gum resin from the box or cup and transferred it to barrels loaded on wagons. Teams of oxen, mules, and sometimes horses pulled the wagons to the turpentine still near the camp.

A turpentine camp was a community unto itself. Each family lived in a small home, usually with a small garden space. A communal barn provided shelter for the work animals and perhaps a milk cow or two. Barrels were made in the cooper's shed and larger camps had a wagon shed and blacksmith shop. Quite a few camps remained long enough to start a cemetery, but when the camp moved the graves stayed behind and the locations have often been lost. Workers received their wages in scrip or tokens redeemable at the company store. Because prices were high—and there was no other choice—getting out of debt was almost impossible and ensured that the workers were more or less bound to the camp.

Some camps posted night guards to keep workers from leaving because "Cruiters" from other camps were always looking to coax good workers to their operation. An arrest warrant followed those who left owing money. On rare occasions, an operator might pay off a laborer's debt.

Those left behind had their chores too. If there was a school, the children attended. Yards needed sweeping, water needed carrying from the communal well, clothes needed mending and washing, gardens needed weeding, equipment needed repair. The chores never ended.

The cooper's shed—where wooden barrels were made—attracted children. The cooper held an exalted position. Each barrel was made by hand to strict standards; a capable cooper would make six or seven barrels a day. By the late 1800s mass-produced turpentine barrels were readily available but coopers still needed to fashion barrels for crude gum and rosin.

Off-hours meant social events. If the play turned rough and people were hurt or killed the operator and woodsriders handled the incident. Rarely, if ever, did a true law enforcement official enter the camp for the simple reason that if one did some of the hands would up and leave. Owners preferred to handle matters on their own.

Distilling the crude gum was a delicate process and had to be watched carefully. The gum was poured into a large kettle and heated with a wood fire to produce a light, volatile oil called spirits of turpentine. Rosin, a by-product of distillation, is quite different from resin. Tar is a thick, dark mixture made from distilling lightwood. Pitch is the viscous liquid or residue obtained by distilling tar. In colonial times crude gum or resin was used to manufacture soap. Native people used gum to treat arrow wounds.

Dr. Crook's "Wine of Tar" sold well in the late 1860s as a sure-fire cure for consumption, coughs, colds, sore throats, asthma, croup, diphtheria, dyspepsia, weak stomach, diseases of the kidney and bladder, nervous disability, female irregularities, and much more. At the dawn of the twentieth century doctors recommended a mixture of honey and tar to treat colds and prevent pneumonia. My grandmother always said that turpentine could cure a chest cold.

Turpentine was used as a solvent for paint and varnish and as a paint thinner known as mineral spirits, once a staple in most American homes. In the camp, turpentine was used to whiten clothes in the laundry, clean furniture, floors, porcelain, silver, and windows and to treat bites, burns, stings, boils, croup, worms, sore throats—almost everything. By the 1940s the pharmaceutical industry used turpentine in a plethora of disinfectants, liniments, medicated soaps, salves, and the like.

By the time B. C. Williams, my great-grandfather, died in 1913, the age of wooden ships was coming to a close and synthetic materials would soon lessen the demand for turpentine. Camps operated into the 1940s, but one by one the operations shut down. Thankfully, the longleafs hang on.

Plan a trip to the Apalachicola National Forest, St. Marks National Wildlife Refuge, or the Blackwater River State Forest. Walk among the longleaf pines. Listen to the breeze sifting through the long needles. Examine a cone. Hear the birds and try to find a gopher tortoise burrow and maybe a tortoise too. If you are very lucky, you won't hear the noise of modern life. Close your eyes and imagine this forest as it once was, stretching for miles and miles. Listen for the creaks of harnesses as teams of oxen and mules pull heavy wagons loaded with full barrels of crude gum for distilling at the fire still. Smell the exquisite air. Appreciate beyond measure what survives.

GAIL FISHMAN

GAIL FISHMAN, *a Florida native, lives in Tallahassee with three cats and a dog. She is the author of* Journeys Through Paradise: Pioneering Naturalists in the Southeast.

GOLD IN THE PINES

Wakulla Manatee

At Wakulla's lower bridge, the river spreads wide
and warm. Here, we know, a handful of manatees
browse among the aquatic grasses in the late summer
months. We seek the convergence of a staggering
sunset, air-breathing manatee, cautious raccoon,
caroling frogs, and a full moon rising. But there
is a price to pay: battalions of no-see-ums, and
bloodsucking mosquitoes so thick a few are inhaled
on each breath. Bats veer close; the insects we attract
offer them a dense buffet. The unrelenting insects
drive us to paddle steadily downriver.

The gathering force of the moon seems at first the
glow of a far-off city, or a fire lit on the horizon. Soon
it burns up through the tree trunks and the round
palmetto canopy, becomes a single inarguable eye.
Mullet jump from the silver river, then slap back
into place, reenter. The moon tries on and discards
fragments of cloud—a wisp, then a wrap of cirrus— but

finally decides to simply hang in the empty night, a huge pendant set in a black velvet box. Then we spot what we thought we came to see: a bouquet of bubbles and the whiskered snout of a manatee surfacing to breathe. A single miracle among the many. When it's time to go, we try to paddle backward upstream to keep the moon and the manatee in view. The kayaks resist, twirling us to face upriver over and over. Reluctantly, finally, we obey, and paddle toward the dark, and home.

SWALLOW-TAILED
KITE

Wakulla County

Free for the Taking

CRYSTAL WAKOA

"I'll work for this land. I'll really work hard."

That's what I told my partner, Freedan, when we first stood on the bank of the sinkhole. A sapphire bowl of springwater, glassy and still, mirrored the sun-sparkled silhouettes of trees. In the center of the pool, one white cloud floated in a blue shimmer of sky, a reflection so true it hushed our thoughts. A pileated woodpecker hammered halfway up the loblolly pine on the far bank. Apart from love, I never wanted anything so badly in my life.

After long minutes, I spoke. "Do you really think we'll be able to buy it?" My voice was a whisper of longing and doubt.

"He shook on it," said Freedan. "Let's hope that will be enough."

"He" was one Gerald Harris who, with his business partner, was selling a hundred-acre tract of land in Wakulla County, none of it timbered in at least fifty years. It included a half mile of river frontage and was exactly what Biophilia, the land cooperative we'd joined forces with, had been hoping to find. We'd met many times in potluck supper style, getting to know one another and hammering out by-laws, but this one-hundred-acre plot was the first piece of land we had looked at with the possibility of buying. But like a bride that sits in the choir room, frozen in ambivalence, her wedding guests leaving the church, the Biophilia group, at the final hour, declined Harris's offer. Harris realized there was more profit in carving up the land and did just that, creating eight long, skinny tracts east of Tiger Hammock Road, each with its few precious feet of river frontage, and seven pieces west of Tiger Hammock.

131

Freedan and I were searching for a place to settle and raise our beautiful three-year-old daughter, Lumin. Since her birth, we'd moved eight times, from Tennessee to New Mexico to the Caribbean. We found loveliness everywhere, but no place called to me until we landed in north Florida. Here, a yearning set hold in me like I'd never known before. I itched to put down roots on Harris's westernmost five acres that cradled this sinkhole in its corner.

"What do you mean you didn't give him a down payment?" I had nearly jumped down Freedan's throat when he walked in the door. I'd been at work when Freedan and Mr. Harris brokered the agreement.

"He wouldn't take it," Freedan had said, pacing the room. He'd plopped down into a battered old chair we had purchased at a yard sale. "I don't get it. Harris said he's waiting until all fifteen lots are sold. Then he'll do all the closings at once. I tried to give him earnest money: one hundred dollars. Five hundred dollars. Whatever he wanted. But he refused."

"He's waiting for a better offer, it's gotta be," I'd moaned.

"Maybe so," Freedan had said. "But I asked him, so we have a deal? And he said yes. I couldn't force him to take the money, so I told him it's a rare thing these days to commit with one's word and I respect that. I gave him my hand and he shook it. Let's hope that will be enough."

I called Harris for updates many times in the four months prior to closing, trying to sound as if I really did trust him to make good on his word. Once on a visit to the sinkhole, which had become a sort of sanctuary to me, I met a close-lipped man poking about. Doubt plagued me. Harris was, after all, in the business to make money. I worried right up until closing day, when pure relief gave way to pure joy, mixed in with a bit of chagrin at my apparent misjudgment of Harris's intentions. I simply could not believe my good luck.

I've been blessed to call this sandy patch of woods and water my home since 1986. Although Freedan and I parted ways a year later, he first settled me and Lumin on the land I loved.

Two years after we purchased the land, a consultation I had with William Webster, a Crawfordville attorney, turned to friendly chatter. I watched his eyes round when I told him where I lived and how I came to own the land.

"You're not going to believe this," Webster said. "Gerald Harris came to me all in a quandary about that same time. He told me people were swarming out of the woods wanting to buy that sinkhole. He had no idea it carried such

CRYSTAL WAKOA

value and wanted to sell it to the highest bidder but he'd shaken hands on a deal with somebody. That somebody must have been you and Freedan. Gerald asked me if a handshake was legally binding. I told him that would be up to a judge if the buyer decided to sue for breach of contract. I always wondered what Gerald did with my advice!"

I about fell out of my chair. "My intuition was right all along!" I practically shouted. "I never really believed we had a deal until we signed that deed." I showered a belated profusion of thanks on Mr. Webster.

We live in a web of relationships so finely woven and crisscrossed that just a quiver in one strand has the power to rewire the whole web in a configuration we could have never dreamed possible. Who knows how many other invisible threads conspired to bring me and the sinkhole together in a bond of mutual stewardship?

The sinkhole is set like a jewel in a limestone cup amidst a splendor of hickory, beech, magnolia, laurel oak, loblolly, and white oak. The water's surface is about forty feet across from any spot on the shore; there's a wider opening below, fanning out into a broad cave beneath the ground where a huge laurel oak was downed in Hurricane Kate and where my deck sits now. If the aquifer got too low, this is where the land would collapse, revealing the sinkhole's truer size. The nearly vertical bank—a mesh of roots, rock and native flora, drops fifteen feet to a narrow rim of sandy shore. Giant boulders form the limestone shelf beneath the water's surface. Beyond the ledge, it's a straight drop, fifty-five feet at the sinkhole's center.

There are three ways to enter the sinkhole. You can wade in slowly and register the shock of the sixty-five degree water, one body part at a time. This is the prayerful way or the cowardly way, depending on your intentions. In either case, you'll be chest deep by the time you reach the stepping-off point. Then there's my daughter Lumin's favorite—immersion via the rope swing. I've watched her literally thousands of times take her stance on the thick grape vine root that juts out of the ground near the top of the bank to form the perfect launching pad. In my mind's eye, I can picture her at age seven, extending her arms as high and as far from her body as she can, securing her hands above two of the rope's knots. She balances there momentarily, lifts onto her tiptoes, and in a split-second of grace, leaps forward and up to grab the rope's next highest knot. I watch her soar with the ease of a heron, legs

FREE FOR THE TAKING

trailing, over the rocks and the water. She lets go at the exact apex of the rope's trajectory, and drops like an arrow into the sinkhole's open heart. Now Lumin is twenty-two, an older wood nymph, but she still swings her way into the sinkhole whenever she's home.

The third way is the quickest—my favorite. Perched atop a limestone boulder on the shore, I take a deep breath and launch, gliding out over the limestone ledge, the cold shock hitting me all at once. When acclimated, I float on my back and look up into a bowl of sky framed by the lacy branches of pine and oak and hickory. If I'm lucky I spot a swallow-tailed kite floating high in that bowl; relaxing into the sinkhole's embrace, the kite and I are kin, suspended in primary elements.

Floating is one of my most favorite activities in all the world. As a water-crazed kid growing up in a lakeless, riverless patch of Ohio farmland, I'd drape my legs over the side of the municipal swimming pool every day of the too-short summer, lie on my back with ears barely submerged, close my eyes, and float, disappearing into pure sensation. A natural and spontaneous meditation, this is one magical childhood art that has not been lost in my adulthood. The sinkhole wraps her arms around me and I'm a goner. Gone to sunlight and green leaves. Gone to silence and the present moment. Once, floating under the spindly ironwood branch that extends out over the surface of the water, I watched a female cardinal alight smack in the middle of the four-foot length of oak snake sprawled out on his favorite afternoon branch. The snake nearly fell onto my raft as he sprung to strangle her, catching himself with the tail of his body, wrestling his feathery meal into his unhinged jaws. We both digested something wild that day, something essential that feeds our sense of belonging to a place.

The watery gem in my backyard is one of thirty or more sinkholes dotted across the Wakulla County landscape. The technical name for them is "karst window sinkholes," so named because they offer a glimpse into the cave system that underlies our bioregion. My sinkhole's window is a narrow crack in the limestone wall that runs the length of the back of the wide-mouthed cave below my deck. Other sinkholes, like the "river sinks" off Greenlea Road, offer a picture-window view. All of the karst window sinks are fed by the Floridan aquifer that underlies most of our state. Wakulla Springs, three miles north of my home, pours 220 million gallons of the aquifer every day into the spectacular headspring and river so many of us hold dear. Like an ancient mother feeding her children for eternity, Wakulla Springs sings her lullaby: "You will always have enough." Until now, that message was never doubted.

A business proposal recently put to the Wakulla County Commission made me sit up and take notice. Two miles as the crow flies from my sinkhole and just two miles west of Wakulla Springs, resides another landowner, a couple, I'll call them the Lowes. Their designs on the aquifer running beneath their land are to pump it (340,000 gallons per day) and truck it (three tankers per hour) ninety-five miles to Madison, Florida, and sell it to a water bottling company. In early January 2004, Wakulla County Commissioners voted 3–2 in favor of the Lowes' enterprise. It was a pro-development vote that could have set Wakulla County down the next step on the slippery path to an intrastate pipeline. Luckily, groundwater removal requires the approval of four commissioners, arresting the exploitative plan, at least for now.

What are the rights and responsibilities of all of us who are privileged to live in water-rich north Florida? What does it mean to say "my" sinkhole? To own land that harbors a spring? Always to me it's meant using common sense: don't use petrochemicals on the lawn; don't cut down the trees whose roots help hold the bank in place; use cedar and cypress for decking instead of treated lumber; don't disturb the old raccoon who has cut her den in the side of the bank; be careful of the musk turtle eggs on the shore. Treat the sinkhole with respect and be grateful for the delight it brings. Under our system of laws, land ownership comes with boundaries defined by a perimeter of orange survey flags. Cross the line and you're trespassing, a punishable offense. If land comes blessed with an opening into the aquifer, does the owner have a right to pump all he wants? If so, why can't anyone drill a well and do the same? Where is the line that says, "this much is yours and no more?"

The bottling plant in Madison that would buy the Lowes' Wakulla County springwater is owned by the Nestle Corporation, headquartered in Switzerland. We know Nestle as the world's largest food conglomerate, but it is also aggressively buying water rights around the world to sell local waters to non–local markets. Some of their labels are familiar to us: Deer Park, Zephyrhills, Perrier, Ozarka, Poland Spring. The 1.47 million gallons of water Nestle bottles every day in Madison carries the Deer Park label. You might buy a bottle from the convenience store next time you gas up your car. How could you know the source of that water to be the Withlacoochee River's Blue

Spring? You may have taken your kids there to swim one hot summer day, or paddled your canoe downstream twelve miles where the river spills into the Suwannee. Who gives Nestle the right to bottle up the Withlacoochee's water and sell it to you? How is it that Nestle can take up to 2 million gallons out of Blue Spring every single day of the year and not pay a penny for it? Why isn't this called theft? How does such a thing come about?

My husband David and I are welcomed out of the January rain by Tom and Mary Beth, the hosts of tonight's study group on corporate globalization. It's warm inside, the living room's ochre-painted walls boasting an assortment of original art, including Tom's photomontages. Mary Beth hands me a cup of tea in a bright orange mug as ten or twelve friends settle into a circle of motley chairs. Every Thursday evening we meet to try to understand the world economic philosophy and the alphabet-soup of organizations and trade agreements it has birthed. Tonight's topic is globalization and water.

Norine, our facilitator, presents a synopsis of the first article: She tells us that the Canadian-based company Global H2O signed a thirty-year contract with the town of Sitka, Alaska, to export 18.2 billion gallons of glacier water per year to China. There it will be bottled in a "free trade zone" where labor is cheap. My hackles go up.

Norine continues: Sun Belt Water, a California corporation, is suing the Canadian government because British Columbia banned the export of bulk water, which voided Sun Belt's contract. Sun Belt Water claims that British Columbia's law violates investor rights protected under the North American Free Trade Agreement (NAFTA), and is claiming $10 billion in compensation for lost profits.

"Unbelievable," says David in disgust. The rest of our group is stunned into silence. We're usually animated this early in the evening, but tonight the mood is somber. Our goal is simply to educate ourselves about globalization. After six weeks, all of us feel like we're getting it. Our feelings mirror the state of our world—small, fragile.

Kitty jolts us out of our silence: "What is it about Americans that prevent them from speaking out? In Germany we have just as many distractions to put us to sleep, but people rally around issues like these; they're out in the streets with banners and puppets." Kitty's voice is passionate, entreating. I'm glad she's in the group.

Mary Beth protests: "But how are we supposed to know that Sun Belt is suing Canada? The WTO [World Trade Organization] hears that fight, not the American people, and we all know their dispute resolution board doesn't exactly publish their minutes in the daily paper. It's a three-member secret tribunal and whatever they decide trumps any law of the land."

"If people knew this stuff, they'd be outraged." Barry leans forward in his seat and his hands begin to talk, too. "I'm feeling tremendously frustrated. I don't know how to talk to people about any of this. No one has a clue and it's all too bad to be true. I'm afraid they'll look at me like some kind of conspiracy nut."

After a pause Norine says, "If we could find just one really big success story that showed the people winning over corporate globalization, maybe we could use it as an educational tool."

"I know one," replies Dubravko, "Cochabamba, Bolivia. It was the biggest story of 2000, even though we didn't hear about it in this country." Dubravko explains: "Bechtel—yup, the same group rebuilding Iraq—well, Bechtel bought Bolivia's water system and immediately jacked the rates up 35 percent. To the peasants, that meant paying 20 percent of their income just for water. Thousands of Bolivians marched to Cochabamba, not just once, either. The director of the World Bank called them rioters and the police came out en masse. People got shot, some kids were blinded, but in the end, Bolivia kicked Bechtel out and the local communities control their water again."

Karla jumps into the conversation: "This is what gets me: that three giant corporations are positioning themselves to take over not only our public water systems, but our springs and groundwater, too. It's a no-brainer for them—America's water, free for the taking, courtesy of Joe taxpayer and Mother Nature. Think about it—Suez, Vivendi, and RWE, the three biggest water dealers, have already bought up the three leading U.S. water companies. Those corporations care about one thing and one thing only and it's not whether our grandkids are going to have anything to drink other than Coke and Pepsi. Money is the bottom line in the corporate takeover of the world's water. It's happened all over the rest of the world and we're next, unless we do something now, or yesterday."

"It's happening right now in our backyard," I say. "The water Nestle pumps out of Blue Spring for free costs us, the consumers, five to ten times as much as gasoline. Really! I did the math. And now it looks like anybody

FREE FOR THE TAKING

137

with a well can do the same thing." I fill the group in on the Wakulla County proposal.

"We're doomed," Jeff says, only half-joking, and the rest of us laugh to keep from crying. We're learning things we'd rather not know.

On a January morning, I rise early to stoke the fire. It's a shimmering bed of coals inside the wood stove. I leave the door ajar and the damper open while I step out the back door and head for the woodshed. And there it is—a pool of mystery, silent in the morning air, alive, breathing mist that lifts in waves of lace off its liquid blue skin. I stand there in my robe and slippers, my breath visible, too, and bow in gratitude to this holy place.

Winter's first hard freeze always dazzles me just like an unseasonably early snowfall once did in my youth. I wake to find, not the dust of virgin snow on barren trees, but a similar, shocking delight—the sinkhole has turned from green to startling blue overnight. Cold night air chills the surface water. As the ambient temperature continues to drop, the water cools to a greater depth until, at some point, the scale is tipped—the top waters become cooler than the bottom waters; the sinkhole turns top-heavy and inverts. Microscopic algae that live in the light-infused surface water, giving the sinkhole its green hue most of the year, sink to the bottom and disappear. Oxygen-starved water rises in its place, reflecting all colors but a brilliant azure. By early afternoon, the sun sends its rays on a chase down the watery depths, and the sinkhole's center, unshaded by its wooded banks, becomes a crystal, cerulean pearl.

It's hard to fathom that our region's fresh water, seemingly unlimited, is not. We only have to look to the southern half of our state for proof that without proper foresight, planning, and management, our fresh water will not last forever. Wakulla Springs's maternal mantra "You will always have enough" comes from a natural intelligence predating and uncorrupted by private corporations that make a business of water exploitation. What has always been viewed as a commons, a resource belonging to all life forms that depend on it for survival, is now being viewed as a commodity, "a useful thing, an article of trade, a product."

It won't be long before south Florida water barons come to the Panhandle to strike a deal in water. The politically influential Council of 100, a group of power brokers promoting economic growth in Florida, was careful to avoid the words "pipeline" and "commodity" in its September 2003 Water Management Task Force Report. Yet the report turned the concept of stewardship on its head by accusing [North] Florida's water management districts of acting protective of the water within their natural watershed boundaries. The districts, says the Council, "think they own their water." The solution they promote is to establish a political body to oversee all of Florida's water management districts and "develop a system that enables water distribution from water-rich areas to water-poor areas." Sounds like a pipeline to me, with a select group tied to money, not place, to oversee it. The Council of 100's report highlights what is most disturbing about the Lowes' plan to ship aquifer water from Wakulla County to Madison for bottling. Their proposal, relatively small as it is, sets a precedent that involves transporting bulk water across county lines. Once that tap is open, most likely we will never be able to shut it off.

To avoid the pipeline issue, the Lowes could decide to bottle "their" water on site. But what kind of sense does it make to take groundwater, pump it into plastic bottles (most of which end up in landfills where they leach toxins into the groundwater), truck it all over the nation, market it back to us, leading us to believe it's now healthier than tap water, and sell it for enormous profit? Who benefits from this?

Nestle pockets over $7 billion a year from its bottled water industry. Their research department hit pay dirt when they targeted Blue Spring—plenty of water in a poor rural county with permissive water use rules. For the promise of jobs, Madison County fulfilled Nestle's wish list: build us a road with taxpayer money, pay for our water and sewer lines, and exempt us from your comprehensive plan. Most significantly, Nestle gets up to two million gallons of Blue Spring water every day, three hundred sixty-five days a year, free for the taking. In exchange, three hundred Madison County residents get decent paying jobs.

"We expect three hundred trucks a day in and out of that site," says Madison County Economic Development Council Executive Director Keith Mixon. "In three years, that plant, if the projections are accurate, will total 1 million square feet. In a county like Madison, that's a miracle."

Miracle or monster? We need to decide *before* a corporate water giant comes to Wakulla County, *before* the next water business plan is proposed, who, if anyone, owns the water beneath our feet and who is entitled to take it. Because if we don't address these two basic questions, it will all be decided for us. We cannot allow private corporations to manage our most precious resource. Trade agreements like NAFTA guarantee that corporate profits will rule over the real needs of people and our lands. Citizens are going to have to take the lead, creating the political arguments that demand the right to keep our water in the public commons for good.

"You're dreaming," my brother says over the phone as I explain how the global water scene reflects what's happening in Wakulla County, and my hopes for turning things around. "You're right," I say, "but somebody's got to dream." As I lie in a tube in the sinkhole this summer day, I'm drunk on the sun, mesmerized by the light dancing its wild jitterbug on the curved base of the oak that juts from the bank. A mess of crows is barking overhead. I close my eyes and dream of an Alternate Council of 100; it's a confident and spirited group of hydrologists, geologists, botanists, lobbyists, farmers, and business owners from all over the Panhandle, united in their love for our region's water and passionate in their defense of how best to manage it. With the dollars and prayers of every citizen that benefits from their efforts backing them, they march, with the stamina and persistence of thirsty Bolivian peasants, into our Governor's mansion and the offices of our legislators. I open my eyes to wonder at the crows' sudden silence. A movement on the bank catches my eye. A black racer slivers deftly down the steep side and takes a long drink. I watch her tongue flicker like a Morse code tapping its thanks as her thirst is slaked. I watch her belly back up the bank more slowly than she descended and disappear. In this moment, the world seems perfect.

CRYSTAL WAKOA *currently lives in Tallahassee with her husband and step-daughter. She hopes that she can still recognize the Wakulla County landscape when she and her husband return home there in three years. She aspires to be a voice for Florida's water.*

CRYSTAL WAKOA

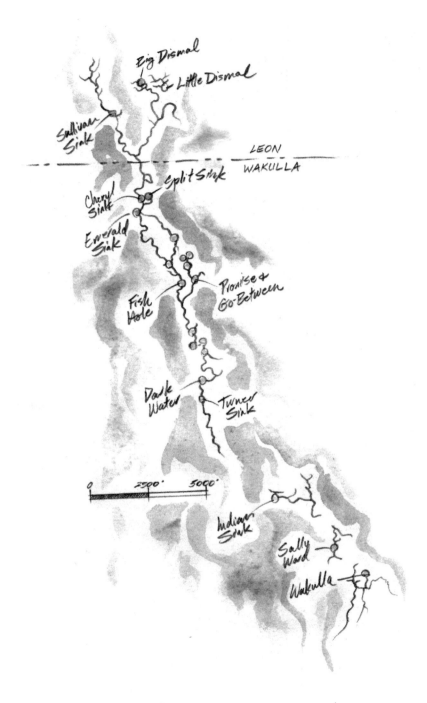

Big Dismal

Little Dismal

Sullivan Sink

LEON

WAKULLA

Split Sink

Cheryl Sink

Emerald Sink

Promise & Go-Between

Fish Hole

Dark Water

Turner Sink

0   2500'   5000'

Indian Sink

Sally Ward

Wakulla

FREE FOR THE TAKING

Wakulla Springs

apple snail eggs-small + pink

hydrilla

The Silence
of the Limpkins

SUSAN CERULEAN

From the top of the tower, where dripping wet children generally contemplate their next trick dive, the chalice of Wakulla Springs wells deepest midnight blue. The water must be clear enough today for the glass bottom boats to run; I see one gliding toward me across the empty swimming area. Closer by, a bull alligator growls, and a pair of common moorhens cluck and bleat.

But as I look more closely, I see that the shoulders of the spring, even sixty feet below the water's surface, are weighted with somber reefs of an ominous watery weed. It is as if an enormous, dark-as-death animal has fitted its body to the run of the river, blotting the passage of fishes and the sun. As far as I can see downstream, the weed coagulates at the water's surface in scuzzy yellowish mats. I train my binoculars on two tricolored herons picking along this unnatural platform. I wonder if their long, slender toes will get hung up in the stuff, locking them in place.

The waterfront at Wakulla Springs State Park, Florida, is closed to swimmers, divers, and dabblers this morning: it's a day appointed for herbicide treatment. I've come to observe the effort to revive our area's most beloved river and to talk about its lost flagship bird, the limpkin, with

143

longtime colleague, Dana Bryan. Dana, now Chief of the Florida Park Service's Bureau of Natural and Cultural Resources, is running a little behind, so I clomp down the steps to the tower's lower level, where a group of workers confer. I recognize the man in charge—Jesse Van Dyke; he's with the state's Bureau of Invasive Plant Management. He's dressed in blue work shirt, boots, and close-fitting sunglasses; according to Dana, when Jesse heard that hydrilla had invaded Wakulla Springs, he had only this to say to the park's managers: "You are toast."

Eight enormous plastic tanks line the dock, each holding 250 gallons of an herbicide named Aquathol K. A crooning battery-operated pump meters the weed poison through clear plastic tubing the thickness of a spaghetti strap.

"Any leaks?" Jesse asks a coworker.

"Dry as a bone," the other replies.

"Good," says Jesse, staring out at the styrofoam balls that buoy the plastic tubing the entire width of the spring boil. "We don't want any hot spots." He explains the procedure: "For the next forty-eight hours, we'll drip a half gallon per minute of this herbicide into the spring run. We want to treat the entire river evenly, all the way across. We want to get it right. The park's been spending so much time and money on mechanical control these last few years: this hydrilla we're after is one of the world's most aggressive weeds."

A lean and energetic red-haired park ranger identifies himself as Mike Nash, and elaborates. "Last month, the boat lanes were so full of hydrilla, we couldn't run our tours. We pulled out five thousand pounds of the stuff four times a day, for several days in October alone. We even had to clear a path for Henry the Pole-Vaulting Fish; people count on seeing that on our glass bottom boat tours."

By now, Dana Bryan has joined us on the dock, and he jumps into the conversation, explaining the short, dreadful history of hydrilla at Wakulla Springs. "When we found it, in spring 1997, it was still mostly restricted to the headspring. But then it took off like a shot, and we've never been able to catch it."

The park staff surely has tried. Since 1997, they've muscled around 6.5 million pounds of the stuff from the swimming area and boat lanes, using dip nets, booms, hand pulling, and mechanical harvesters. The scary weed has far outpaced these physical control measures, so the park has turned to periodic herbicide treatments.

SUSAN CERULEAN

"I don't relish the thought of putting herbicides in this river," says Dana Bryan as we make our way to the boat dock, where Ranger Nash is preparing to give us a downriver tour. "But it's either that, or face ecological collapse."

How did the river used to run? I remember standing at the edge of this swimming area just last May on an annual Mother's Day outing. The immense spread of the azure spring still seemed a perfect stage for my sons David and Patrick and their friends, beautiful long-bodied teens, who leaped from the diving tower, over and over, and then raced to the low dock to warm themselves in the sun. We, their mothers, watched them from the cypress-shaded shore, as we've done ever since they were babes. The chill of this water must have informed their cells even during our pregnancies, when we'd cool our heavy bellies in this spring during the hot summer months. But as I eased myself deep into the river's crystal chill last May, I kicked up murky clouds of khaki-green algae that hung over the lime-rock bottom, and I saw that the eelgrass meadows were gone. It can't have been that long since these lovely rightful grasses still grew. I remember how they flowed with the current like a woman's long hair, spring green or gold, the sun lighting their lengths. To swim from the dock to the tower, you'd have to push past that ribboning grass, your extended swimming body just inches above the shimmer of the plants. Our little children thought its tickling an unwanted intimacy, wondered what might be lurking in its thickness, ready to grab or nip. But I'd slip on my mask and snorkel and stroke over it towards a small column of clear water and a certain large limestone boulder where I'd briefly perch. A squadron of bluegill might scatter at my approach, or a startled soft-shelled turtle. Then I'd swim hard for the deep water along the guard rope, where the fish would be larger and sleeker at the edge of the spring's blue chasm. It's some combination of the freezing cold and the loveliness that attracts me so to Wakulla. For the minutes I am immersed in that water, I am fully present. Not in my head. Nowhere else.

We board the *Limpkin*, one of four river cruise boats used to tour up to forty-five visitors at a time, about a mile down the Wakulla and back to the headspring. This is where most everyone around here takes out-of-town guests on a holiday visit when you want to show them the best our area has to offer. It's almost required.

The Silence of the Limpkins

As I settle into a seat near the *Limpkin's* bow, I watch the dozens of black vultures that bead the branches of the rusty-needled cypress trees. Familiar river residents slip past our boat: a kingfisher, four Suwannee cooters on a single downed log, wintering teal, and wigeon. Over the side of the boat, I can see how the hydrilla plants, up close, resemble enormous bouquets of bottle brushes packed tightly together, stiff to the touch not soft and feathery. They also look very familiar, as though I've seen them in a hundred aquariums before, and I probably have. Hydrilla was imported to the United States from India for the indoor aquarium trade in the 1950s. No one knew it would become a major invader of Florida's lakes and rivers. I watch a foot-long alligator struggle through the hydrilla mat, coming to rest on top. It holds the tiny reptile like an unnatural sling.

"Hydrilla is all about territory and light," says Dana. "Left unchecked, it forms a canopy that shades out and eventually displaces the native vegetation almost completely. This plant is not so much affected by the underwater flow of the spring run; it molds that flow."

I ask Dana (an impressive birder long before he was promoted to an indoor job) how he believes the river's renowned wildlife populations have responded to the hydrilla invasion.

"Well, we didn't see any purple gallinules last summer, and I'm sure there are fewer anhingas," he says, beginning to tick through a mental list.

Ranger Nash nods, "I used to see six to eight anhinga and yellow-crowned night heron nests on this boat tour. People loved looking at the baby birds rearing their heads up out of their nests."

"It used to be almost anytime you went out, you'd see eight or ten wood duck families," continues Dana. "I haven't seen them in a while, either."

"And of course, the limpkins have disappeared."

According to the Park's surveys, the Wakulla's limpkin population has been drifting downward slowly for some years, although they were reliably tallied in the double digits until the summer count of 1997, when only a single bird was spotted. Rare, chocolate-brown limpkins stand about as tall as a small egret or heron; a spangling of white flecks their heads, necks, and shoulders. Though the limpkin is far less showy than most of our wading birds, none can match its astonishing cry. The eerie resounding *"Kur-r-ee-ow, kow, kow, kow, kr-ow, kr-ow"* of male limpkins proclaiming their territories surely has bolstered Wakulla's jungly Tarzan mystique; but all on its own, the bird's wail evokes in us a powerful, wordless longing for the wild.

"Used to be, you'd always see at least one limpkin camped out on a cypress knee around here, cleaning out an apple snail shell, or opening a mussel," says Dana Bryan wistfully as the *Limpkin* engines the left-hand turn that will circle us back to the dock. This man has been keeping tabs on Wakulla's limpkins since the late 1970s, when he rode every boat tour that left the dock, collecting data for his master's thesis.

"Do you think most visitors see what's going on at Wakulla, what we're losing?" I ask him.

He says: "Maybe 95 percent of the folks who take the river boat cruise or a glass bottom boat tour are still completely happy just to see some alligators and birds close up. Not everybody knows or cares about our lost limpkins, or apple snails, or even the eelgrass forests."

But the limpkin is already so thoroughly missed by Park staff, they've erected an interpretive audio station in the waiting area for boat tours to tell the bird's story, so it won't be forgotten. If you press the square white button on the exhibit, a recorded wail will startle the birdwatchers at the end of the dock, causing them to whip their binoculars to their eyes, hoping to glimpse that rare and vanished bird. The silencing of Wakulla's limpkins, Bryan and other scientists agree, has much to do with the loss of key food items from the river run: the apple snail in particular. We've seen less than a handful of the snail's easy-to-spot eggs on today's tour. Apple snails, whose broad spiraled shells match the milk-chocolate brown of the bird that so loves to eat them, are equipped with both gills and lungs. Mostly, though, they breathe with their lungs. It'd be hard for the snails to work their way from the river bottom through this impenetrable mat of hydrilla to reach the necessary air.

"But there's no single smoking gun that explains the loss of apple snails and their eggs from Wakulla," says Dana Bryan.

You can still see limpkins on the nearby Wacissa River. We launch our boats into its headspring on a Saturday afternoon, just to be certain. My husband Jeff and I take the canoe; our two fifteen-year-old boys and a nephew sprint downriver in sportier kayaks. The river channel, broader than the Wakulla's, is filled with interesting gabbles of birds. I hear a pileated woodpecker drumming, duets of common moorhens, a strident red-shouldered hawk, a creaky roost of blackbirds. Do I imagine, or is this river so much more alive than its sister to the west?

I've visited both of these rivers almost equally over the past two decades. If I want solitude and the wild, I generally take my kayak to Wacissa. If I want to play or picnic or lounge with family, Wakulla is more often my choice. If you'd asked me even a year ago which river was less protected, more in need of help, I'd have said the Wacissa. I've seen its alligators brutalized by gaff hooks and left to die; ducked my kayak between dueling airboats; skirted nasty piles of trash in the parking area; knew its uplands to be pine plantations ditched and drained by the St. Joe Paper Company.

But that's not what I'm thinking today. Jeff and I maneuver our white canoe under the shade of the cypress, behind a seeding stand of wild rice. We scan the waist-high cypress knees that cluster like children about the stiff wide skirts of their mother trees. Immediately, we notice clutches of apple snail eggs, a foot or two from the water's surface, all around. While I study the pinkish eggs, a reproductive miracle I'd always noticed on our rivers, and always taken for granted, Jeff leans over the canoe's edge, drops morsels of our fried chicken lunch into the shallows, and reports on the ensuing competition between crayfish and minnows. The snail eggs have been laid ten to thirty at a time, glued in small drifts to cypress bark, or rigid bulrush stems. They resemble plump berries the size of a pea. Quite a few have yet to hatch, and these are dark with the embryonic bodies of the apple snails-to-be.

When we head back against the current, upstream, our slowed pace allows us a good look at Wacissa's underwater geography. Hydrilla has colonized this river, too; long stringers of the stuff finger toward our boat. But unlike her sister, the Wakulla, Wacissa still opens to the sky, blinking back shaggy eelgrass eyelids to reveal sandy stretches of bottom studded with all manner of apple snail shells, and other mollusk shells, as well. The leaves of the native underwater grasses are strappy, about as wide as amaryllis, dipping and moving like a run of slim-bodied eels.

I'm so taken by the watery sun-bright meadows of mostly natural vegetation, the hopeful flow and light of the place, that I almost miss it: a limpkin flies close, trailing its long legs like a crane, then teeters into a marshy stand of plants. We must be too close for this bird's comfort: it eyes us closely, begins to click its bill. As it slowly relaxes, it probes its thick bill into the trampoline of water lettuce, eelgrasses, asters, and hyacinth where it stands. Two noisy little blue herons work the same beat; all three execute quick lifts of

SUSAN CERULEAN

the head as we paddle past, lowering our eyes, trying not to spook them away.

Minutes later, we spot a second limpkin belly-deep in the dazzle of sun and water lighting the body of the river. We actually see it fish a fat brown apple snail from the marsh and quickly dig out its flesh. When the bird moves on, I explore with my own hand where the limpkin had just stood, brailling how an apple snail might easily wind its life through this still-loose tangle of vegetation to reach the air.

On the Wakulla, when we reach the "back jungle," Ranger Nash cuts off the motor, and we drift. "This is where we do the Tarzan thing on our boat tours," he says. "You can see that there are still mats of eelgrass back in here."

But here's another disturbing sight: what eelgrass remains appears to be cloaked with a spectral, brownish algae. Even the hydrilla bears khaki-colored capes of the stuff. What's that all about?

"The whole spring bowl has started getting draped with this algae periodically," says Ranger Nash. "It takes a pair of us scuba divers two tanks of air just to clear the significant features of the spring bowl for our tour boats." I'm touched again by this man's concern for the effects of Wakulla's invaders on park visitors.

"What we do first is jump off the tower and clean the limestone ledge where the Creature from the Black Lagoon emerged," Nash continues. "Then we swim to the mastodon bone site, strip off the algae, and reposition the bones. Then we go to Mother Nature's fish bowl, on to the hollow log, and finally, to what we call the bee tree," he finishes, traveling in his mind's eye past the underwater curiosities that have delighted patrons of the glass bottom boat tours for decades.

"This algae is new here," emphasizes Dana Bryan. "We didn't see it at all until just a few years ago. It's correlated with the increased nitrate load coming out of the spring. Between the total replacement of eelgrass with hydrilla, and this nutrient-gobbling algae, our spring run now has all the signature of an unhealthy system."

Can this be Wakulla Springs we're talking about? Can this be the spring described by an anonymous traveler in 1835 "to be of such perfect transparency, that the smallest object is seen at the immense depth of water below, and the spectator upon its surface, sits and shudders as if suspended on empty air?"

THE SILENCE OF THE LIMPKINS

What is this, that darkens our spring's perfect heart?

The pollution at Wakulla that feeds the hydrilla and the algae is measured in clumsy-big increments—the number of days each year the spring is clear enough to run the glass bottom boat tour—and measures so small we can barely comprehend: milligrams of nitrate per liter of water.

The limestone that underlies our bioregion is like an enormous rock sponge saturated with the freshest of water—our aquifer. As water pushes and struggles through the miles of belowground caverns and conduits, it springs to the surface where it can, responding to the unique geography we call "karst." This aquifer is the free and abundant source of the water we pump to meet all of our needs: drinking, washing, irrigating, industry. We're incredibly lucky this way. But it's just as easy to dirty this underground water, and we do. Along the way from Tallahassee to the coast, we withdraw what we desire, and we flush our wastes.

A Northwest Florida Water Management District study in 2002 found—not surprisingly—that the cities of Tallahassee and Woodville, suburbanized Leon County and of course, Wakulla County, overlie what's called the spring capture zone. In other words, most of the water that wells out of Wakulla Springs is funneled first below all the pipes and wastewater treatment facilities and septic tanks that we care to build. The City of Tallahassee's wastewater spray field on Tram Road is very possibly a source of the increasing nitrogen at the springs, says Wakulla County. But what about all your rural septic tanks, and future influxes from those enormous new proposed subdivisions? retorts the City of Tallahassee.

We can argue about the source of Wakulla's pollution, but we can't dispute the impaired purity of the place. Are we content as a people to simply steer our cars the length of Wakulla's heat-dusted road to spot the historic lodge and behind it the lake-like expanse of spring boil, and an alligator or two? Is that enough? To blur our eyes to what is, and wipe our memories clear of what so recently was?

If we fully believed in the sacredness of our springs, all of them, and honored them, wouldn't we draw a line around the ground that recharges them and figure out how to clean up after ourselves, and a better way to live?

After the *Limpkin* nudges into its stall at the boat dock and Ranger Nash ties her safely in place, we walk back to the herbicide operation at the dive tower. The men discuss a trial reintroduction of apple snail eggs they've begun, a joint experiment between Jesse Van Dyke's shop and the Park. Despite the complex forces challenging the spring, hope and even excitement lift their voices.

"I miss the limpkins," says Jesse Van Dyke. "Their silence disturbs me. But we're going to work hard to get a boot on the neck of this hydrilla and bring back apple snails to the river."

Two weeks from now, the men tell me, the hydrilla plants here will start to brown, then disintegrate bit by bit, dropping to the river's bottom. "By December 15, the river should look much more clear," says Jesse. "I think you'll like what you see."

So I return to Wakulla again in mid-December, on a low-ceilinged, heavy-clouded day. It's warm in the way north Florida can be in winter, just before a rainy front pulls colder temperatures in from the west. Again, the waterfront is empty; I go to the dive tower and sit, watching a mist swirl and rise from the surface of the river. The reefs of hydrilla are gone, topkilled by the herbicide treatment, beaten back for some months. Across the boil, a good-sized alligator tails through the clear water, holding its place against the current. I count twenty-nine white ibis working their way around the edge of the spring, sorting urgently through the duckweed and what must be small hillocks of decayed hydrilla. Their backs are bent low, and they continuously contact one another with an urgent, gruff honking, as they bobble along the collar of the spring bowl. On the dock, a lone cormorant spreads its back to take in the low winter sun.

I hear people approaching: three young mothers and their four little children are first through the gate, laden with buckets and baskets and towels.

"Will you help me make the biggest sand castle ever?" says a small one to a slightly older sister, her voice piping with excitement. "I think it's going to take up the whole world! Or at least the whole beach!"

A blond German couple strolls arm in arm to the water's edge, apparently daring each other to swim. The young man wades knee-deep in the water, mock-poses with flexed biceps, laughs at himself. His companion snaps his picture, using her expensive camera to shield against being pulled into the cold water.

One of the mothers strips her little baby to his diaper. He sits down hard, patting the water's surface with the flat of his hand, grinning. It's clearly not his first time at Wakulla: I remember how my son David's eyes went dark with shock the first time I lowered his six-month-old feet into this very water. The older children move sand into water, sticks into water, bodies into water.

"Watch this, Mommy!" says the biggest girl. "One, two, three . . . Mommy, I can go under!" She surfaces quickly, hair streaming into her eyes. "It's freezing, isn't it? It's like ice!" The children cry out as the sky begins to mist: "It's raining!" They splash springwater high in the air to meet the raindrops.

The German emerges from his swim, shivering, and the couple wanders back toward the lodge.

A school of mullet fins in close now, since most everyone's evacuated the cold water. One fish heaves clear of the spring run, two, three, four times, like a heavy skipping stone. Out beyond the dock, a glass bottom boat circles the headspring. "Henry," calls a ranger to the fish on the bottom of the river. "Henry, are you there? Come on out and give these people a show!"

Writer and activist SUSAN CERULEAN *lives with her family in Tallahassee. She loves to edit anthologies of personal essays: her collections include* The Book of the Everglades *(Milkweed Editions, 2002) and* The Wild Heart of Florida *(with Jeff Ripple, University Press of Florida, 1999). Cerulean's latest book, a nature memoir entitled* Tracking Desire: A Journey after Swallow-tailed Kites, *will be published by University of Georgia Press in 2005. Her essays have appeared in five anthologies and a variety of magazines and newspapers, including* Orion, Hope, *and* Defenders.

SUSAN CERULEAN

Cows eating
vegetation
in the spring
circa 1924

THE SILENCE OF THE LIMPKINS

Garden Pollinators

My garden trembles under the attentions of the lovers of late summer. Ruby-throated hummingbirds lower into the salvia bed, stroking like sleek fishes through an azure framework of flowers. Enormous yellow and black bumblebees clasp the open-lipped blooms, whole-bodied, hairy, indelicate. From a pink version of the same plant near my garden shed, sulfur butterflies hang folded—lemon-painted fans.

Let us praise the pollinators! They have never abandoned the garden, as I have, when the simmering rasp of cicadas drives the thermometer's mercury to a boil. All these summer months, I've mostly stayed in, testy, neglecting the real life outside. Overgrown weeds tell that truth.

But look at the fury of activity around the summersweet. The rosy, bottlebrush flowers of this small native shrub crawl with bees, tiny wasps, and beetles, drawn to the fragrance of the flower nectar

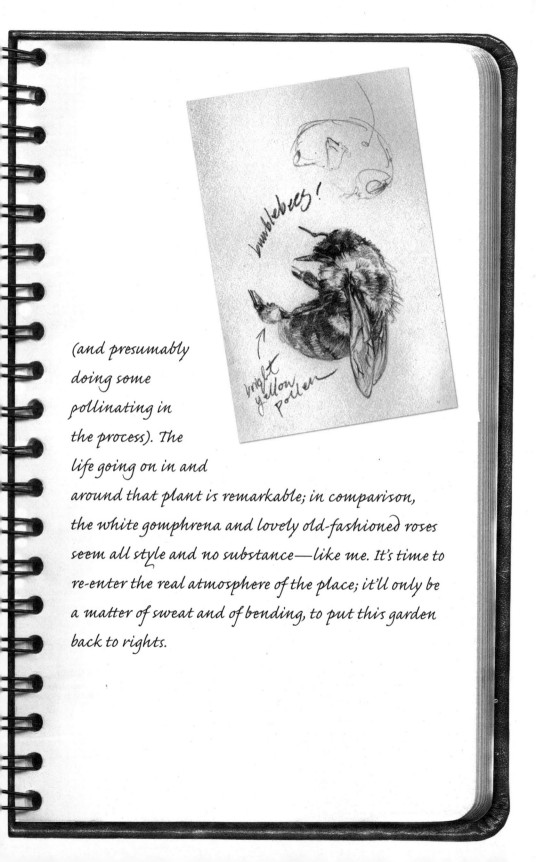

(and presumably
doing some
pollinating in
the process). The
life going on in and
around that plant is remarkable; in comparison,
the white gomphrena and lovely old-fashioned roses
seem all style and no substance—like me. It's time to
re-enter the real atmosphere of the place; it'll only be
a matter of sweat and of bending, to put this garden
back to rights.

sketch in
1834

Tallahassee

Postcard, 1912

creek as
it's routed
through
Cascades
Park 5/04

The Cascades,
Tallahassee, Fla.
213527

Florida's Lost Waterfall:
Cascades Park

JULIE HAUSERMAN

When schoolchildren visit the Florida State Capitol, the governor likes to tell them a story. First, he asks them, "How did Tallahassee become the capital of Florida?" Their small hands go up, and the governor calls on the kid who looks like he's going to explode with the answer. The kid says, "Because it's halfway between St. Augustine and Pensacola!"

And the governor says, "That's right! One man came from St. Augustine and one man came from Pensacola and they met here and decided this is where the capital should be!" Well, kind of. The governor leaves out the other part of the story, the one that might lead to some uncomfortable questions from the fresh-faced schoolchildren.

Questions like: Why would anybody turn a pretty waterfall into a town dump? And: What's toxic waste?

It isn't pretty, what the grown-ups did. Better to leave it like it is, a tangle of vines behind a fence with a sign warning you to keep away. No, it is time for the truth. The truth is that a waterfall—a waterfall!—beguiled the men who were assigned to find a site for Florida's Capitol.

Imagine it: a bubbling stream through deep green woods, and then a waterfall, cascading twenty to thirty feet through the wet air into a deep pool, perfect for swimming. It was right downtown. Locals called it the "Cascade," or sometimes, the "Cascades." It flowed near the hillside where the Capitol is now, most probably on the east side of South Monroe Street where the railroad bridge passes over the road. Using today's landmarks, the Cascade would have been behind Buddy's Marine, across South Monroe from an old square, pointed-roof building that was a bar and then a fruit stand. It was fed by a stream known today as the "St. Augustine Branch," which started near present-day Leon High School and ran down the canal that's now in the center of Franklin Boulevard. According to historian Jonathan Lammers, who did an exhaustive history of the Cascade, the stream historically wound through the valley at the eastern edge of Tallahassee before falling into a ravine created by erosion.

Of course, there's no waterfall there now. You have to go to Falling Waters State Park, halfway across the Panhandle, to see anything like it. The truth: I have wept for this lost place, felt fury in my belly that men could turn a stream into a concrete ditch and silence a waterfall with truckloads of garbage.

Why did they do it? I can't tell you. I can't possibly imagine any realistic justification for such behavior. It is an old Florida story, really. Why throw old washing machines into a woodland spring? Why drain the Everglades? Why fill the hole in the bottom of Lake Jackson with concrete? Why dig up Florida's ancient limestone and phosphate bones and sell them off? Why trash a perfectly good waterfall?

The white men who came upon it in 1823 must have heard the soft music of water tumbling over stones before they saw it. Can you see them, standing on the hillside?

"Gorgeous," one might have said.

"Yes," the other would agree. "It's big enough to turn a mill. The governor will love it."

They must have been tired. It's a long trip from where they started, St. Marks. Plus, they'd had a tense encounter with an Indian chief, who wasn't happy to see them. In his journal, one of the men wrote: "Here, the chief picked up a handful of dirt, held it out, and angrily declared that this was his land." Well, they'd deal with that whole thing later.

For now, they were focused on the errand that Governor William DuVal sent them on, setting up a capital. DuVal asked two guys—one was a lawyer, and the other was a doctor—to find a capital after Florida became a

JULIE HAUSERMAN

158

territory in 1822. Legislators kept dying on their way to the annual sessions in Pensacola and St. Augustine, and back then, they thought that was a bad idea. The doctor set out on horse from St. Augustine. The lawyer took a boat from Pensacola, and he had a lousy trip. In the Gulf, he got into a huge fight with his boat captain and was so furious he asked to be let off in the middle of swampy nowhere. The captain later cooled down and went looking for the lawyer. When the captain picked him up, the lawyer was half-blind and starved, trying to cross the Ochlockonee River on a piece of driftwood. Imagine how it felt, then, when he met up with the doctor in St. Marks, and eventually came up on that glen and waterfall.

Travelers described the site three years later in an 1825 edition of the *Pensacola Gazette:*

> Our party was not long in selecting a camping ground, and pitching their tent about midway of the southern slope, which might be taken for the land of the Fairies: to the southward and westward, the country opened to their view . . . at their feet a crystal fountain, gushing from the declivity of a hill; to the eastward the view was more confined by the thick foliage of the undergrowth, which served to screen the view, though not the sound of a beautiful cascade, which was formed by the rivulet above described, falling over the ledge of rocks into a deep glen, which forms a circle of about seventy yards in diameter.

On November 1, 1823, the lawyer, John Lee Williams, wrote

> Doct. Simmons has agreed that the Site should be fixed near the old fields abandoned by the Indians after Jackson's invasion, but has not yet determined whether between the . . . old fields, or on a fine high lawn about a mile W. In both spots, the water is plenty and good. . . . Directly east of the old fields runs a . . . stream of water which you must recollect. This stream, after running about a mile south, pitches about 20 or 30 feet into an immense chasm, in which it runs 60 or 70 rods to the base of a high hill which it enters among clefts of Amorphous argilaceous . . . rocks full of shells and other fossils.

But Florida's pioneers didn't think land ought to just sit there looking pretty. It had to work for a living. Settlers built a mill along the stream. And later, those lovely rocks full of shells and other fossils were gouged out and carted off to produce mortar for Florida's second Capitol in 1826. The lovely waterfall now had a rock quarry next to it, the first chapter in this story of lost opportunity.

For the waterfall, things got much worse. In the 1850s, railroad surveyors decided that the easiest route over hilly Tallahassee was to follow the valley of the St. Augustine Branch. That brought the tracks directly over the ridge where the Cascade waterfall flowed. Worried that the V made by the waterfall would undermine the new tracks, they started filling the natural chasm with railroad ties and other junk to make a level place for the tracks to cross.

"It was a shame it was done," wrote Elizabeth Brown, who moved to Tallahassee around 1828 and lived the rest of her life here. "The (rail)road could have gone on one side without any trouble."

Even after the railroad tracks destroyed the waterfall, the Cascade pool remained.

In 1890, the editor of the Tallahassee *Weekly Floridian* offered an excellent suggestion: "A good investment," he wrote, "would be the purchase of the 'Cascade' south of Tallahassee. If enclosed and cleaned out it could make an excellent swimming pool."

People did still swim there. It was also apparently a place where men met to drink, fish, and gamble. Old newspaper articles describe a few accidental drownings there, including "two small negro boys. . . . Their names were Charley and Lewis, aged respectively eight and nine years—the first belonging to Dr. Barnard and the last to Mrs. Sheppard. They had gone to the cascade to swim—jumped into the water without knowing it had greatly increased in depth."

The water was probably still clean then. But in 1895, the city actually started poisoning the Cascade. Officials built a coal gasification plant on the west side of Gadsden Street near what is today Cascades Park to provide natural gas for Tallahassee. It was a dirty business. Workers dumped tar and toxic chemicals into the beautiful St. Augustine Branch. The poisons seeped underground, and they never went away.

The deep Cascade pool was cut off from its waterfall, poisoned and injured. The city fathers decided that it was a dangerous mosquito breeding ground—wasn't all of Florida, really? They started filling the sinkhole with trash. After a while, it officially became the town dump.

From gorgeous waterfall to town dump—did anyone notice? Did anyone speak up? When the city plugged up the Cascade pool with garbage, the water still wanted to go there. It backed up, and that whole low area around South Monroe Street turned marshy. In 1924, city fathers built a ballpark for Tallahassee's centennial, on the east side of South Monroe Street near the lost waterfall. To keep the field from being spongy, crews got to work obliterating the last of the charming watercourse. They turned the meandering St. Augustine Branch into a concrete-lined ditch to route water away from the ball field.

"When these ditches are completed, many objectionable water holes will be done away with," the Tallahassee city manager wrote in 1928. My God. Is that Florida—or what? *Many objectionable water holes will be done away with.*

I keep thinking about an 1823 account by Williams, one of the explorers who scouted the Capitol site for Governor DuVal. He described "innumerable springs and small streams of water" around downtown Tallahassee. Think about how lovely those springs and rivulets would be downtown today, instead of concrete drainage systems that drown in a hard rain. Think about how nice it would be for the old Cascade pool to be a park. We'd have a marker there to commemorate the founding of Florida's capital and the waterfall that drew us here.

You can hardly find the Cascade anymore. One day, when it was raining like it meant business, I went looking. I drove along the old course of Cascade Creek to see where the water goes now. In the confines of the concrete drainage ditch in the center of Franklin Boulevard, the old Cascade Creek bunches up in an angry rush. I crane my neck to see it, cars hard on my bumper, people wondering what I'm looking at.

I follow the stream to where Franklin dead-ends into Lafayette Street, behind a bunch of hulking white state buildings. The water buckles up here in an urgent swirling wave, running fast enough to float a whitewater raft. The giant gray culvert can hardly contain it. The stream begins to spread out over a green expanse in front of the Department of Transportation.

Look at that, I think: *The stream still lives. That's why Franklin Boulevard floods in a hard rain. It's a stream bed, not a road!* With lightning flashing, I drive a block over to South Monroe, just south of the Capitol. I turn into a short driveway behind a concrete building with "Buddy's Marine" painted on its side. There's a chain-link fence there, keeping me out of the Cascade, ground zero of Tallahassee history. Giant electrical lines march up the hill. Old junked boats poke through the kudzu.

This was an oak-magnolia forest, with redbuds stepping out in the spring and vines blocking out the summer sun. People had picnics along the creek, and baptisms in the dark, cold pool. Before that—who knows? Was it a place for tribal ceremonies? A mastodon watering hole?

Cars splash past on Monroe Street, wipers furiously clearing away rain. Water roars through the culvert under Monroe beneath the railroad bridge. I never noticed it before when I drove here. I never noticed the stream, rushing under my wheels. The last gasp of a place I'll never get to see.

Or will I? I am not the only person interested in Florida's lost waterfall. In 1971, then-Secretary of State Richard Stone became captivated by the Cascade's story and persuaded the legislature to dedicate a piece of downtown land as Cascades Park. The state moved power lines and earth and built bridges across what's left of the old streambed, a green park near the headquarters of one of the biggest environmental spoilers of all: the Florida DOT.

Stone built support for a plan to restore the old waterfall and pool, even hiring a pair of architects to design the site. The architects proposed a thirty-foot *artificial* waterfall as the park's centerpiece. Imagine it! It seems like a theme park fix to one of Florida's saddest natural disasters. Maybe it would be better than nothing.

Today, a copy of that grand plan languishes in the Tallahassee attic of one of the architects, Sam Hand. "People perish, and towns perish, for lack of a vision, and we've never had one in Florida," Hand said sadly. Stone's plan sputtered a few years after it began. Work stopped for two reasons: one, Stone moved away to serve in Congress, leaving Cascade Park without a political champion. And environmental officials found the massive contamination from the old coal gasification plant. The site, the U.S. Environmental Protection Agency (EPA) says, "may present an imminent and substantial endangerment to public health, welfare, or the environment." The EPA says Florida and the City of Tallahassee need to clean it up.

Some people are working to salvage something out of this mess. The

Trust for Public Land has a plan to create an urban park called the Capital Cascade Greenway. It would have a paved trail running along a restored version of the old Cascade Creek. The greenway would start where the stream once began, the site of today's Leon High School ball fields. It would go along the old watercourse, which is now a series of ugly drainage ditches. The idea is to clear them and put paths and benches along them. Make the water an asset, not an eyesore. People could bike and walk through old historic neighborhoods, between the campuses of Florida A&M and Florida State Universities, down the meandering hills that so captivated the capital-hunters. Eventually, the Capital Cascade Greenway would connect to the St. Mark's Trail, a modern echo of their historic path from the coast to the waterfall.

It's a great plan—a bit of hope in a story that desperately needs it. But the waterfall? It is lost to us. Even if the water did flow, it would be filled with poison. I read a depressing EPA technical plan called "Request for a Removal Action at the Cascade Park Gasification Plant and Cascade Landfill Site, Tallahassee, Florida." Tucked among pages that describe a list of horrible poisons underground, the report notes cheerily: "Because of the area's former natural beauty that included woodlands with a waterfall and running streams, the area was designated as Cascades Park by the former Florida Governor, Reuben Askew, and Cabinet on November 9, 1971." EPA hazardous waste experts say that Florida needs to carefully line the old Cascade Creek with concrete so the poison won't move even farther. The experts say that the old dump, and the waterfall beneath it, must be buried under a heavy clay layer.

"A sod-covered clay cap will provide an effective barrier from human contact with the waste," the engineers note.

Oh, I get it. A tomb. Maybe we could raise some money and put a headstone on top. Show some respect for the dead. Maybe then the governor would send the schoolchildren over to the gravesite, to honor the lost waterfall. Maybe he'd tell them the truth about what the grown-ups did. Maybe he'd say: we're sorry, children. We're sorry. We won't let it happen again.

Julie Hauserman *has been writing about Florida's environment for eighteen years. She was a Capitol bureau reporter for the* St. Petersburg Times *in Tallahassee for seven years and is a national commentator for National Public Radio's "Weekend Edition–Sunday" and* The Splendid Table. *Her work is featured in several Florida anthologies, including* The Wild Heart of Florida *and* The Book of the Everglades. *She has won numerous awards for her investigative journalism, including two nominations for the Pulitzer Prize. In 2001 she won the Scripps Howard National Journalism Award's top environmental prize for her stories about arsenic leaking out of pressure-treated lumber. She lives in an intentional community in the countryside outside Tallahassee with her daughter, Colleen.*

Julie Hauserman

FLORIDA'S LOST WATERFALL: CASCADES PARK

OLD TOWN

BACKYARD OAKS

DK3

22

Tallahassee

Brevard +
Dean St
Frenchtown
Tallahassee

Growing Up alongside Tallahassee

HOPE NELSON

I'm somewhat of an anomaly among my friends and colleagues. I, unlike many of my neighbors, classmates, and co-workers, am a lifelong resident of Tallahassee, Florida. They're often fascinated with this tidbit of knowledge, and many who hail from bigger cities—Miami, New York—have one question in common:

"But . . . what could you have possibly DONE here for twenty-three years?"

I always look at them, raise my eyebrows, smile, and respond: "You have no idea."

Upon first glance, Tallahassee probably seems like a sleepy town populated mostly by college students and seasonal legislators, with a sampling of state workers thrown in for good measure. Flying into the smallish regional airport, it's difficult to make out the skyline for the trees. But beneath the branches of the canopy oaks and nestled among the seven hills of the city, the real Tallahassee shines through. The one I'm familiar with. The one that I call my home.

Tallahassee is an interesting fusion of several distinct cultures. So close to Georgia, its ties to the rest of the Deep South are as thick as the red clay that turns to mud on a rainy day. Eight hours from Miami, it has its share of metropolis-dwelling transplants and other people of many rich, diverse heritages who add their own experiences and cultures to the mix.

But unlike Miami, Tallahassee's personality exudes a quintessentially Southern subtlety, a soft melody of birds singing and cicadas whizzing through the breeze on a summer night—a far cry from the cacophony that pierces the air in a larger city. But that quiet, that natural sound of birds and bugs, reaffirms each day the existence of myriad forms of life—indeed, of a bustling, busy existence that has carried on throughout time. State government may convene and protesters may shout, raising their signs for Capitol workers to read; football fans may cheer for their hometown college teams; the exuberance of university life may at times appear to be a rat race all its own. But through it all, the natural beauty of this town prevails, and the cicadas continue to buzz incessantly each summer dusk.

These facets—natural beauty, Southern charm, opportunities of a larger city nestled in a small-town atmosphere—make many visitors to Tallahassee never want to leave: visitors like my parents, who arrived in 1970 to attend Florida State University. From generation to generation, Tallahassee wins over a plethora of converts.

What amazes me about my hometown is the number of "old Tallahasseeans" who live among us, residents who have witnessed the advent of automobiles and remember when downtown roads were barely paved. Despite their advanced age, these residents are called "old" for a different reason: their wisdom, an insight that can be gained only by experiencing the pleasure and pain of extensive change. These "old Tallahasseans" watched from their sprawling front porches as their tiny town expanded into a bustling city, complete with new roads, new buildings, and new worries—with many old live oaks and antique homes still intact. And as the city grows, the older folks sigh, shake their heads, and do their best to keep their homestead, their little niche in the world, unchanged, unaffected by the goings-on around them.

At twenty-three, I am certainly not an "old Tallahasseean," despite my native roots. But like the older generation of city residents, I have watched my hometown turn into a developer's paradise over the two decades of my life, have seen up close the struggle of many residents to maintain the natural beauty and culture that are synonymous with Tallahassee.

I've seen two-lane roads widened into six. I've witnessed the decimation of some of my favorite childhood wooded areas—a tree-filled spot near my neighborhood lake, a vast expanse of pines and oaks near what was originally a two-lane road—in the name of home building and road widening. I've sighed—sometimes cried—to watch the natural landscape change, disappear, and see new, harsh buildings take its place.

But I've also smiled at the sight of concerned residents who time after time defend the wide, looming trees that dot the landscape. I've oftentimes silently—and sometimes more vocally—rooted for the denial of a building permit or variance that would allow for more development in my favorite natural spots. I've supported the struggle to fight the sprawl that is quickly becoming the law of the land. Through all of the growth, through all of the changes that my town undergoes year after year, I have slept peacefully to the sounds of crickets and tree frogs, with the flicker of fireflies outside my window.

A lot has changed in the twenty-three years I've been here. In 1979, when my parents moved to the house I grew up in, Tallahassee's hospital, now next door to a six-lane road that leads to a main artery of town, was thought to be on the outskirts of the city. Our own home was nestled in what we lovingly referred to as "the boonies"—indeed, our house was encompassed by woods, with one two-lane street leading south into town. As a child, I was frustrated by the lack of nearby sidewalks, which impeded any would-be bicycling to anywhere other than around the block. I was enamored with my father's tales of his childhood in small-town Panama City, a childhood filled with adventures involving Dad careening through town on his own two-wheeler, stopping for a drink at the soda fountain, or dropping in after school to visit his father at work. In the boonies, I longed for connection with the "outside world."

Now, my wish for sidewalks has been granted—but much more has changed, too. With a Wal-Mart Supercenter devouring a beautiful wooded area near my childhood home, and Thomasville Road expanding into a gargantuan highway, the Foxcroft area—my old stomping ground—is witnessing a startling sprawl. No longer isolated neighborhoods, Foxcroft, Killearn, and their ilk on the once-quiet northern side of town have metamorphosed into the heart of a sprawling community with a dense population and all the "comforts" of city life. Grocery stores, strip malls, gas stations, and the aforementioned Wal-Mart now make their presence known with bright signs and busy parking lots as suburbanites come to consume. The lush wooded areas that once lined two-lane Thomasville Road have been obliterated in favor of a six-lane highway and buildings created for the convenience of the thousands who now live in the many neighborhoods that have popped up over the past two decades.

This growth has not been limited to the north side of town—indeed, all of Tallahassee has been subject to new streets and road extensions, and there is a proposal to build a slew of condominiums in the heart of downtown—but growth reigns supreme throughout the north area as more families settle in the newer neighborhoods that are the result of urban sprawl, as the existing schools become more crowded while new ones continue to be built. I suppose the sprawl was a long time coming, but it appeared to take hold almost overnight; in my memory, one day the roads were small and the location remote, and the next, the roads had become akin to the Indy 500, and the north side of town was suddenly the place to be.

The prevalence of northbound sprawl in Tallahassee makes me wonder what will happen to the older, personality-filled neighborhoods and locations in the central and southern part of the city. What will happen to the homes, the communities, that have cultivated so much character throughout the years?

The historically black neighborhood of Frenchtown is tops on my list of concerns. An economically depressed area for nearly all of my life, Frenchtown is home to many wonderful old houses and businesses—oftentimes passed down in families from one generation to another—that have only suffered more in the face of the migration north. These structures, many of which are now dilapidated and in need of extensive repairs, are nestled in one of the oldest neighborhoods in Leon County. Created as a place for Marquis de Lafayette's French peasants to live, Frenchtown later became an oasis for African Americans in a heavily segregated Southern city, a community where blacks could feel a little safer, a little more protected from white violence and scorn. However, after integration finally took hold, and businesses no longer catered solely to one race or another, many Frenchtown businesses found themselves facing stiff competition, and as the housing market opened up for more affluent African Americans, the property value in Frenchtown fell, along with the tax brackets of its inhabitants.

For my entire life, though, Frenchtown has remained a culturally rich portion of Tallahassee despite its poverty and violence. Elderly men and women still live in the homes they've owned for years, eager to tell stories of a different time, a different community. "Nobody was really strangers," said one lifelong Frenchtown resident in a May 2003 Tallahassee Democrat article. "Even when college students moved in, they were part of the community. It was like a big family." Now, though, "It's almost like there's nothing to associate how it was when I grew up. Everything is something else now." But some family businesses—barbershops, restaurants, and the like—are still going strong despite the influx of competition. And by drawing on its deep-seated history, Frenchtown lives on, hoping for better, more affluent days ahead.

What can be done to save this wonderful part of Tallahassee? The city government has embarked on a revitalization effort to beautify Frenchtown and revamp its buildings and homes, but by doing so it may eviscerate the trails and traces of the neighborhood's rich culture, its heritage. For as buildings are torn down or completely renovated, as new businesses are encouraged and fostered, the property values are bound to rise, but the residents' pay is not nearly as likely to follow suit. The city will have created a wonderful, updated neighborhood, but the present tenants will be forced to move elsewhere, to lower-paying housing yet again.

Certainly, the history of Frenchtown cannot be lost in the mire of dire economic straits or neglect. But instead of revitalization, the neighborhood would benefit more from preservation. Frenchtown desperately needs advocates, internally and externally, to ensure the preservation of the community without negatively affecting the lives of those who live there. Revitalization would only drive the current residents away. Preservation, on the other hand, would help Frenchtown's inhabitants preserve the buildings, the homegrown businesses—indeed, the community—they've called home for decades.

While many Frenchtown residents live in dilapidated homes and face financial woes at every turn, another side of town—the Midtown/Old Town district—is thriving. The dichotomy between these two neighborhoods, mere miles apart, is startling. While the west-side community suffers, the centrally located Old Town and Midtown area succeeds, with renovations sprucing up house after house, some of which now sell for $380,000 or more.

The affluence wasn't always this way, of course. When my parents came to Tallahassee and began their hunt for a home, they found many properties in the Midtown area with asking prices of forty thousand dollars or less. Then, many of the houses they looked at were 1940s-era homes with little to no renovation work completed—making a hefty home project for any would-be inhabitants.

Now, however, nearly every house in the fairly small community sports various renovations, and since the homes have maintained their World War II-era charm in the process, buyers embrace Old Town and Midtown as the best of both worlds.

Nestled among crape myrtles, pines, and blooming wildflowers, Old Town and Midtown—separated from each other by Miccosukee Road—boast a truly North Floridian charm. Built at a time when functionality was king, the houses in the area have maintained a simple beauty, a reminder of the possibilities of the 1940s in the face of war and in the glory of the soldiers' return. Unlike so many of the homes built today in shiny new subdivisions, none of these houses resembles any of the others, but instead complement each other in myriad ways, juxtaposing wood and brick; green paint and white; lush, grassy yards and wooded enclosures. Though white picket fences are the exception rather than the rule, their presence harkens back to the seemingly carefree days of years past.

Though the property values continue to rise in Old Town and Midtown, the boundaries of the community maintain the same tautness they've had for years. As popular as the neighborhoods are, they have no room to grow, no way to expand—and this rigidity effectively combats sprawl. Despite the growing fascination with the area, potential homebuyers must wait their turn for a house to become available, knowing that there's little to no chance of any more homes being built there.

It's a comforting feeling for someone who lives in Midtown or Old Town to know that in the face of an ever-expanding city, the area's homes will stay as they are, with no surprising bursts of growth, no stretching out or abandonment of elastic boundaries. I know from personal experience: I've had the pleasure of living in the neighborhood for a year now. And behind my tiny, 1940s duplex, my backyard overlooks a wooded area that is too small to develop but too large to see through, offering a wonderful oasis of privacy. The front porch offers a view of butterfly bushes and a crape myrtle that blooms with mad abandon every spring. A menagerie of birds spends its days dive-bombing mischievous squirrels, and every so often I see a hawk flying high above me.

Hope Nelson

The Midtown and Old Town section of Tallahassee holds more than an old-city charm. This part of town paints a dramatic portrait of how humans and nature can coexist, how buildings can be built and the natural landscape can endure. How trees can grow, bushes can bloom, and owls can hoot from their far-flung perches while human life continues alongside. The scenario I face in my neighborhood each day reminds me of life in Tallahassee fifteen or twenty years ago, before the rapid development throughout the city. While new subdivisions are developed each year and while residents try to eke out every single bit of useable space within the city and county limits to build their homes, Old Town and Midtown stand in the same place they always have, a relic of times past and one, unlike Frenchtown, that has had no trouble with preservation.

Directly east of my neighborhood, however, new construction has taken hold. The road next to the hospital where I was born, Centerville Road, is being widened from four lanes to six. Street additions, such as that of Blair Stone Road, a highly controversial project, are continually forging through what was originally wooded land, sparking years-long protests from environmental groups and costing taxpayers money in construction and upkeep. But most startling to me, mainly because of its quiet yet forceful impact, part of one of the more lengthy thoroughfares in town, Park Avenue, has undergone a metamorphosis from a two-lane, narrow street to a huge road that can easily accommodate four lanes of traffic.

The expansion from two lanes to four is seemingly innocuous. After all, in a city where six-lane roads are becoming the latest trend to help suburbanites and new residents shuttle to and fro, a small change such as the one on Park Avenue seems like nothing doing. But the effects of the Park Avenue expansion, more so than some of the other transportation projects around town, have a ripple effect that is far greater than a new, larger road.

From my earliest memories, those days of riding shotgun in my father's little orange Datsun pickup, I have always been enamored with the vast expanse of trees and shrubs lining both sides of Park Avenue. When heading west, toward downtown, it was always a treat to see the landscape change from woods to older homes and houses-turned-businesses to the taller buildings in the heart of downtown that face a chain of public parks. Because the sights were so ingrained in my mind, I didn't even blink when, in my teenage years, I learned of new plans for the road's growth. Indeed, long after construction started, the trees stood tall and lanky, offering shelter for wildlife and shade for construction workers.

Then, one day, they were gone.

I say it happened in one day, but the sweeping change actually took place over a series of weeks. But imagine my surprise when I turned onto Park after not using it for a month or so and faced vast gaps of barren, tire-scuffed land where my beloved woods used to be. Where would the wildlife go now? What would happen to Tallahassee's prized trees?

The answers, to me at least, are unclear. The owls, birds, and other creatures that inhabit this city are being jostled into smaller and fewer spaces with each new subdivision and each road widening developers embark on. The ease with which Tallahasseans are accustomed to coexisting with other species of animals has faced significant challenges in the past decade or so. As the city continues to expand with new roads, strip malls, and neighborhoods, the problems of coexistence are sure to worsen.

The solution to such an issue is a tricky one to pursue. To demand that developers cease construction on new structures would be futile. To place some sort of population cap on the city reeks of isolationism and elitism. What residents, businessmen, local politicians, and developers alike need to do is take a long, hard look at the history of our city—starting with its humble roots and cobblestone streets and ending with today—and chart the balance between humans and nature throughout the years. When was there an equal balance? What allowed us to coexist for so long with minimal problems on either side? How did we as a community somehow rock the boat, causing the balance to shift? And most importantly, what can we as a city do to repair whatever damage has been done, to soothe the growing pains of an ever-more-populated area and restore harmony?

The answers to these questions, the fruits of extensive research, may not be altogether pleasing to the eye. But to ignore the city's lack of balance in the name of construction, and to lose some of Tallahassee's most precious natural and cultural resources in the process, would be a shame.

Despite the rampant growth, however, Tallahassee is filled with areas that have escaped the bright light of development and have remained untainted for years—and, in some cases, centuries. When I feel a pull to escape from the fast-paced world around me, when I need some solitude, I hop in the car and head to Lake Jackson Mounds Archaeological State Park, which for hundreds of years served as the home base for the Native Americans who moved to this area.

Without fail, a trip to the mounds restores me. Nearly every weekend, families pack picnic lunches and plop down on the grass or at one of the covered tables to enjoy the sun and the company. Children play with Frisbees or footballs on the long, flat stretch of grass in the middle of the area, their echoes of laughter resonating throughout the woods and down the short, satisfying trail that leads through part of the property.

Aside from the mounds themselves, the trail is what draws me to the park. As the sun filters through the slits between the myriad trees, I am able to put one foot in front of the other, draw a deep breath, and smile. Particularly in my college years, when exams and deadlines loomed without respite, I spent hours on this trail, examining plants and watching for wildlife, to gain a sense of myself again amid the classes and the coursework. Growing up with an appreciation of the outdoors—one passed down to me through my parents and their families—allows me the luxury of realizing exactly how special moments like the ones spent on the Mounds trail, away from honking horns and unrelenting construction, away from desk work and air-conditioning, really are.

The small, looping trail is a representation of what Tallahassee is all about. Only here can visitors find a capital city with not only preserved greenspace but also wooded areas that are more conducive to pausing in thought than to playing tag. Far removed from the land of the legislators, the history of the Lake Jackson Mounds goes back much further than Tallahassee's government background. Indeed, the Indian mounds reconnect Tallahasseans with the area's true history, a history so deep and complex that it is difficult to even begin to unravel.

The mounds themselves are a sight to behold. Looming, rounded artifacts of an entire culture's life and livelihood, they could easily be mistaken for some of Tallahassee's Seven Hills. But even a layperson such as myself can take one look at these mounds and feel the history that exudes from them, the successes and pains of the Native Americans who once walked the land I call my home. When walking among these mounds and down the trail that leads away from them and then back again, I am often awestruck by the rich heritage of this land I love so much. Long before the likes of Midtown and

Old Town, centuries before Frenchtown came into existence—long before Florida was Florida, before it was a state—another community was thriving, one whose legacy lives on through artifacts and strikingly incredible additions to the natural landscape.

But the mounds at Lake Jackson aren't the only relics of a way of life that precedes the town itself. From years of private ownership by prominent Tallahassee families, to the year the state purchased the property in 1983, to today, archaeologists have been uncovering artifacts from the Apalachee Indian tribe and excavating what is now known as the Mission San Luis de Apalachee site, bringing to light an entirely new knowledge of a culture that has been dead for four hundred years. The Apalachee Indians who lived alongside the Spanish missionaries at San Luis died before their time. Casualties of a colonial tug-of-war between Spain and England, they lost their land, their identity, and in many cases their lives when the mission was burned to the ground and they were forced to choose whether to go with one of the fighting countries or whether to strike out on their own and join up with another tribe.

Today, the mission site is truly sacred ground. Each year, archaeologists make new discoveries and learn more about the Apalachees and the Spaniards who lived with them, and each year, the Native Americans who walked on the very land I live near today gain a more solid place in history and cement their culture, their way of life, with every new excavated item, every bead or toy or remnant of food.

As a child, I loved going to San Luis on field trips; sure enough, my class would go nearly every year. In second grade, for instance, my classmates and I heard many stories of the Indians and Spaniards and played near land that was neatly cut away into rectangular blocks as part of a new archaeological dig. We loaded up in cars or on buses and ventured to San Luis frequently—after all, it isn't every city that has such a historically significant site so close to home. But even with the regularity of such excursions, I learned so much more with every visit. Tallahassee's children, especially the ones who take field trips to places that are teeming with living history, are taught at an early age that they, their families, and even the "Old Tallahasseans" that are so revered in town share their community with a long lineage of inhabitants, many of which have long died out, effectively stanching the flow of the cultural ways from long ago. By visiting sites such as San Luis, Tallahassee's children are taught that they are certainly not the first, nor probably the last, to be residents of this area—which, for me, was a daunting realization at seven years old.

Probably because of those early field trips to the mission site, I still feel a sense of wonderment when visiting San Luis, which has been revamped in the last ten years to include a wealth of artifacts and hands-on exhibits for visitors to interact with. Whenever I venture to the west side of town, past the Capitol and the universities, and set foot on that land, I try to see the world the way the Spaniards and the Apalachees would have—and with a cell phone in my car and a picnic lunch in my hands, my mind boggles at the task.

In fact, the very existence of the San Luis site and the Indian mounds at Lake Jackson offer an interesting correlation with the growth of Tallahassee over my lifetime. Like other areas of town, as abundant growth overtakes the land, turning it from greenspace into asphalt, these relics of another time, another century, loom large despite their small stature, which is itself nowhere near as tall as the twenty-two floors of the Capitol, the tallest building in town. And despite road widenings, new neighborhoods, and new businesses—not to mention a population that is growing by leaps and bounds—the Indian mounds and mission site remain stunningly silent, unpopulated save for the visitors that venture to the property for a glimpse at what came before.

Despite the myriad changes that have taken place throughout my twenty-three years of life, the natural bounty of Tallahassee remains strong, unrelenting, in the face of human expansion and newly paved roads.

To be sure, Tallahassee is ripe for growth. However, as a native, I have always felt an immense pride in the way the city has developed around its wooded areas and animal habitats, placing a concentrated emphasis on the ecological beauty of this area. Up until the past decade or so, the human-environmental balance was surprisingly successful. As more people discover Tallahassee's beauty, though, and as more people are welcomed to the Land of the Seven Hills by accessible greenspace and friendly residents, more of the city's heritage—its trees, its small-town feel, its alluring privacy amid tall, sweeping live oaks and pines—is in danger of disappearing at the hands of its own popularity.

So, to answer my metropolitan friends' question—I can do, have done, a lot here for twenty-three years. I've watched buildings pop up with startling speed, watched my forests change shape or disappear in the face of construction and "improvements." I've played among the ruins of a long-lost Native American culture and hiked to the top of mounds that precede my existence by hundreds of years. I've moved into an older, charming neighborhood and lobbied for the preservation of a kindred community. And through it all—through the construction that continues to recreate the landscape, through the upward surge in Tallahassee's popularity in the mere two decades I have been on the Earth, through growth and change and everything, good and bad, that comes with them—I marvel at the wealth, the goodness, of the land I call my home.

Hope Nelson, *a Tallahassee native, is a professional editor and writer whose work has appeared in national publications. She has enjoyed teaching courses in American and Florida Studies at Florida State University and works with young, aspiring journalists to produce a weekly teen page in the* Tallahassee Democrat.

orchard oriole

GROWING UP ALONGSIDE TALLAHASSEE

Migrating Eastern Kingbirds   Late August

I slipped my kayak into Buckhorn Creek, searching
for signs of fall. Saw grass stood six feet above my
head; only the rising song of cicadas broke the silence.
Even though the air temperature veered near ninety,
light breezes promised something of autumn.

But there was more: the marshes downstream were
salted with Eastern kingbirds, restless hundreds of
them, preparing to migrate south. I hadn't realized
that kingbirds gathered up like this; indeed,
nothing about them was as I have kingbirds filed
in my mind—quarrelsome and noisy, territory-
and nest-defending, springtime pairs. It was as if
I were a child used to seeing my parents yoked to
the predictable tending of kitchen and home and
unexpectedly caught sight of them wild and dancing
at a bar.

In silent charcoal clutches of eight or a dozen,
the kingbirds sallied over the salt marsh, lighting
on flexible tips of cypress or bay trees, riding those
branchlets as if they were tiny trampolines. I watched

one bird with folded wings, studying the air-wrestling of its conspecifics. How easily it startled into flight when a clapper rail beat alarm through the grasses. The bird gathered up its thin shoulders and hopscotched to yet another perch, displacing its neighbor, all in an eerie, most unkingbird-like silence.

The continent's kingbirds have set aside their householding; fall is stirring their bodies. Here, at the breaking edge of our coast, they cut broad invisible trails through the upland tree hammocks, lacing the cedars and palms and oaks together just as robins and waxwings will do in the winter months to come. They skim the creek's brown surface, filling the wide yellow gapes of their mouths, catching small insects on the wing, taking what they must have from this landscape.

When they choose the spent spike of a saw grass flower to perch, arching that plant like a bow close to the face of the creek, they themselves become the arrows, using the last of our summer marshes to propel themselves on their southbound paths.

CHOCKSACKA NENE

Noah at the creek

mosquitofish

A Sabbath Outing

SHARON RAUCH

Noah and I are ready for the creek walk. He has a net in one hand and a clear plastic container with a handle in the other. I'm toting a white garbage bag he insisted I take so we can pick up trash. I have a small notebook in my pocket and we're both wearing water shoes.

It's Shabbat, the day of rest, a time to leave work behind and tune into what's important. But my mind is racing. As we step down into the creek at Koucky Park in Indianhead Acres, I decide to let go, to focus on what's in front of me: the limestone creek bottom, the ankle-deep water gurgling past me, the damsel fly with black wings and iridescent-green body landing on a nearby elephant ear.

Eight-year-old Noah is already scooping the water with his net, trying to catch minnows—mosquito fish, to be exact. It's one of the few kinds of fish that live in this water. He hops over the rocks, skirting a waist-deep pool of water with ease. He's been visiting this creek since he was a toddler.

I wish I had known a similar patch of earth as a child. Even one, tiny piece. A chunk of land I had dug my toes in, rolled around in, smelled deeply; where I had listened to the wind rush through its trees, tasted its rain water, cupped its bugs in my hand. A place that would pull me back, even years later, whispering: "You belong here."

But I have no such place.

I'm among the many rootless Americans who have a tenuous tie to the land. In the Chicago suburb where I grew up, I saw little wildlife. Trees—certainly good climbing trees—were scarce. I never got near a natural body of water. After moving to Florida when I was thirteen, I never returned.

Fort Lauderdale wasn't much better. In 1970, it was booming—new developments popping up everywhere, land razed and carved up. A true paved paradise.

Then twenty-seven years ago I came to Tallahassee, rumbling in on a Greyhound bus late at night, and caught my first glimpse of the live oak trees along Park Avenue. In the dim light of the streetlamps I could see the outline of their thick girth and the dark sprawling branches with clumps of Spanish moss hanging down and swaying in the breeze. I couldn't see them, but I knew their roots went on forever. I wanted to call this place home.

But it's not that easy. Knowing a place in a deep, in-your-guts way takes time. I've claimed this land, but I'm not sure yet that it's claimed me.

I reach down and pick up the tiny notebook that has fallen out of my pocket into the creek. I dab the pages with tissue, irritated that the ink has started to run.

"Sorry, Mom," Noah says, putting his arm around my waist. It's not his fault. I shrug and let out a long sigh. That's when we hear the "Plop!"

Noah looks up at me, his eyes shining, and then rushes over to the bank where the sound came from. He plunges his net into the water and brings up his prize—a large bullfrog and a tiny crayfish.

"We bingoed!" he cried.

If my notebook hadn't fallen out and we hadn't stopped, we would have missed it. My irritation gives way to gratitude.

The bullfrog isn't that unusual, but the crayfish is. Although this creek looks sweet, it doesn't support very many small organisms—about six at tops: crayfish, mosquito fish, snails, damsel fly larvae, midges (called blind mosquitoes), and worms. That's because it's not really a creek, at least not any more. It's a ditch. Other "real" creeks in the area support upwards of thirty-five species of animal life.

This creek was once one of those, originating near the present-day electric substation on Chowkeebin Nene, one of Indianhead's major north-south roads. Water would seep out of the ground near there and start flowing south through the floodplain that edges Optimist Park. When the heavy rains came, the water would overflow the banks, creating a swamp until the water slowly sunk into the ground. At one time the creek was dammed up just north of Hokolin Nene, forming a lake. People used to canoe and sail boats in the water.

Then that all changed. After a heavy storm in the late 1950s, the dam broke and was never repaired. Today the original creek is almost dried up, and thirty feet east of its remnants runs a huge ditch dug by the City of Tallahassee. Rainwater could now gush into the ditch and be quickly transported south. During big storms, Noah and my older son, David, beg me to let them go down to the creek. They love seeing the water, which is usually about ankle-deep, turn a coffee-and-cream color and rise to over ten feet, swirling and swooshing under the street culvert, racing downstream.

The ditch solved the flood and mosquito problem, but the creek paid the price. The gushing water scoured out the habitats of many organisms, allowing only a few sturdy ones to survive. The water also eroded the ditch's bank, causing some parts of the ditch to now be ten feet wide. The real creek—which you can still find along the greenway trail behind Optimist Park—is stagnant.

You can't change the natural flow of things without consequences. Don't I know. As I stood looking at the crayfish that Noah promptly put into his plastic container, I was grateful that at least this small animal had survived. I've changed the natural flow of things more than once in my life and I pray that despite the disruption, not everything is destroyed.

I was raised Catholic, but totally rejected the religion as an adult. I felt it was too patriarchal, too rigid, so I threw it out in one fell swoop when I was barely eighteen. Later, in my thirties, I forged a whole new path by converting to Judaism. This religion seemed more open and expansive. It welcomed intellectual rigor, yet had deep roots and a rich history. This was a place for me.

But again, it's not that simple. As the years go on, I grow to love Judaism more, but I also mourn what I let go. Nothing I do in my Jewish life resonates with my youth. When I light Shabbat candles, put on my *tallit* (prayer shawl) or recite prayers in Hebrew, nothing feels familiar. The Jewish melodies, even though I may like them, don't awaken old childhood memories, tying me to

A SABBATH OUTING

past generations. I'm like the new ditch that replaced the creek—more water runs through it, but I'm scoured clean of my former life.

I like to think that new life is coming back to my spiritual river. But I want to do better than the Indianhead ditch. Six species isn't enough for me—I want all thirty-five.

The garbage bag is getting heavy. We've barely gone a few hundred yards down the creek and we've already collected so much trash the bag is ripping.

"Look at this!" Noah yells, pointing to a half-submerged basketball. He pulls and yanks and digs around it until he finally lifts it out of the creek bottom. After emptying it of water and sand, he puts it in with the other garbage: soda cans; beer bottles; a strip of garden hose; a red, white, and blue flannel shirt; white and brown plastic bags; broken glass. We decide to leave the bag on the side of the bank and retrieve it on our way back.

Garbage isn't the only thing "unnatural" around here. So is a lot of the vegetation. Among the native hickory, black cherry, pine, and oak trees you have the mimosa tree, which sprouts pink powder puff balls in the spring. It's from Australia. Covering a lot of the ground, particularly near Optimist Park, is green wandering jew, a green-leafed plant with small white flowers blooming from spring through fall. It's from South America. In this country, it's considered invasive, taking over forest floors and not allowing native species to grow. Then there's Chinese tallow and skunk vine from Asia, kudzu from Japan, and air potato plants from Africa and Southeast Asia.

The vegetation is all mixed up, a jumble of native and non-native, so much so that the average person doesn't know the difference. We may long for the pristine, for the authentic, but we have a hard time finding it in the natural world. The same can be said of our own bodies and souls. Sometimes it feels like we're a mix of fragments, each pushing and pulling against one another, competing for ground space. It's hard to figure out which ones really belong here.

That's why every morning I recite the Jewish blessing: *Elohai Neshama she-natata bi tehorah hi.* Oh God, the soul you have placed within me is pure.

There is a piece of me, beyond the Catholic or the Jew, the native or non-native, that is pure in its essence. Most of the time I can't feel it. Most of the time I don't even know it's there. But for a few short moments in the morning, wrapped in my *tallit,* I affirm this purity in myself.

SHARON RAUCH

Walking in the creek I suddenly stop. Noah is way ahead of me now, trying to catch minnows again. I close my eyes, tilt my face toward the sky and feel the sun's warmth pour over my cheeks. When I open my eyes, there's a cardinal perched on a nearby branch. Its feathers are stunning, bright red, pure.

"Mom! Come here!" Noah yells from the large concrete culvert that runs beneath Holokin Nene. I'm down below, at the edge of the embankment, which has been covered in cement to prevent erosion.

I shake my head *no,* and sit down on a huge tree limb that's running parallel to the ground.

"Oh, come on, Mom!" he yells again. "Please?"

Now I understand. He wants to go through the culvert to the other side. I stand up and climb my way up to him.

He grabs my hand and starts pulling me through the tunnel, baby step by baby step. I'm slightly bent over, looking down at the water, which is getting blacker and blacker as we get farther away from the culvert opening.

"Are you scared?" I ask Noah.

"I can't see the bottom," he says. "What if there's snakes in here?" But he continues on, holding fast to my hand. As the light from the other side of the tunnel gets brighter, his grip lessens.

"I can see the bottom now," he exclaims, then lets my hand go.

Going into dark, unknown places. Who wants to do that? But if someone's with you, it's not so bad.

I think of the Hebrews, wandering in the wilderness for forty years. Which way should they go? This way? That? They had to rely on a cloud by day and pillar of fire by night.

Then one day the sky darkened, lightning flashed, and God spoke from a quaking mountain. It was so awesome, no one person could withstand it.

But they weren't alone. They had each other. Being together allowed them to listen to the Voice.

Going back through the culvert, Noah doesn't hold my hand. He practically gallops through, his fear of snakes suddenly gone. Looking down the long tunnel, I see his silhouette when he reaches the other side. He never even looks back.

A SABBATH OUTING

187

It takes us two hours to explore about a block's worth of creek. That's Sabbath time for you. Elongated and unrushed. My racing mind has finally settled down.

On our way back, Noah sees a zebra longwing. Governor Lawton Chiles designated the longwing as the state butterfly in 1996. The black butterfly with yellow stripes roosts in flocks and sleeps so soundly you can pick it off the roost and return it later without waking up any of its family members. Every night it returns to the same perch. During the day, it flies slowly and doesn't startle easily. A Sabbath butterfly.

But the one Noah found isn't just slow. It's dead. He picks it up and asks me to carry it home. Further down the stream, I also pick up the brimming garbage bag that we had placed on the bank earlier. In a few minutes, we will climb up the embankment near Chocksacka Nene and walk a few houses down to our home.

But before we get there, a huge bird suddenly swoops down near the water and then flies up to a low branch in a tree. Another one follows. Noah stops dead in his tracks and motions me over. We're not more than thirty feet away. I can't believe my eyes—it's two red-shouldered hawks. In all my twenty-seven years in this area, I've never seen even one so close.

We hold our breath, not wanting to scare them away. We stare. One of them, which had its back turned to us, suddenly turns around and looks down at us. We get a full view of its russet-colored chest.

"It's like he wants us to get a good look," Noah whispers. I nod in agreement. The birds take off again, swooping down and then up to another branch. They continue this way, flying and perching, flying and perching, until they finally take off over the trees and out of sight.

My heart is pounding. I look down at Noah and he wraps his arms around my waist. We stand this way for several minutes, feet in the ditch's water, surrounded by garbage and invasive plants. But part of us is also up there, flying high beneath the hawk's wing, listening to a voice that says: "Welcome home, o soul."

SHARON RAUCH

SHARON RAUCH *has been a reporter for the* Tallahassee Democrat *since 1991. For the past eight years she has written features and columns focusing on family and community life, spirituality, and nature. She lives with her life partner and their three children in Indianhead Acres.*

firebush in bloom

ruby red
sweet!

3pm

A SABBATH OUTING

magnolia leaves
3/9 most look old
russet underneath
not these only where
shadows fall from
above where light
es thru bright
lime green

Tallahassee

Miccosukee Road

The City in the Trees

MARY JANE RYALS

I'm driving back from the airport, basking in the shade of my recent summer in Spain. I have seen Picasso's most famous, two-room-large painting, "Guernica." I've also seen Goya, Velasquez, El Greco paintings in grand cathedrals and museums, Gaudi's crazy, Moorish-influenced architectures, rooms, homes, parks. And, the *Sagrada Familia,* the largest cathedral in Spain, which has been under construction for a hundred years and will be for another hundred.

Yet as I turn on to St. Augustine Road, one of our region's seven famed canopied roads, I realize *these* are our riches. This, these trees. The largest of all plants, the oldest known living things. Shall I list them, too? They stand, lean into the road, these trees, some older than any famous paintings or cathedrals in Europe, these grand live oaks, hickory trees, bald cypresses, and cedars.

I can't get over it. I have not had the luxury of driving through this canopy for four months. It's August, hot, humid, the kind of weather required for these trees to survive. This is our cathedral, the steeped roof of trees growing over us. The sun filters through the leafy greens down onto the shaded road. I roll down the window and breathe deeply. I feel richer now than I ever have in my life. These old ones give us so much.

They keep wind and water from taking our topsoil. They give the food of life—oxygen. They absorb our garbage—carbon dioxide. The first spears, boats, wheels came from their hardy stems. They gave us tools, buildings, art.

Nowadays, trees give us fuel, baseball bats, alcohol, and plastics. We get apples, nuts, chocolate, coffee, cinnamon, and clover from their mysterious fruits. They keep us supplied with latex, and they shelter our wild animals.

I turn onto my own road, driving past horses, goats, and sheep down the rutted and nasty-for-your-car-suspension road toward home. Turning onto my own road I discover the prettiest picture I've seen this year: this deep woods and sloping hill, a dirt road cut and curving gently through it, swampy land on the east–southeast side of Leon County.

It's gorgeous. Cooler, wetter, greener here than in any museum. It's as precious as Spain's gold, France's cuisine, or Italy's art. I breathe in again. I've not had this much oxygen all summer in urbanized Europe. Suddenly I realize we will lose this if we're not careful. Very careful.

This country is still a child. A wild child. We can decide we don't want to kill off all our wildness, all our deep woods where birds don't need to eat from a feeder because they're sustained by the place. We can maintain a green difference. Our European friends caution us against doing what they did hundreds of years ago—cutting down the forests.

As I write this and as you read this, hundreds of our region's trees are being destroyed, are about to be or are dying. I'm not trying to be symbolic here; I mean to be literal.

Here, I mean to speak to most of our Tallahassee region's readers—we love our trees. And we can change the urbanized, commercialized, legalized logging of our city, our county, and our region. The place that our sister-city citizens from Russia referred to us as "the city in the trees."

I spoke with Ann Bidlingmaier, a local tree advocate who herself was like any tree lover, no different from any of us: she saw bulldozers behind her property near the Tallahassee Mall in the 1980s on their way to plowing down huge old live oaks. She stopped the driver and asked him to show his permits for the tree removal. There were none, and the removal was halted for the time being.

The incident landed her in a news article, and she received two hundred calls from local tree lovers cheering her on. She went on to found Tree Watch in 1983 and was appointed vice chair of the Environmental Ordinance Management Committee in Tallahassee when the city decided to create its own ordinance, separate from the county ordinance her group revised earlier.

MARY JANE RYALS

She sees several main problems that have solutions if our tree lovers will only pay attention, speak up, and (to use a cliché) save our trees.

First, we have ordinances to save individual trees that are "too big." Incidentally, Bidlingmaier says the county protects trees better than the city does. She says where we've gone wrong is to not protect smaller trees and clumps of trees and roadside buffers. For instance, Governor's Square Mall recently cut back their buffer. One big-box store, Target, thins out its understory trees. Small businesses often will cut down trees for customers to see the businesses, for instance, along Capital Circle Northeast.

As is so often the case, we're all so busy thinking one way that we struggle against the obvious opposite: wouldn't most people love tree buffers that shelter their favorite businesses? Wouldn't it tend to attract business rather than to repel it?

What if tree people spoke out about wanting to save the trees as a way to promote better business? Most of us support places of business that keep their trees. Think of the most pleasant business areas in town: Lake Ella and Betton Place, to name two. Think of the places in town that feel pleasant to us: both Florida State and Florida A&M campuses are surrounded by trees. We love the Capital City Country Club area for its dripping moss and old oaks. The Tallahassee Museum is fruitful with trees. Frenchtown and San Luis Park bloom with trees.

Why not encourage businesses to develop tree-plentiful areas that will make us want to go there? And build ways to protect the trees that already give us comfort? Why kill what protects us unless it's absolutely necessary?

Another problem Bidlingmaier sees is with the Environmental Management Ordinance, which the city passed, and the Environmental Management Act, which the county adopted. The city and county both are too understaffed and not really managed to actually enforce and check on protecting all the trees in jeopardy in the area. One person should oversee the Notices of Violations and problems with trees, to centralize enforcement, considering all the construction, housing, road, and commercial and utility pruning going on—not to mention the trees that could be damaged already. Nowadays, Bidlingmaier says, it's "hit or miss" with protecting trees by sending out different inspectors instead of one who is looking at the whole city's grid who can assess needs and get enough workers out to deal with varied situations.

THE CITY IN THE TREES

Another problem is the strange lack of balance on the Environmental Management Ordinance Revision committee. With thirteen members on the supposed "watch-dog" team of our beloved trees, isn't it strange that eleven of them are developers and only two are environmentalists? *Why?* we need to ask, and *Change it,* we need to say.

Yet another problem not impossible to solve is the fact that the city and county have spread out the duties of permitting, inspection, calls about damage, and all the rest among several departments. Savannah has consolidated its tree facility into one division, and we could do the same, Bidlingmaier says, by sheltering it under Parks and Recreation. Why haven't we done it?

Politics: growth management would lose a piece of their budget.

Meanwhile, we're losing forested corridors. A designated "Tree City USA," Tallahassee has no singular tree agency. There's pressure to four-lane our canopied roads. We have more and more out-of-town developers—Wal-Mart and Target from Arkansas, to name two, and others from south Florida—developing in our area and going back home with little evidence that they care about the trees they've mown down here in Tallahassee.

I wish more of us felt as connected to trees as does Georjean Machulis, who said when I called her, "I would chain myself to a tree if it meant saving its life." Machulis is true to her words, having made it into the paper once by standing next to a giant tree alongside Riggins Road to keep it from being chopped down. The tree stands today.

We love our trees, Georjean says, but we don't have a representative to save them, either in state or in local government. She reminds us that trees are considered sacred by the native peoples. The cypress tree is sacred, and Machulis and her husband Cliff Thaell planted seventeen trees in south Florida where their daughter was killed in a car accident. They took a place of terrible tragedy and turned it into a place that was sacred, she says.

Can't we do that with all our places? Aren't all our asphalted and cemented places a bit tragic, and don't we deserve to give them back a little of the sacred?

We still have the gift of trees. We have a long growing season and plentiful rain. We have people who appreciate trees profoundly. My call is to you and to me. I'm just a writer. I know little about biology or trees. I just know that my mother wept bitterly when we had to take a tree out of our two-

MARY JANE RYALS

194

and-a-half acres of sacred, treed land when I was an adolescent. I was both embarrassed by her open emotion and cut to the very heart by the truth she spoke, even if only I heard it.

When I returned from south Florida where I was attending college for the first time and saw across the swamp on the way to my home big streetlights instead of woods, I wept just as instinctively as my mother had. Another piece of ancient, silent, but life-giving, history destroyed. It's time for us wipe the tears and begin to shout for the trees.

MARY JANE RYALS *has lived in the Tallahassee area for most of her life. She co-edited the poetry anthology* North of Wakulla *with Donna Decker, and she wrote* A Messy Job I Never Did See a Girl Do, *a short story collection. She serves as the fiction editor of the* Apalachee Review.

ST. MARKS
NWR
ST. MARKS
FL 32313
PT 334

MAIL

butterfly tag
close-up

The Monarchs of Eden

CLAUDIA HUNTER JOHNSON

I am slogging through snow on the Upper West Side, on my way to see butterflies. Big wet flakes fall quickly, lining the ledges of brownstones like the snow-white tips of a French manicure. It's early March–springtime in my hometown of Tallahassee—but a book tour has brought me to wintry New York. I slip on the sidewalk, regaining my balance on a section some kind soul has salted, but I'd walk through worse to see butterflies. Once, visiting an abbey in Ireland when I was just twenty—younger than my children are now—a yellow butterfly lit on my hand and stayed with me while I toured the chapel. Since then, though I'm not what you'd call a religious person, butterflies have been my mystical symbol. Seeing them is, for me, as it was for Nabokov, a moment of grace. Not that I know much about them. So on this, my last day in the city, the snow notwithstanding, I'm bound for the Butterfly Conservatory at the American Museum of Natural History.

Thanks to the storm, there aren't many visitors. I'm the first to step through the vivarium's double-door entry, designed to keep butterflies in and predators like wasps and flies out. And just like that, I've gone from winter to summer, stepping into a hothouse of tropical plants—bromeliad, orchid—and hundreds of butterflies nectaring, flitting. It's eighty degrees—I'm dying in my wool turtleneck, but I sweat it out for more than an hour while a lepidopterist (an entomologist specializing in butterflies and moths) and her volunteers show me exquisite blue morphos, paper kites, painted ladies, owls, monarchs, white peacocks, question marks.

I have plenty of questions, mostly about monarchs. *Danaus plexippus.* For years I've clipped articles about them, intending to read about monarchs and to visit St. Marks National Wildlife Refuge on the Gulf coast south of Tallahassee where they mass each October as they migrate to Mexico. My husband has even given me *The Handbook for Butterfly Watchers* by Robert Michael Pyle, one of the leaders in monarch research, but I've only flipped through it. Still, one fact stuck with me: It takes more than one generation to complete their migration from Canada and the northern United States to Mexico and back. This stuck with me not just because it's intriguing but because it reminded me (once a playwright) of Olga in Chekhov's *Three Sisters* who says at the end of the play, "Time will pass, and we shall go away for ever, and we shall be forgotten, our faces will be forgotten, our voices, and how many there were of us; but our sufferings will pass into joy for those who will live after us, happiness and peace will be established upon earth, and they will remember kindly and bless those who have lived before."

When I mention the monarch migration, a gray-bearded volunteer in a Monarch Watch t-shirt lights up. "I've just been to Mexico to see them!" he says, ecstatic. I ask if it's true that it takes more than one generation to make the migration. "Three generations." He tells me that monarchs live four to five weeks in the spring and the summer when they're reproducing, but the ones that fly south in the fall live six to eight months, flying thousands of miles to overwinter in Mexico where they go into *diapause,* clustering with reduced energy (west of the Rockies, they overwinter in southern California); then, when it warms up in March, they head north, the females laying eggs as they go, and both males and females dying soon after. "So it's their grandchildren that make it back up north where the migration started," the man tells me.

"That is stunning," I say.

He smiles. "Everything about monarchs is stunning."

In mid-April, when my book tour is over and I return to the warm Red Hills region of Tallahassee, I call St. Marks Wildlife Refuge and speak with Robin Will, the Refuge Ranger who oversees the fall monarch festival in October. "It's a real spectacle," she says. "Thousands of monarchs flying in, roosting in bushes and trees right here on the beach by the lighthouse, nectaring on the goldenrod before they cross the Gulf." But some monarchs, she tells me, are trickling through right now, returning from Mexico. "I've seen some on the beaches where they're easy to see flapping along." She suggests I call Richard RuBino, Professor Emeritus in urban planning at Florida State University. "Richard heads our tagging operation here in October, but he also tags in the spring."

I blink. "How in the world do you tag a monarch?"

"With a sticky circular tag about the size of a hole punch. We tagged 1,500 last season; in fact, we're one of the most significant tagging spots in the Southeast and on the Gulf coast." She gives me RuBino's number. "And you might want to raise your own monarch. Native Nurseries sells milkweed. They might even have some with monarch eggs on them. You could tag your own butterfly and release it. If it's found you'll find out where your monarch has been."

I thank her and call Richard RuBino, who thanks me for my interest in monarchs and says when he's back in town in ten days he'll be happy to take me with him on his rounds at Eden, the farm north of town where he raises, tags, and releases monarchs each spring to augment the population during their journey north.

In the meantime, I start to raise my own monarch. At Native Nurseries, my friend Mary Ann sells me a milkweed (a monarch's sole larval plant which provides toxins—cardiac glycosides—that protect it from being eaten by birds) complete with a one-inch-long monarch caterpillar—black with yellow and white bands—and a "Happy Home" screened enclosure. "So it can't go off—and it would—to places unknown to pupate," Mary Ann says. "Just wait. The chrysalis is lovely to look at. Jade green with gold threads. Just gorgeous."

That evening my husband, Ormond Loomis, and I sit on the porch overlooking our butterfly garden and contemplate our caterpillar in its Happy Home. Its mouth moves so fast as it eats milkweed leaves, it seems to mow more than chew. When one leaf is gone, the caterpillar attaches its mouth to what's left of the stem and seems to be drinking. We watch until dark, two people with more than plenty to do mesmerized by one caterpillar.

For the next two days, the caterpillar grows as we watch. I get a ruler and measure—two inches long. "Its girth increased from three-sixteenths of an inch to three-eighths," I inform Ormond.

"Did you use your caterpillar caliper?" he deadpans. He studies the fat caterpillar and pronounces, "I think it's big enough that it needs a name." We kick ideas around. A monarch reminds me most of stained glass—in Frank Lloyd Wright's palette but with Tiffany's graceful Art Nouveau lines. "Then we'll call it Frank," Ormond says. I point out it may be a female. "In that case, Tiffany. But for now, Frank."

The next morning, Good Friday, we wake to a noxious odor, some insecticide our next-door neighbor has sprayed. I grab the Happy Home from the porch and move it inside, shut the doors and windows, and turn on the fan. Frank still looks fat and happy, but Ormond suggests I buy a second plant for backup before we leave for our farm in Live Oak, where we'll spend Easter weekend. I buy another milkweed with an inch-long caterpillar. When I get home, the noxious odor is gone, so I put both caterpillars out on the porch and pack for the farm.

When I wake Easter morning, I find the new caterpillar lying limp in the fork of the milkweed. Dead. Our neighbor's insecticide, I suspect. I can't tell if Frank is dead or alive; he's attached his back-end to the top of his Happy Home and hangs motionless in a J. I tap the top of the screened enclosure. He curls up tighter. Alive, but who knows for how long?

Around three o'clock, a neighbor, Mike Conners, drops by to visit. We sit on the porch overlooking the meadow, our backs to Frank, while Mike talks about changing careers. Suddenly Ormond shouts, *"Oh, Claudia, look!"* And there Frank isn't. A soft green blob hangs where he used to be, and as we watch--utterly speechless--it hardens into a jade-green chrysalis.

"The caterpillar's skin isn't elastic enough to accommodate how fast it grows," Mary Ann explains Monday morning, "so it sheds its skin five times. Each stage is an instar. The fifth instar caterpillar fastens itself into a J and sheds its fifth skin, revealing the green chrysalis."

"Amazing," I say.

"You think *you're* amazed. This lobbyist—a short gray-haired man— came in before Easter all agitated because his wife made him buy a caterpillar for their son. Just then, one of our caterpillars started morphing right before his eyes. He was transfixed. Said it was the coolest thing he's seen in *years*. Now he's signing up for butterfly workshops."

"Jaded lobbyist transformed by jade-green chrysalis."

"Really," she laughs. "The caterpillar morphed, and so did he."

I tell her about the dead caterpillar, our neighbor's insecticide. "I'm afraid

CLAUDIA HUNTER JOHNSON

our monarch will emerge with eight wings and bucked teeth."

She scowls. "If it does, you take it over to them and show them that's what their insecticide did. And think what it's doing to *you*."

In the interest of science—and monarchs—I decide I have to ask my neighbors what they sprayed—and ask them please not to spray it again. They're good neighbors; I don't want to offend them. I ring their doorbell and realize I'm wringing my hands. Smiling, Pat answers the door, registers the look on my face, and says, "What happened?" I explain. "Oh, no!" she says, truly sorry. "I have a close friend who raises monarchs, so I know how passionate people are about them, and how wonderful—and wondrous—they are." Her husband, Vince, says he sprayed Malathion to kill mosquitoes. He tried to be careful, avoiding the hedge between our two houses. "But it drifts," Pat reminds him. "Maybe that's why we never have any butterflies."

"Maybe you could find an organic alternative," I suggest gently. Vince says he will. I thank them. "I knew you'd want to know." A pause, awkward. "So I guess that's the, um—"

"The environmental minute," Pat says, and we laugh.

I spend the rest of the morning reading about the monarch's migration—floods of butterflies turning blue sky to orange—what Pyle describes in *Chasing Monarchs* as "the grandest butterfly spectacle on the planet."

> This is how the sky river floods North America each spring. Wave upon wave of orange insects, whose grandparents ebbed out of their summer range the previous autumn, now pour in . . . Eddies occur as the sky river gives off another generation and then another, each of which will live just weeks . . . Then the current turns back again, to become not a meandering, chaotic mob like their northbound ancestors but a single-minded, gathering onslaught on the southern reaches. So the sky river runs two ways, north with the spring, south with the fall.

Over lunch, looking at our one chrysalis, I say to Ormond, "To be a small part of something so big and wonderful is, well, wonderful."

After lunch, Richard RuBino swings into my driveway in his black Honda Accord. He gets out to greet me, a tall thin retiree with wavy gray hair and

THE MONARCHS OF EDEN

beard and kind brown eyes behind tinted wire-rim glasses. As we head north to Eden, he underlines the importance of augmenting the monarch population. "As the entomologist Lincoln Brower has shown, over the years we have a lot of peaks and valleys in the overall number of monarchs, but he's projecting that the overall number is beginning to decline because their overwintering habitats in Mexico and California are getting smaller, and their summer habitat is being destroyed by urbanization." And heavy spraying of pesticides and insecticides is causing harm, too, he tells me. I mention losing a caterpillar to Malathion. "Well," he says, "you have a good example right there."

Take away the pesticides and the politicians, and Tallahassee is paradise. Even our neighborhood is Edenic (never mind the Satanic leaf-blowers), our backyard full of cardinals, wrens, Carolina chickadees, jays, bluebirds, owls, hawks. Twice I've seen a bald eagle, and beyond our backyard a kingfisher fishes alongside blue, green, and white herons that high-step the lip of the pond, content to share their peaceable kingdom with wood ducks, mergansers, and Canada geese. It's no wonder Colin Phipps chose the name Eden for the Native Species Horticultural Park he began developing in 1994 "to bring back the dominant upland plant community of Longleaf Pine and Wiregrass," as it says in the brochure Richard RuBino gives me when we arrive at Eden's office.

After introducing me to Phipps and his staff members and dogs, Richard unfolds a three-panel cardboard display—the kind kids use for science projects—titled "Eden Spring Monarch Migration Project." The mission is clearly stated: *To augment the population of monarch butterflies during their journey north in the spring season.* Augmentation, Richard explains, means attracting monarchs to hundreds of planted milkweeds and nectar plants; capturing and tagging free-flying monarchs; gathering eggs and early-stage larvae; placing them in screened enclosures to protect them from predators; keeping the enclosures clean and well-managed during the maturation of monarchs from egg or larva to adult; and tagging and releasing the monarchs after they emerge as adults.

"The project was Colin Phipps's brainchild," he says, setting the board on a table. "He felt that an awful lot of attention was being given to monarchs in the fall migration—and that's very true—but there was very little attention that he could find given to the monarchs as they went north—which was even more true." Phipps thinks if you add monarchs, increase their survival rate in the spring, then you'll have a greater number going north, and a greater number populating during the summer, and a greater number coming back in the fall, and that will help out the sanctuaries where they overwinter. "He feels that he's at the—can I use this metaphor?—that he's at the handle of the faucet." Richard laughs. "So he sees this as a very critical link in the monarch migration process and the monarch life cycle, and I agree with him, so we put it together in the spring of 2000. He funds it, and I manage it."

He points out the monarch flyways on the marked map of North America, red arrows that swoop from different parts of Canada and the northern United States east of the Rockies and converge at Mexico's Transvolcanic Mountains. When I ask how new generations of monarchs find their way every year, he says, "Nobody knows. There are a number of theories—orientation by magnetic fields and so forth—but I prefer the Altitude Angles of the Sun theory put forth by Chip Taylor [University of Kansas] and David Gibo [University of Toronto]. Simply put, the theory is that spring and fall migrations can be predicted by the angle of the sun as measured at solar noon." I must look blank, because he adds, "Which basically means on June 21 the sun is at its farthest point north, and as it begins to move southward, the monarchs will eventually begin to move down with it. I like that theory best of all, because the same thing works in terms of coming north in the spring." Most of the monarchs that survive the winter in Mexico migrate north to the greater Midwest, he explains; fewer monarchs take the longer sub-flyway skirting eastward along the Gulf coast south of the Appalachian Mountains and then turning northward along the Atlantic coast. "But some spring migrants come this far east," he says, "and Eden lies near the southern terminus of the Atlantic sub-flyway, so it's a good location for attempting to augment their spring migration."

For the next couple hours, I follow Richard on his daily monarch management rounds, stopping first at the greenhouse—new this year—a wooden structure with gray screened sides and long benches lined with pots of tropical milkweed *(Asclepias curassavica)*. "What's been going on out here this year is that we have a greater number of caterpillars, chrysalides, and adults coming out of our first generation—those returning from Mexico—than we have in past years," he says. "Two-and-a-half to three times more." He attributes it to more milkweed, "a bigger buffet" because of the greenhouse. "The plants were here when the first monarchs came through. With enough tender, young, fresh plants—about two-hundred-fifty—the big buffet was just waiting. More milkweed is a critical aspect. We have nectar plants to support and sustain life, but the fresh young tender milkweed is the key. And the other is that there are a fair number of monarchs migrating out of Mexico this year as opposed to past years. We observed seven faded migrating monarchs this year, five females and two males." The significance of this small number is lost on me until he explains that each female lays four hundred or more eggs. "Last year we only observed two monarchs, and none in 2001." And this year they appear to be coming over a broader span of time. We've had monarchs before in the area for a week or maybe two weeks, but now it's been over a month, because the first lady appeared on March 16. She laid eggs, and we took those eggs and put them in the shelter on milkweed that we put inside."

I spot a good-sized caterpillar on one of the milkweeds. "That's a fifth instar," he says. "You can tell because a crook appears in the antenna, and the bands get larger, more distinct." He plucks the leaf it's on and cradles it in his hand. "I like to get them in the first stage or as an egg because there's less chance of parasites bothering them, but we'll take it with us." The caterpillar taps the leaf with its head. I ask what it's doing. "Tapping!" he says, and we laugh. "It may increase their sensing ability, but I'm not sure." I offer to hold it so he can drive.

The caterpillar taps in my hand as we drive along a wooded ridge recently planted with rhododendrons and azaleas. "Colin is bringing back wild azaleas and rhododendrons," Richard says. "Longleaf pines. Wiregrass. It's a major conservation effort." The woods open up to rolling grassland with brontosaurus-necked live oaks and relatively new longleaf pines.

Richard parks in front of Hut A, an 8 x 12 building located on the eastern side of a live oak so it will get sun in the morning but not in the hot afternoon. We step through the same double-door system they used in New York into the screened area where jade-green chrysalides hang like stalactites. The hut is lined with pots of tropical milkweed where different-stage caterpillars are having a heyday. "My first task is to sweep," he says, rounding up the black droppings—*frass*—because they could introduce harmful bacteria. "My second task would be to water the milkweed, but today it might rain. If it doesn't, I'll water tomorrow." His third task is to remove the chrysalides that have "failed" because of bacteria or a protozoan called O.e. *(Ophryocystis elektroscirrha)* or predators like the tachinid fly, though he doesn't see the

CLAUDIA HUNTER JOHNSON

"telltale strings" left by fly larvae. He places them in the dustpan. I ask about a desiccated caterpillar in its J. "Poor creature," Richard says. "Could've been a spider just sucking the juices." He adds it to the dustpan. "Oh, yes, spiders are not good for caterpillars. They have their good sides, but not for caterpillars." I notice a smaller insect on the side of a fifth instar caterpillar crawling along the edge of a pot. "Good spot," he says, and kills the hitchhiker. "The plywood floor is carefully caulked, but predators still get in. So there's a loss, but not like outside." He dumps the dustpan a safe distance from the hut, and disinfects it with Clorox.

When he comes back in, we count. We each take a different section of the hut and count the chrysalides on the screen walls and roof, sliding on our backs under the benches (I'm glad I wore overalls) to count the chrysalides attached under there. I count thirty-eight in my small section, and he counts ninety-seven in his—a total of 135. "It was 133 yesterday," he says, checking the data.

Outside, Richard shows me new milkweed planted in two butterfly gardens close to the hut. "Ladies prefer laying eggs on young tender plants. Easier chewing for the children. But eggs can be tough to find. They're white but the size of a pinhead." He hunkers down next to one of Phipps's longleaf pines. "I've got an egg!" he says, triumphant. He shows me the white dot on the underside of a milkweed leaf. "There it is. Tiny. Easy to miss. The lady lays them on the underside of the leaf to protect them from rain—and predators." He finds a second egg, then stands up. "I'll get them tomorrow when there's no danger of rain."

I see a flash of orange on the other side of the garden. "Is that a monarch?"

"That's the lady I've seen trying to lay the last couple of days, but I haven't found any eggs." He watches her flutter from milkweed to milkweed. "This gal, if she's back from Mexico, has had a trip that started last September. She may be wrung out, too old to lay eggs. She may have laid four-hundred-plus eggs without being mated again. May be just habit." He smiles. "I'm guessing. But I'm sure it's toward the end for her. She's pretty faded."

I feel a wave of compassion for this faded lady at the end of her long hard journey.

"It takes a new female four to five days before she's fertile with eggs. Males, two to three days. Females move from plant to plant looking for places

THE MONARCHS OF EDEN

to lay. Males just fly along, back and forth, looking for females."

"Cruising."

"Yes, cruising," he laughs. "Just like in north Florida towns."

We follow the same routine in Hut B, a smaller 8 x 10 building. I count seventy-nine in my section, he counts ninety-four. Frowns. "That's a total for both huts of 308. Yesterday I counted 311." We count again. 308. "Well," Richard says, "we took three chrysalides away, so that must be right."

We go out to the garden, and he shows me a caterpillar he's just found, a big fat stage five. "Oh, he's a beauty," he says. I ask if he judges that from the girth. "And the differentiation of colors. The white bar is real white—whiter than the other we put in Hut A."

"That's a sign of health?"

"Yes."

"This must never cease to be thrilling."

He smiles, beatific. "It's a wonderful way to be in retirement. A whole new arena has been opened up to me, and it sort of rejuvenates life. Like the monarchs." He takes the caterpillar into Hut B.

"So that's the adventure of a day at Eden," Richard says as we get in the car. "I'm just sorry we didn't have any new monarchs emerging. We should by this weekend." He shows me the small hummingbird feeder and watermelon Gatorade he'll use to fill them when he hangs them up in the huts. "Once monarchs start to appear, they'll need nectar before I can get to them and tag them. And I'll put in a potted nectar plant or two. Pentas or something like that."

His door ajar to catch the breeze, he pulls out photos of St. Marks National Wildlife Refuge so I'll understand the other half of his work on behalf of the monarchs—the fall tagging project—and St. Marks's crucial role. "St. Marks is essential," he says. "You should try to get down there, see the lay of the land." He shows me a photo of the lighthouse on the edge of Apalachee Bay. "There's a series of dikes where goldenrod grows. The principle fall nectar plant for the monarch is wild goldenrod. When the goldenrod go in Nova Scotia, the monarchs begin to go, too, the angle of the sun affecting both. The last dike is right on the edge of the bay. So say it's late afternoon, and we're both monarchs"—he squints into the distance—"and we're following the bloom of the goldenrod and suddenly see this big blue thing that's the Gulf, so we head downward to spend the night, because this is the last land we see."

In October and November, Richard and his volunteers go to the refuge on Wednesday and Saturday mornings to count and tag monarchs. They start before dawn, when the butterflies are inactive, capturing as many as they can in large nets. "We take them to the parking lot and tag them," he says. "We may do some measurements and weights and things of that nature, and then we take them back to their roosting sites."

Since 1990 they've tagged thirteen thousand, but only four tags have been found in Mexico, a much lower ratio than monarchs tagged elsewhere. To Richard, this may mean that not many survive the Gulf crossing. "It's six hundred to nine hundred miles," he explains, "and generally people estimate that monarchs fly fifty to sixty miles a day, then come down and feed and get enough energy to keep on going. However, we found one a couple of years ago that came from Cape May, New Jersey, to here in ten days; that's about twelve hundred miles. It must have picked up a major frontal system to carry it on through." He points to the sky. "When they migrate, they migrate up there. They'll catch thermals, just like eagles and hawks, and go up four or five thousand feet or more. They'll ride those thermals because they can't flap all that way. It uses up too much energy, so they glide on the wind like hawks and eagles. Apparently they don't fly at night, which gives the sun angle theory even more credibility."

"Evolutionarily speaking, isn't it kind of dumb to try and make such a difficult if not impossible crossing?" I ask. Lemmings, of course, leap to mind.

He must notice the mournful look on my face. "Only four tags have been found, but more may have made it," he says. "Those that travel on west and go through the coastal states have a good chance of getting to Mexico. And some go straight down the Florida peninsula and overwinter there. Some tags have been found in both places." He puts the photos away. "So there you have it—our two monarch projects. We're the only operation in north Florida and in the Southeast doing this kind of thing. And the Eden project is unique, the only one, to my knowledge, that attempts to augment the northward migration from Mexico."

"If my monarch survives, could I tag it?"

"Sure," he smiles. "And should your monarch be found, you'll get a certificate from Monarch Watch." He pulls out the tags Monarch Watch has provided—a sheet of adhesive-backed hole-punch-size circles with print so small each one says:

MAIL TO
BIOLOGY
UNIV.KS
LAWRENCE
KS 66045
(THE TAG NUMBER)

He gives me two tags, "in case one fails." Then, to illustrate how it's done, he shows me a photo of him tagging a monarch, holding its wings together with his left hand while he applies the small tag with tweezers. "You can also use a toothpick," he says, "but you don't want your finger to touch the tag because it might remove the adhesive. Place the tag on the end of the distal cell in the center of the underside of the right hind wing."

"For balance?"

"That's right." The tag, he assures me, only adds five percent of a monarch's weight (their average weight is about half a gram), so it won't affect flight. "When the tweezer's removed, take the wing between the thumb and index finger of your left hand and give it a good press. Not a crushing press, but a good firm press to make sure it sticks. Then release the monarch. And call me with the date, location, gender, and tag number."

I promise I will.

When I get home, I check my chrysalis—still a healthy jade green—and call Robin Will at St. Marks National Wildlife Refuge. She invites me down for a tour the following Tuesday. I do a quick calculation: the chrysalis will be nine days old; Richard said they emerge in ten to twelve days; I can visit St. Marks without missing the monarch's emergence. If it emerges at all.

"As far as I know, we're the only wildlife refuge involved in the monarch research program," Robin Will says, unlocking the doors of a U.S. Fish and Wildlife Service–Department of the Interior white SUV. A St. Marks's Refuge Ranger for twenty-five years, she's slim and tan with short dark hair swept back from her face and green and gold dragonfly earrings. Sunglasses hang from a cord around the neck of her beige short-sleeved ranger shirt. She slides them on as we begin the seven-mile drive from the visitor center down to the lighthouse. "When the monarchs funnel down the eastern seaboard and begin making their cut toward the Gulf of Mexico, we seem to be in the right place for them to drop off. It's probably because there's not a lot of development not just along our forty-one miles of coastline, but also the Big Bend Preserve all the way to Cedar Key. There must be a hundred miles of undisturbed coastal vegetation, which is what monarchs want. They want to rest, they want to eat, they want to be left alone and not be hit by cars or mowed down by a tractor or whatever. So I think that poises us perfectly to continue to be a very significant keystone in their migration."

We pass the series of dikes Richard described and park by the white 1829 lighthouse, next to a car with the windows rolled down. A grackle hops from the open window into the car's front seat. Robin laughs. "I see a banana in there. I think that grackle wants that banana." We close our windows and get out of the vehicle into the parking lot where Richard and his volunteers tag the monarchs. "They weigh them and palpate their abdomen to see if the females have mated," she says, "and they'll look and see if their wings are torn or bitten or chewed, or if they have any other kind of damage, and they'll note that, then they tag and release them. On a good morning, they might have five hundred to a thousand monarchs."

We walk along the dike on the other side of the lighthouse. It's unlike any waterfront I've seen in Florida—a narrow beach next to dense vegetation. "We don't have pounding waves like St. George, so it's actually much better for monarchs. Pounding waves make wonderful mounds of sand, but they don't permit all this vegetation to survive," she explains. She's right: the bay, the confluence of five rivers—Aucilla, Pinhook, East, St. Marks, and Wakulla—is calm and blue, barely making a wave.

She touches the leaf of a thick, thorny bush. "This is saltbush—prickly ash—one of the monarch's favorite foods, and do be careful because it has spines up and down. They love this because it provides a safe place to hang at night, and they don't get attacked by anything because of the big sharp spines." She smiles. "I'm anthropomorphizing a little bit, but it does add extra protection. And it has this huge white puffy bloom that smells almost like cotton candy—very, very sweet. And it buds up and blooms in early October, just as the monarchs are showing, so it's a perfectly adapted bush for what they need. They nectar on it profusely. You might see fifty monarchs

THE MONARCHS OF EDEN

on a bush this size. They'll be on the lee side, so if the wind's blowing out of the north, which it usually is, they'll be resting here where we're walking, nice and sheltered, with the gray underside of their wings showing. They're camouflaged because when their wings are closed they look like a leaf." We walk back to the lighthouse, past cedars and oaks Robin says Richard's volunteers planted. "They're wonderful roost trees for the monarchs. They get camouflage and protection from lizards and dragonflies."

"Dragonflies are predators?"

"Oh, I've seen big dragonflies—not these little tiny ones, but these really big ones we get in the fall—push a monarch to the ground and start eating the abdomen while it's still alive." We both make a face and walk on. Along the dike on the other side of the lighthouse, she points out early goldenrod and Spanish needle. "A wonderful plant that blooms almost twelve months a year. Monarchs, skippers, fritillaries, they all love it," she says. A small brown skipper lands on the tiny daisy-like flower. She laughs. "Right on time to show us how much butterflies like it."

We arrive at a shelter at the end of the dike and sit in the shade on a bench overlooking the bay. Robin gazes out at the water. "Apalachee Bay is one of the most pristine—if not the most pristine—estuaries that we have left in Florida. There's so much public land wrapped around it. We have the combination to be a very significant aquatic zone for years and years to come." She points out the houses of Shell Point around the bay to the west, and tells me that two hundred one-acre lots have just gone up for sale to the east.

"Couldn't St. Marks buy them out?"

She shakes her head. "We can't afford it. And Congress is not in a mood to spend a lot of money to buy public lands. It's kind of amazing when you think about Teddy Roosevelt back in 1903 when the first refuge was declared. He actually set aside something like fifty national parks and twenty or something national wildlife refuges, and who would have cared about public lands back then? That's a hundred years ago! But he had some kind of vision to say it might matter down the road. I wish we had visionaries working in the government now," she says wistfully. "I mean, fifty years from now, what do we want the United States to look like? And how will we salvage these significantly unique pieces of the U.S.? I think that's where wildlife refuges need to play a bigger role in the community and community decisions than we

CLAUDIA HUNTER JOHNSON

210

have in previous decades."

I suggest that monarchs might be a good link.

"Oh, gosh, yes," she says. "It's incredible how excited people get about monarchs. I would have never believed it. I mean, I think they're fascinating, but we have lots of critically endangered species here on the refuge that don't generate that kind of support. People must have some intuitive connection to monarchs. They call from New York, they call from south Florida, and they'll want to know, 'Have you seen monarchs? Have they shown up yet?' And every October four-thousand-plus people come to St. Marks from all over the country—even from Europe—to see them. Experience them. Witness them and their migration."

"Why do you think people are so taken with them?"

She muses that it's their mystique and migration and the ease of being able to participate in that phenomenon. "You don't have to rent a boat. You don't have to fly to an exotic location. You don't have to have any equipment. You can just be there, and they'll be resting and feeding in large numbers, totally absorbed in what they're doing. They're not worried about you. They'll land on your head, on your shoulders. And I think people find that captivating. Even mystical. Something that's not interrupted by the hand of man."

Before I leave St. Marks, I watch their monarch video. It shows stunning footage of the orange sky river of monarchs flowing into the Transvolcanic Mountains, "a certain kind of paradise," one visitor calls it, but the narrator adds a sobering note: Of the hundred million monarchs that start the migration, only half will make it back to the States, and of the many dangers along the way—birds, dragonflies, pesticides—civilization is by far the worst. Not just urbanization in the United States. The impoverished villagers— *ejidatarios*—who live on the edge of the forest of oyamel fir trees where the monarchs roost every year need the wood to build homes and fires, to shelter and feed themselves and their children. So they cut down the trees, critical to the monarch's migration, slowly destroying the overwintering site—a cruel irony, it strikes me, since the monarchs—*Mariposa monarca*—have great spiritual significance for them: according to local legend, the butterflies are the returning souls of the dead. "The species won't become extinct, but the phenomenon of migration could very easily become extinct," says the shaggy, sad lepidopterist, Lincoln Brower. "It would be a great tragedy to lose the mystery of how the monarchs migrate here, the beauty of it. If all of this were lost, it would be like having one of the great art museums of the world burning down. It would just be the end of it."

The next day, the last day of April, Richard picks me up around two. I've begun to see lines in my chrysalis—faint wing patterns—and I'm concerned I'll miss my monarch's emergence while I'm helping tag his. "Should I bring it along?" He looks at the chrysalis—still jade green—and assures me the monarch won't emerge for another day or two.

On the drive up to Eden, I tell him about my trip to St. Marks. "The festival we have there every year in mid-October has become a major draw," he says. "The monarch is becoming a symbol of this area." He turns into Eden. "The monarch is no more important than other creatures, but it has sort of an aura. A mystique. It gets people interested, and it becomes a symbol for a larger thing, not just for the monarch, but for a larger thing."

"Critters at large?"

"Critters at large. The environment at large."

We drive through Rhododendron Ravine into the rolling grassland, another beautiful day, albeit warmer, the high close to ninety.

"We've got monarchs!" Richard says when we get to Hut A. Monarchs indeed—twenty in Hut A and twenty-three in Hut B. A few hang from the screen with their wings closed, the gray underside showing, but most are flapping like crazy. Backlit, their bright orange outlined in black looks even more like stained glass. "Oh, they're ready to go," Richard says.

"They're *gorgeous*," I say. "They're so *vivid*."

"They are quite vivid when they first come out," he says, clearly proud. "It gradually fades. It's not quite as bright in Mexico. If they get whipped around, the color fades faster. But this early color is so vivid. I like your word—vivid."

I spot one nectaring on a potted milkweed. "That one is crippled," he says, "and there's another crippled one on the other side." The first has a crimp in its wing, the second has almost no wings at all. "They didn't unfold properly," Richard says. "It probably didn't get the fluid pumped through them properly, so the wings didn't come out right."

"Will you release them?"

"I do let them go, but I don't tag them. They don't survive very well." I ask if two deformed monarchs out of forty-three is about average. He says it is. *And that's without Malathion,* I think. "Now," he says, "let's get ourselves a butterfly." He reaches for one and plucks it off the screen, holding its wings together. "It's a male. How do I know?"

"The black spots along the vein on the hind wings," I say. Pyle calls them "androconial (or sex) patches, black velvety pads of specialized scales also called alar (wing) pockets."

"You have to look at the abdomen, too," Richard says. "That's the only way to be sure. The male has two claspers he uses to hold the female during mating. The female's abdomen is smooth and rounded." He sits on the edge of a bench, the monarch in his left hand, the tweezers and sheet of tags in his right, and rolls the sheet until the edge of the tags is exposed. He picks the first one off with the tweezers, places it on the distal cell of the right hind wing, removes the tweezers, and gives the tag a firm press. "Done," he says. He takes the monarch outside—I follow—and sets it on the back of his hand. It opens and closes its wings a half dozen times. He blows on it gently. The monarch takes off, flapping hard, and lands on a nearby longleaf pine.

We go back inside. Richard suggests I get the next monarch. I try, but it hangs on to the screen. "Go ahead and tug. It won't hurt it." I do, and he tags it. I manage to tag the next, but not very gracefully. He smiles. "I certify you as qualified to tag by yourself."

One by one, I take forty tagged monarchs outside and release them. Some take off right away. Others stick around until I blow on them gently, then they fly swiftly into the trees or beyond. "Is this the payoff for you?" I ask Richard as he records the data.

"No," he says, "the payoff would be having them found and knowing where they got to."

We tag until five, until the grass turns chartreuse in the late afternoon light, and the sky fills with cumulus clouds touched with pink. Thunder crackles off in the distance. "Cumulus clouds are formed by thermals, an upswelling of air," Richard says. I ask if this will help the monarchs fly north. He says it might.

We get back in the car and head south. "This has probably been the peak day right now, the most monarchs emerging. I expect the numbers to start decreasing." But he predicts the total will be more than 300, compared to 104 in 2000, 47 in 2001, and 91 in 2002.

"You must feel very successful," I say.

THE MONARCHS OF EDEN

"Oh, it's a joy. I feel like I'm making a contribution. And Colin had it right: all the attention has been on the fall migration—where do they come from or where do they go? This is even more important," he says.

I return to our farm the next day, the Happy Home in the passenger seat beside me. The chrysalis has darkened a bit, and the wing pattern is much more distinct. By evening I can see orange in it. Only the top is jade green. The ridge is still gold.

By morning the orange-and-black wing patterns are perfectly clear. The jade green is gone. Richard said they usually emerge in late morning, "after things have warmed up a bit," and I've promised to spend the morning with my friend, Sharon, who lives near the Ichetucknee River, so I take the Happy Home with me. Sure enough, shortly after I carry it into Sharon's kitchen, the monarch emerges from the chrysalis, its abdomen swollen, its wings small and folded—*like the crippled one I saw at Eden,* I fret—but fifteen minutes later the abdomen's sleek and rounded—no claspers—and all four wings are full-size. She's perfectly normal. I'm as relieved as any mother might be. "It's a female," I tell Sharon. "Tiffany."

For two hours Tiffany hangs from the chrysalis with long graceful black legs, but she doesn't flap her wings once. The air-conditioning, I realize, may be retarding her progress. I move the Happy Home outside, and in half an hour she's not only flapping her wings, she's flapping around the small screened enclosure. I know she'll hurt herself if she stays there much longer, so I take her inside and tag her, placing the tag on the distal cell of her right hind wing with the tweezers and give it a firm press. Then I take her outside to release her. "Goodbye, Tiffany!" Sharon sings out. "Good luck on your journey!"

When I set Tiffany on the back of my hand, her feet feel like the brush of a feather. She opens and closes her wings, revealing that vivid orange outlined in black, as exquisite as any stained glass by her namesake. "You need to get going," I whisper, but she doesn't budge. I blow on her gently. She hesitates, then takes off—a bittersweet moment of grace. She heads due north as if she knows what she's doing, then doubles back as if she isn't quite sure, and lights on the dogwood next to Sharon's herb garden—black and orange amid the green leaves. A few minutes later she takes off again, flies a circle around me, then banks around the house to the north.

<small>CLAUDIA HUNTER JOHNSON</small>

214

After lunch, I say goodbye to Sharon and get in the car, the Happy Home now empty beside me, except for the dangling transparent chrysalis top. I drive the forty miles back to our farm—just shy of a monarch's average distance per day—past ponds and pecan groves and fields of pink phlox and gold coreopsis. I'm heading north, the same direction a spring monarch would go. It's a perfect spring day, warm and breezy, with fair weather clouds, and a few cumulus clouds getting started. With luck, maybe Tiffany will catch a good thermal.

"Go, baby, go," I say to the stonewashed blue sky. "Fly, baby, fly. Do your thing, lay your eggs, so others can continue the journey."

CLAUDIA HUNTER JOHNSON *is the author of the memoir* Stifled Laughter: One Woman's Story about Fighting Censorship, *nominated for the Pulitzer Prize and winner of the inaugural PEN/Newman's Own First Amendment Award, and two popular screenwriting books,* Crafting Short Screenplays That Connect *and* Script Partners: What Makes Film And TV Writing Teams Work *(written with Matt Stevens). She recently finished a new memoir,* Taking Ross To Texas: A Mother-Son Road Trip.

Filmy Dome Spiders Mid-September

This morning is so foggy—
100 percent humidity, the
weatherman says—I have to use
my headlights to travel south to
Leon Sinks, even at 8:30 a.m.

As I strike out on the trail, I'm
enchanted by a ghostly encampment of small, igloo-
shaped domes pitched on the forest floor, as far as I
can see. It's as if the whole of the forest is sieved by
spiders. I settle on the ground next to one web, the size
of a half grapefruit. Others nearby are no bigger than
a Ping-Pong ball. The spider has woven her silken
tent between a small native blueberry shrub, the
leaf of a bracken fern and a seedling longleaf pine.
Now, I spot the spider herself, dime-sized, suspended
upside down, legs spread in the dome's apex. The lacy
network of threads that make up her web are strung
with droplets of fog, and the lightest breeze makes the
whole construct shimmer and tremble. She floats.

I continue on my walk, noticing that the tents of the filmy dome spiders march only to the brink of the dry sinkholes. They seem to prefer the sandy upland habitat. As I hike up and down the string of dry sinks laced by the trail—Tiny, Hammock, Magnolia, and the others—I see that the shape of the dome spider domiciles are perfect mimics of the conical sinkholes. It's as though the animals have built their silken webs to balance the slump of the sinks, as if they would pull those limestone depressions with all their concerted strength, back to the level of the land.

web

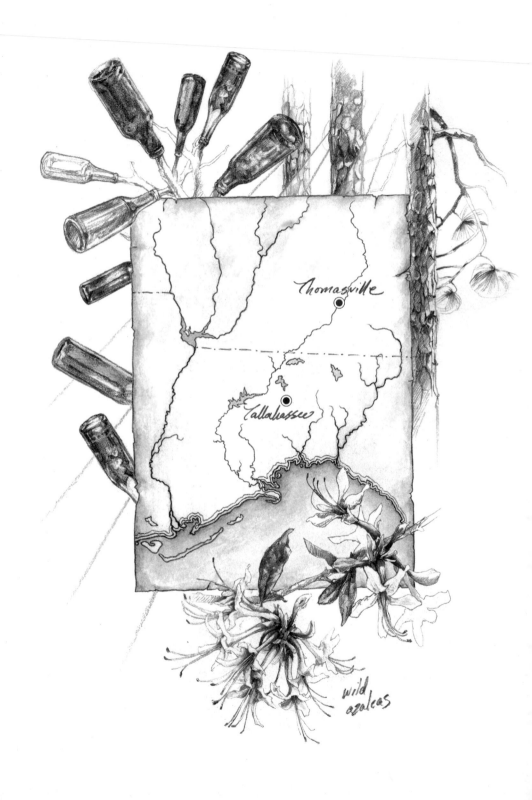

Thomasville

Tallahassee

wild
azaleas

Tobacco Prayers

MONIFA A. LOVE

*To the East, to the New Day . . . I Call on
Your Power and Spirit to Come in . . .*

When I was a child, my grandparents had a place in Carver,
Massachusetts, which hummed with the smell of marigolds, honeysuckle,
pine, scuppernong, and mint. The woods embracing their home were alive
with Japanese beetles, monarch butterflies, owls, chipmunks, and a variety
of poisonous and benign snakes. During Carver summers, between my
chores, I lolled in the thick and tickling carpet of grass and watched water
lilies unfolding on the pond. I studied hawks sailing in the cumulus clouds,
and geese parading and lifting off in signature Vs. I inspected the snakes
that took special pleasure in the warm bed of day lilies by the front door.
I was captivated by one snake that had been partially devoured by some
foe; a broken twig was my necropsy tool. I ran from skunks launching their
overwhelming weaponry and was lulled to sleep by the calls of whippoorwills
and bobwhites.

During my chores, I learned to feel worms moving inside apples, watched
ladybugs handle aphids, marveled at the insect life that teemed amidst
the compost, and gradually came to appreciate the odor-filled beauty of

regeneration and interdependence all around me. As a child, when I looked at old pictures of Carver and thought about the tales my grandparents told about our people, I imagined runaways on their way north and Massasoit retreating from the happenings at Plymouth Rock sitting among the trees and flowers.

When my own family moved to Tallahassee in 1990, I was not aware that I was looking for my version of that sacred, Carver place; yet we did find a home as fragrant with life and as animated by those who came before us as the northern haven of my childhood.

We lived in northeast Tallahassee, surrounded by towering water and live oaks, wildly exuberant bamboo, massive chartreuse and ivory azalea, delicate wisteria, and jasmine whose tender breath woke us at night. The full moon shone into our glass house and transformed our living quarters into a cathedral where we whispered in response to that divine light. We shared our property with possum, fox, deer, bats, armadillo, mice, skink, and insects of such incredible size and constitution that they looked like miniatures from 1950s mutant horror movies. Hooting owls, droning crickets, heavy-footed scavengers, and singing frogs punctuated the night; the darkness indeed held a thousand eyes. In the summer, mosquitoes were relentless, the flies as determined, and milky-white, trigger-happy scorpions made our trips to the trash receptacle an exercise in fleet-footed care. In the late fall and spring, the sun cast razors of light across the woods and showed the world in such stark contrast, it took my breath. The play of light and shadow was one of my favorite lessons.

At that home, my husband's sculptures found a place to live in peace. My husband looked forward to thunderstorms and the metal's dance with lightning. The sound of torrential rain against the steel was musical and comforting. He built a blue, steel teepee frame for me to cover with bottles. Inside that arbor, he hung a bell he had made to honor my mother. He also made a table that sat at the eastern entrance and held candles, water, and our little offerings. The dwelling was a place for daily prayer and our ceremonies of thanksgiving and praise.

Our blue, green, and amber glass temple was favored by God. Despite the often heavy rain and powerful winds, the bottles did not break, the hornets did not invade the bell as they did the other bells around the house, and the fire ants that lived below were as well-mannered as their aggressive temperament would allow.

MONIFA A. LOVE

While living in Tallahassee, I dreamed of a steel woman and a pot of coins. In the dream, each coin was a thing I feared. I gave the woman the coins. As she grew heavy with my fears, I grew lighter with courage. I shared this dream with my husband who made me a three-foot high, female-bodied bank, a pot, and coins the size of my thumb and finger touching. Over the course of many weeks, I prayed over the coins, and placed them, one by one, in the slot in the back of the bank. In the front yard, I dug into the red clay to bury the steel, guitar-shaped surrogate filled with the coins of my distress and sorrow. I planted flowers on her grave. Each day as I walked by her station, I was reminded of what she and the earth held for my relief.

Not long before I left Tallahassee, we established a small shrine amidst some sheltering branches. There, my offerings were taken up by the spirits and animals that responded to my small acts of devotion.

I am getting ahead of myself.

> *To the South, to the Little Mouse, to the*
> *Good Road Home, to the South . . .*

In 1988, I flew to Tallahassee from Miami to serve as a visual arts judge at the Harambee Festival. My plane was a small commuter prop plane. It should have prepared me for the bungalow-sized terminal. Coming from the pastel glitter of Miami, I was startled by the airport's World War II appearance. As I walked across the tarmac, I wondered what was this place—part capital, part outpost. It felt more southern than Miami. I was a little afraid. I found my way from the small airport to a hotel on Apalachee Parkway, and to a place that felt surprisingly like home. The city was alive with a sweet and sour smell. The slant of late afternoon light turned the landscape into origami. The folds of shadow and color moved me. Minutes after I had placed my bag on the luggage rest in my hotel room, I was outside, walking down the busy highway, anxious to take in everything.

Near the capitol buildings were markers commemorating Hernando DeSoto's travels through the region. I read the signs. I stood in the grass. Visions of long ago people passed through my body. I felt them in my hands, in my legs, weighing down my eyes, filling my ears and mind. Nearby, a black community held on. The modest houses were hot pink, lime, lemon, blue-gray, and white. They were filled with desire, disappointment, fury, stubbornness, and faith. I read the footprints on the weary steps. I stood by the porches. I touched the thin, tender walls. The sounds of juke joints, babies born at home, and great aunts and uncles on cooling boards filled my ears and mind. An expanse of land divided the community from itself. The area was lush. "No Trespassing" signs were posted. I respected those signs.

Around the corner was a tree. Three streets met it. The tree stood resolutely. Something in me wanted to climb up and be held in its branches. Something in me wanted to light a candle. I reached to touch the tree. Something drew my hand away. When I later discovered this was one of Tallahassee's lynching trees, I was not surprised.

I made my way to the Civic Center where the festival was taking place. Vendors were unloading their wares, musicians and dancers were preparing to perform. Artists were staking out territories and vantage points. Curry, barbecue, fish, and fruity smells hung in the air. The swirl of activity was deeply enticing. Instead of finding where I was supposed to be, I went back outside to watch the sunset and ponder how deeply the lives of people and the life of the land are intertwined.

The next morning, before the festival resumed, the organizers took me and the other judges to the Indian mounds in the northwest portion of the city. A guide took us up to the highest mound and relayed the history of that ceremonial place. I cared very much what the guide had to say, but I found it difficult to hear. The smell of cedar was so strong that I could not concentrate. I saw the guide's lips moving but all I heard was *cedar.* One of the judges took my hand and placed a small piece of cedar in it. "Keep it in your wallet," he said, as he started down the steps built into the terracing. I rubbed the cedar in my hands until it and my hands were warm. I tucked the cedar in my pocket. I closed my eyes and washed my face with my cedar-laced hands. My grandmother appeared to me. She always smelled of cedar and jasmine. She kept her clothes in a cedar closet and believed a woman should always smell like flowers, no matter her work. Feeling her there with me, I knew I would have to return to this town.

To the West, to the Dark Waters of Looking
within, to Beautiful Shell Woman . . .

MONIFA A. LOVE

My family and I lived in Tallahassee from 1990 to 2001, off U.S. Highway 319, twenty-two miles from the Georgia border. When I was not in school, teaching, or writing, I rambled along the back roads between our home and the state line. I was looking for something I came to visualize as a golden key that would unlock who I was born to be.

I also felt as if someone or something was looking for me.

As I was searching and being sought, I often thought of those who ran away, who somehow ventured from the desolation of slavery to the possibility of freedom elsewhere. On summer evenings when mosquitoes were thick, roaches on the wing, and snakes wriggled across our front porch, when banana spiders spun their magnificent nets, when the live oaks with their tangles of poison ivy and mite-ridden moss looked like monsters, I was humbled. Who could do such a thing? Who could walk so far by faith?

Early one autumn morning, I embarked on a small experiment. I decided to walk to Thomasville. Twenty-seven miles. A marathon. I wanted to see if I could just begin a journey that took some runaways thousands of miles away from what they knew. I wanted to see if I could feel them beneath my feet. I wanted to see if I could feel myself walking on their shoulders. It was my homage. It was my test. From Tallahassee, enslaved people most often sought the provisional freedom offered by the Everglades, or attempted to join the rebellious and contentious marroon communities throughout the territory. There were some, however, who made their long way to the north. I was not courageous enough to leave in the night, as one would if one were running away. Although I took a walking cane, I did not feel the threat of dogs. I was not faithful to the period. I powdered my feet, tied on my sneakers, laughed at spoiled me, and began. The day was lovely. The humidity was low. The sky was the color of old turquoise. The air was ripe with the smell of earth mixing with fallen leaves.

I had awakened that morning with the need for traveling shoes. I had not prepared an alternate route to the busy highway. In my mind, Highway 319 ambled north like a nineteenth-century trail, not the flurry of cars, semis, RVs, motorcycles, SUVs, and pickups with boats that it actually was. After I advanced through our quiet neighborhood and reached the highway, I paused for some time, trying to determine if I really wanted to test myself along the fast-moving road. In 1991, 319 was two lanes, one in each direction, with no sidewalk.

TOBACCO PRAYERS

223

I walked about ten miles, jumping into the tall grass and brush when a vehicle came too close. After five hours, my tired arms and legs were scratched and swollen from my sudden movements to dodge the traffic. As I brushed myself off and considered the foolishness of my enterprise, I noticed a dirt road on my right. I veered down the road and saw a majestic, sheltering tree. Beneath the tree, a roughhewn bench and a handmade sign that read, "Wait Here. See God. Acts 9:18." I thought I must have been dreaming, but I sat and waited. The thrum of 319 traffic sounded like a river.

Beneath the tree, I saw things: deer, snake, one adult fox and pup, a field of orange day lilies, butterflies, and birds of many hues. It occurred to me that I had awakened that morning so that I could encounter this tree of life, these beings, this place pointed out to me by some divine kindness. After a long while, I was compelled to rise and head home. The way back felt less fraught with peril. When I reached our driveway, the sun was setting. As I sat in the tub that night, I fell asleep dreaming of how much a runaway might see and come to know.

To the North, to the Old Ones and Those Gone by . . .

In the spring of 1999, my husband died from a massive heart attack. I continued to live in the house for three-and-a-half years. From the kitchen window, I watched a hummingbird and hawk hover in midair next to one another. On the front porch, I studied a snake as it leapt over my head and crashed into the front door. From the front yard, I examined the thousands of starlings that overtook the trees and house for three days before flying on. I examined these happenings and thought of Ed and how my ancestors animated the landscape.

One Sunday morning in 2000, I drove to St. George Island. I left the house early enough to watch the sunrise on the way to the Gulf. I crossed the causeway slowly in deference to the hatchlings making their tentative way through the air and across the road.

When I reached the beach, a congregation was in the midst of a baptism. The group numbered about fifty. Most stood on the shore singing. I recognized their songs from my childhood. Their singing encouraged a minister who held a young man in his arms a few yards out. The minister began shouting. The sound of his shouting mixed with the roar of the water and the clapping of the parishioners. I found myself on my knees in prayer. When I opened my eyes, the baptism was over and the church members were gone. I missed the holiness of their dark bodies against the cloudy-blue water and sky.

Ed's ashes had been scattered where the baptism took place. I was as glad as I was confused. What had I seen? Were there human beings celebrating the meaning of thresholds, or was I watching a reenactment of my husband's reunion with God?

Although I have not always appreciated it, my life has been abundantly blessed with occasions for me to feel one with God, nature, and my ancestors. Those occasions of consonance have brought me unspeakable, and perhaps *unwritable* joys. Tallahassee, like my grandparents' home, comforted me, taught me, and expanded me. The lessons, like most great lessons, did not require my planning, rather they required me to be open to the ways God speaks our names in the rocks, trees, earth, and water.

MONIFA A. LOVE *teaches writing and humanities at Morgan State University in Baltimore. She is the author of several books including* Dreaming Underground, *published by Lotus Press in 2003. She lives in Prince George's County, Maryland.*

I Support the
LAKE JACKSON
ECOPASSAGE
www.lakejacksonturtles.org

Watershed Down:
Lake Jackson's Fall from Grace

ANN J. MORROW

*The surface is carved into watersheds—a kind of familial
branching, a chart of relationship, and a definition of place.*
—*Gary Snyder,* Coming into the Watershed

It's late morning in July and the sun is high overhead when I pull my car
into the U.S. Highway 27 boat landing on Lake Jackson's western shore. The
landing is deserted, partly because it's a weekday, but mostly because the
water's not deep enough for anything bigger than a canoe or johnboat. The
lake is slowly refilling after completely draining and drying three years ago.

From the shade of a live oak, I watch a great egret pick its way along
the water's edge. Beyond, the shallow expanse of the lake stretches two miles
to meet the cloak of green that defines the mostly undeveloped northeast
shoreline. The water glistens in the hazy heat, flat and still on this breezeless
morning. Red-winged blackbirds chatter, tree swallows dip and glide. There's
life here, and beauty, and I wonder for a moment why I have spent so little
time at this lovely four-thousand-acre lake, just four miles north of downtown
Tallahassee.

The blare of a car horn reminds me. The four-lane divided highway
behind me is alive too. Traffic flow is intense and noisy on this major artery.

It's one of the reasons that I have lived in Tallahassee for almost twenty years and, until today, never stopped my car along this stretch of road. Another reason is the landing's popularity, when there's enough water, and its attraction for jet skis, motorboats, and crowds.

But more than that, I have stayed away from the lake because of well-publicized reports over the years of poor water quality, toxic algae, and impenetrable mats of exotic hydrilla. They made it hard for me to believe the glowing historical accounts. Trophy bass—what century was that? Swimming? You've got to be kidding!

Good reports have always accompanied the bad ones, and encouraging changes have taken place in the last few years. But for the most part, whenever I wanted to head out to someplace nice, I rejected stormwater-plagued Lake Jackson. Why go there, I reasoned, when so many quiet, clean rivers and bays beckoned from the coastal lowlands south of town?

Matt Aresco doesn't need anyone to point out the life and beauty to be found at Lake Jackson—or its fragile nature. The herpetologist and Florida State University (FSU) graduate student stopped along this same stretch of U.S. Highway 27 in February 2000 and found the remains of ninety road-killed turtles along a one-third mile stretch of the road. The carnage shocked him into action.

I caught up with him at the deserted landing one hot day and followed after him on the daily turtle trek he's made ever since. He's worn a path on the inside of a two-foot-high silt construction fence that flanks the mowed edges on both sides of the highway. This temporary fence was the cheapest and most immediate solution he could devise to block the turtles from reaching the asphalt and herd them toward an existing culvert that connects two sections of the lake. Aresco patrols this border of black fabric and wooden stakes twice a day, every day. He walks fast, dodging the clawed tendrils of blackberry vine and scanning the path ahead of him.

"I usually find six or seven turtles each time I walk along here, but it's really hit or miss," he tells me. It's probably more *hit* than miss, I think to myself, considering the mortality statistics he has collected over the past three years. They document that his stretch of highway has the highest rate of road-killed turtles in the world.

Animals die because of the road's location. Its two lanes were laid down in the bed of the lake in the 1930s, and expanded to four lanes in the 1960s, effectively snipping off a fifty-five-acre portion of the lake, known today as Little Lake Jackson. Passage between the two sections became a deadly proposition for turtles, snakes, alligators and dozens of other species. Turtles make up the bulk of the animal pedestrians, but Aresco has documented over 9,200 animals of fifty-seven different species attempting to cross the half-mile section of the road in the past three years. Fluctuating water levels exacerbate the problem. Aresco found two hundred to three hundred turtles per day attempting to cross the highway when water levels dropped sharply in the main body of the lake.

The posted speed limit on the road is 45 mph, but traffic moves faster than that, at an estimated volume of 21,500 vehicles per day. It's not surprising, then, that 98 percent of turtles that try to cross don't make it.

Aresco bends down to examine the remains of a turtle nest, a new one since his last patrol yesterday evening. "You can tell it was made by a cooter because they always dig a three-chambered nest," he says, pointing to the line of three holes. " Most of the eggs are laid in the central chamber, anywhere from nine to twenty of them." He digs carefully with his fingers, but this nest has already been raided, probably by a raccoon. When Aresco does find eggs, he takes them to his lab, incubates them, and returns the hatchlings to the lake. April to mid-July is the prime egg-laying season and it's just about over.

"Just a couple of successful nests can mean a lot in terms of population numbers," he shouts over the rumble of a passing tractor-trailer. The more turtles, the better, he says. They help keep the lake clean by eating dead and decaying matter. Plus, they're fond of hydrilla, an exotic invasive that has choked parts of the lake in past years.

Ten minutes later, we come across a male cooter, alternately pushing against the fence and moving along it. Aresco estimates that the turtle is twenty-five to thirty years old. He points to the road. "Without the fence, he'd be dead right there." Back at his lab, Aresco will measure and weigh this individual and do a fecal analysis to figure out what he's eating. The turtle will also get a tag or notch in the shell before release back to the lake. Recaptures provide information on reproduction and growth.

I ask Aresco if he ever tires of these daily patrols.

"Sometimes I just don't feel like coming out," he acknowledges. "And it's very discouraging to have something get hit while I'm here. But I figure that if I move just three turtles every day, that's over a thousand a year, and that's significant."

He's been far more successful than that. To date, the system of temporary fences and daily patrols has spared the lives of over eight thousand turtles. Meanwhile, Aresco is moving ever closer to his goal of a permanent wildlife crossing—what he calls the "Lake Jackson Ecopassage." It's modeled after a guide wall and culvert design used successfully on U.S. Highway 441 across Payne's Prairie in Gainesville. The Department of Transportation has allocated the money for a feasibility study that will be managed by Leon County. Progress has been slow, but Aresco is unwavering in his goal.

"I want zero mortality," he says. "Some people tell me that I can't save all of the turtles; but I can sure try."

The placement of U.S. Highway 27 in the lakebed was a huge blow to the lake's integrity, though it certainly wasn't the first time humans had left their mark on the surrounding landscape. Excavations at the Lake Jackson Mounds Archaeological State Park have turned up bones and shells from deer, birds, turtles, freshwater mollusks, and fish as well as copper breastplates, beaded necklaces, and other elaborate burial objects—all remnants of a thriving Native American culture that occupied the lakeshore when this area was a political and religious center between AD 1200 and AD 1500. The complex consists of the remains of seven mounds, a plaza and a village area on the lake's southwestern shore, just down slope, yet centuries away from the Lake Jackson Trading Post on U.S. Highway 27, where today a chain grocery store and video rental place and other retailers celebrate a different kind of culture.

The Native Americans planted corn that thrived in the fertile soils. Hickories, oaks, and pines have grown up since then, but it's still obvious that views of the lake from the largest mound, which reaches a height of thirty-six feet, must have been spectacular.

These same attributes attracted land-hungry planters to Leon County in the 1800s, when good farmland was priced as low as $1.25 an acre. Historian Clifton Paisley described how lakes Jackson, Iamonia, Miccosukee, and Lafayette encircled some of the choicest farmland. Land around Lake Jackson was particularly attractive. In his book, *Red Hills of Florida, 1528–1865,* Paisley wrote: "Only a few other planters farmed west of Tallahassee. Far richer lands lay north of town, along the thirty-mile shore of Lake Jackson.

Ann Morrow

230

Planters loved the rich lands along its borders, and they loved equally well the high hills rimming the lake. From their houses they enjoyed an almost aerial view of this, the most beautiful of four large lakes in Leon County."

The planters bought up thousands of acres around the lake and set to work building successful enterprises in cotton and corn production and livestock grazing throughout the 1800s and early 1900s. These prominent planters were also leaders in business, banking, and politics and three of them served terms as antebellum governors in Florida.

It was trophy largemouth bass, not farming, that brought other folks to the lake and put it on the national map.

When Arlene and Furman Henderson settled on the northwest shore of Lake Jackson in 1955, it was drying down and the property was bargain-priced. There wasn't much of anything out that way then *except* the lake. The Hendersons had to drive seven miles to Apalachee Parkway to shop. It wasn't unusual, they told me on a recent visit, to make that trip into town without seeing another car, or to take a run around the lake in a boat and pass only a few houses.

The Hendersons still live on the lake in a log house decorated with black and white photographs and some good-sized mounted bass that keep company with a stuffed bobcat and possum. From 1955 to 1975, the Hendersons ran the thriving Trade Winds Restaurant (later adding a bait and tackle shop) on the site of the present-day Red & Sam's Fish Camp. They later presided over a fishing camp at Sunset Landing.

Arlene showed me a faded black-and-white photo in which she is hoisting up two fifteen-pound bass she caught in the lake in 1955, but it's Furman who provides the caption.

"It was nothing to catch a ten-pounder then, or to come out with a string of bream this high," he says, holding his hand five feet off the floor.

The 1950s and 1960s were busy times for the Hendersons. According to Arlene, on a weekend, especially when the bream were bedding, you couldn't find a parking space there.

"We had ten fishing guides running and more than forty johnboats renting out as fast as they would come back in. We had a guy from Texas who would fly in every weekend and regulars from London and South Africa." Arlene gets up from the couch and disappears into a back room, returning with a copy of a popular foldout map they used to sell. Called *Lake Jackson*

Hot Spots, the map shows the lake dotted here and there with splashes of color, coded to direct anglers to the best fishing holes for bass, crappie, and bluegill.

Record-high water levels in 1966 closed things down for about a year. The water was so high, it flooded U.S. Highway 27. "We had geese swimming in and out of the place," said Furman, "but when the water went down, we just cleaned out the snakes and frogs and reopened."

Arlene hasn't fished in almost five years, since the lake went down in 1999, but she's anxious to get back out there.

"I love the lake, as long as there's water, 'cause I live to fish," she says. Others do too. Arlene still receives phone calls from Lake Jackson fans in Chattanooga who used to come down two or three times a year. "They call from time to time, checking on the lake; they can't hardly wait for the water to come back up so they can get their boat in."

When pressed about past water quality problems, Arlene admits that some of the reports scared people away from the lake and that the building of Interstate 10 in 1972 made a mess in the southern end. "You couldn't eat anything out of that part because it just tasted bad."

Fishing will be good again in the future, she thinks—though, in general, the sport will suffer from a decline in interest rather than water quality.

"I think we'll have some big bass in the lake again, but it'll never be fishing like it was," she says. "The younger generation just doesn't seem to care about fishing as much."

She looks wistful as she concludes, "I want the water to come back up. I want to get back out there and catch me some butterbeans—that's what I call the small bream—they're the best tasting."

Arlene is not alone. A lot of folks would like to see the lake fill up and bustle again with activity. The fishermen know, though, that the fishing is always better after a drydown. Organic deposits dry and compact, creating a firmer substrate that is better for fish and the macroinvertebrates that many game fish eat.

But the lake has its own timetable. Since it was first documented in 1907, the water has disappeared from Lake Jackson six times, not including the most recent occurrence in 1999. Normal water levels return in a matter of months or sometimes years.

ANN MORROW

The lake's cycles are a reminder of the complex connection between geology and weather; groundwater and surface water; politics and priorities.

The four-thousand-acre lake has a twenty-seven-thousand-acre watershed. It is a closed basin; water enters through rainfall, stormwater, and several creeks, and exits only through evaporation and seepage into the ground. Water drains from the lake through two major sinkholes, Porter Sink and Lime Sink, which connect to a labyrinth of tunnels and caverns in the underlying lime-rock bed and eventually to the Floridan Aquifer. The basin that forms Lake Jackson today was probably created when water slowly dissolved the limestone and caused a collapse of channels and caverns over a broad area.

Water drains constantly through the two sinks, but that's only obvious during prolonged periods of below-normal rainfall, such as occurred in the years prior to the most recent drydown in 1999. Porter Sink drained a portion of the lake in September 1999. By May 2000, Lime Sink had drained the northwest portion of the lake near U.S. Highway 27, causing the mass migration of turtles and the subsequent road kill that first grabbed the attention of Matt Aresco. By then, more than 90 percent of the lake was dry.

The Lake Jackson watershed showcases the best and worst that Tallahassee has to offer: everything from greenways and unpaved clay roads to malls and interstate highways. The southern edge of the watershed ends only ten or so blocks from the intersection of West Tennessee and Monroe streets. A drive from there, north to the lake, is a journey down a continuous commercial strip. Stormwater from this and other developments to the east enters the south end of Lake Jackson through Meginnis Arm or Ford's Arm.

As water follows its downhill course, it carries to the lake what it picks up from the surface: things you can see like leaves and pine needles, plastic cups, and candy wrappers and things you can't—motor oil and radiator fluid, fertilizers, and pesticides. Unpaved surfaces soak up some of the water, cleaning it as it slowly percolates through layers of vegetation and soil. But water just rolls off pavement. A good rain can scour accumulated pollutants and send them quickly to the lake.

Sediment from construction sites also flows into the lake, a problem that started in earnest in the 1970s with big projects like the Northwood and Tallahassee malls and a section of I-10. The I-10 project, in particular, made headlines when heavy rains sent plumes of silt into the southern part of the lake. Sewage spills from a City of Tallahassee lift station went into Meginniss Arm. All these contributions created a nutrient-rich soup that fueled the massive growth of harmful and invasive plants such as hydrilla, hyacinth, and blue-green algae in the lake's southern end. As the vegetation died and decayed, a layer of organic muck built up in the lake bottom. It was three feet deep in some places and a sure sign of a troubled lake.

In 1999, as the water disappeared and sent turtles and alligators on the move, state and local officials scrambled to find money and permits for lake restoration, something they had always planned to do when the lake went dry again. It's just that it was not expected to go dry until around 2007, based on the average interval of twenty-five years between these natural drying events.

The muck in the lake bottom had to be removed or the nutrients would continue to cycle between the sediment, the vegetation, and the water.

"Even if we refilled the lake with pure, bottled springwater, we'd still have a problem," says Tyler Macmillan, who coordinates the Surface Water Improvement Management (SWIM) program at the Northwest Florida Water Management District. The SWIM Act, passed by the Florida legislature in 1987, takes a watershed approach to surface water management. It addresses the sources of pollution, such as stormwater, that flow into and degrade lakes, rivers, and estuaries.

The program is run by the District in cooperation with the Florida Department of Environmental Protection (FDEP) with assistance from other state agencies and local governments. In 1988, the District listed Lake Jackson as one of its top five priorities for the expenditure of SWIM funds.

Macmillan helped draft the Lake Jackson Management Plan, which included a 1993 expansion of the Meginniss Arm Treatment Facility that the District built in 1983. The facility captures some of the stormwater in this troubled drainage area and cleans it before sending it into a human-made marsh that then flows into the lake. The management plan also called for the eventual construction of regional stormwater ponds, which could handle greater volumes of stormwater. A contingency plan, which was not fleshed out, addressed the need for sediment removal if and when the lake dried.

When it became clear that the lake was going to dry in 1999, officials shifted into high gear. Money was moved around too, and the county had to put the regional stormwater plans on hold.

"The original plan for the watershed called for building the holding ponds first, but we didn't have a choice," says Macmillan. "We had to dig when the lake was dry."

Macmillan coordinated the permitting, funding, and implementation of the sediment removal project, which eventually cost over $8 million and removed muck from six hundred acres of lake bottom—enough to fill a football field one hundred stories high. Leon County covered more than half the cost. Other financial partners included the Florida legislature, the District, the Florida Fish and Wildlife Conservation Commission, and the Florida Department of Environmental Protection. Because water levels stayed low for an extended time, muck was removed not only from the southernmost troubled parts of the lake, but from other large areas of lake bottom with sediment accumulations.

According to Macmillan, the county's money and manpower represented "an extraordinary commitment for local government, and very uncommon in the state." He attributes a part of their interest to the results of a study in the early 1990s, which estimated that spending or sales related to Lake Jackson poured $10 million per year into the local economy.

"I think local officials viewed it as an issue of 'the lake gives us $10 million, what are we going to give the lake?'"

What they gave the lake was extra time—time to build regional ponds to catch and clean stormwater in the watershed so that as the lake refills, the incoming water will be cleaner. The timetable now calls for those ponds to be built within the next several years.

"Did we turn the clock back fifty to seventy-five years? We think we did," says Macmillan. "The lake may look kind of funny for awhile, but it's just going to take it some time to recover from that kind of major surgery."

Dr. Robert J. "Skip" Livingston, Director of the Center for Aquatic Research and Resource Management at FSU, is less optimistic. Livingston has studied area lakes since the 1980s and has published alarming reports about Lake Jackson, citing evidence of toxic algae, heavy metals, and fish kills.

"It's a cesspool, same as it was before and same as most of the lakes in Tallahassee," he states emphatically. He says the sediment removal was good, but it was just the beginning; that nothing has changed because the same dirty water continues to flow into the lake, though he acknowledges that regional ponds will help the problem in the long run.

Another long-term solution is education.

"A lot of people cry about what's happening in the Everglades, but they don't even care about the stormwater in their own watershed," says Russ Frydenborg, a natural sciences manager in FDEP's Division of Resource Assessment and Management. "Most people want to blame pollution on some big business and they think that government will fix everything. They don't make the connection between their own actions and the nearby waterbody."

Every one of us lives in a watershed, though most of us go about our daily lives without giving much thought to which one it is or what it means. Where does that soapy water go when you wash your car? Who stops to think about Lake Jackson when they park their car with its oil and coolant leaks at the Sugar Creek Plaza to catch a film at the movie theater? Do the folks who live off of Thomasville Road, on the shores of Lake Hall, think how the fertilizer they sprinkle on their lawns can affect the lake they live on *and* the distant Lake Jackson?

"I've often wished I could put up a billboard that reads: "You are now entering the Lake Jackson Watershed; please conduct yourself accordingly," says Macmillan.

There would have to be many billboards and plenty of detailed instructions.

Lake Jackson is currently enjoying a quiet convalescence. A lot of good people who grew up here and hold an abiding affection for it are watching its vital signs. Regular rainfall is filling the lake faster than it can drain. Water levels hover around eighty-one feet above sea level on the gauges. When it gets to eighty-five feet, water depth will be back into the normal range, one that will allow jet skis and bigger boats to launch. A stalled tropical storm or slow moving winter front could get us to that point almost overnight.

There are still a lot of unknowns that can't be overlooked. The science of stormwater is imperfect. Money for regional ponds might get diverted once again. Urban growth may completely undermine all the good intentions and expensive engineering fixes. I fear that people may never make the connection between life in the lake and lifestyle around it.

And yet, I put myself in the camp with the optimists.

I paddle to the center of the lake over a hard, sandy bottom visible through clear water. There are no motorboats, and instead of traffic, I hear cawing fish crows, grunting pig frogs, and the hum of a bee diving deep into the yolk-yellow center of a water lily.

Turning my back on the cell phone towers and facing the undeveloped northern shoreline, the timeless nature of the Lake Jackson waterscape seduces me. For the moment, the lake belongs to the small fish that streak through the shallows and the screaming osprey overhead.

For the past seventeen years, Tallahassee resident ANN MORROW *has been writing about Florida's wildlife and habitats for a variety of books, magazines, and newspapers. She especially likes to explore the relationship between children and the natural world and is at work on a young adult novel set in north Florida.*

Hurricane

To live in north Florida is to inhabit a place inviting to hurricanes—the open arm of the Big Bend coast beckons them in and they come, gathering up the Gulf of Mexico into violent chop and surge. Today's visitor is named Opal, but so far all I can see, thirty miles from the coast, is a race of gray clouds across the ceiling of our sky and brief blitzes of rain.

A tearing eastbound wind tests the flexibility of the trees in our clearing, bending their trunks at unexpected angles, checking their rootedness and the grip of their leaves. A laurel oak just threw down a scatter of small dead branchlets in response to the wind's assault as if to say oh all right, here then. Have some of me. But before the night and the hurricane are spent, much more may be asked of these trees, and they know it. The wind is already so strong that even the weeds in the field, only four or five inches tall, are forced flat, turning their hidden white undersides to the sky.

A mourning dove speeds by, and then a crow. Do they feel the drop in pressure, intuit the path of the storm? Will they cling low and tight to the bark of trees for protection? What would I be able to guess about this hurricane if I were uninformed by weather radio and websites, dependent only on my bodily senses?

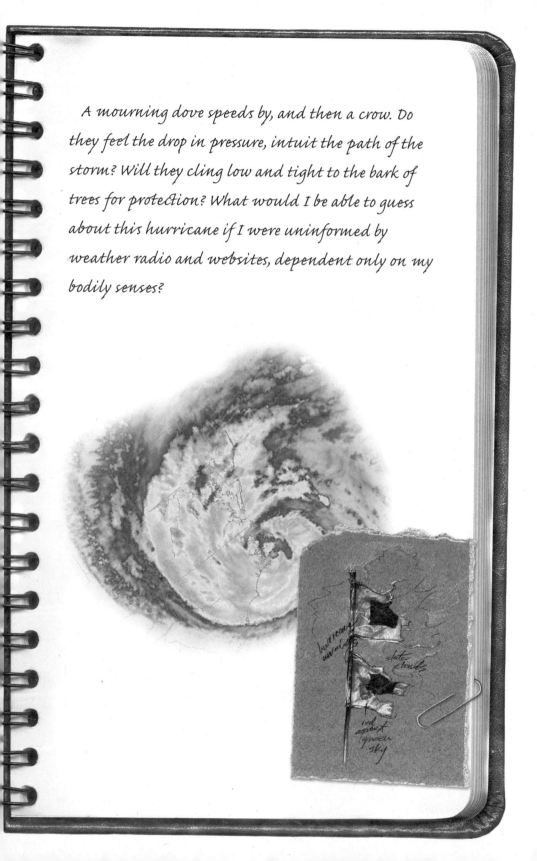

R.C.W.

Thomasville

Tall
Timbers

[Form No. 47.]

Station No. 11

[FOR PLANTER.]

JOINT RECEIPT.

PENSACOLA & GEORGIA

AND

ATLANTIC & GULF RAIL ROADS

No. 182 March 14th 1868

RECEIVED FROM

Bales Cotton,

ton & C.

BALES.

8

5

under the
receipt, which
nce.

Agent.

Kennelhouse
c. 1935

Millpond Plantation

Big Chance. Fat Chance. Slim Chance:
How Caprice Brought Us the Red Hills

JIM COX

It's impossible to lead when you waltz with a two-hundred-year-old tree. A leather climbing belt tethers me to my senior dance partner some sixty feet above the ground. I feel like a seahorse attached to a strand of kelp as I sweep to and fro with this venerable longleaf pine. Our gambol doesn't match the tempo I hear and feel in the swift, steady wind, but there's no room for my dance chart in this setting. The ancient one presides.

I hold an endangered species, a red-cockaded woodpecker, that represents my reason for climbing this tree. I've removed the bird from the cavity where it hatched just eight days ago. It will require attention soon—some measurements, leg bands, and then back in the cavity—but I pause to bask both in the sheer beauty and mysterious improbability of the forest that surrounds us. This bird is secondary to the music, magnificence, and thoughts of providence that waltz through my head.

The magnificence of this old-growth longleaf forest, the Wade Tract, is quickly absorbed. Hundreds of grand old trees with tall, erect postures steeple-stretch toward the sky. Others with gnarled, wrought-iron branches, flat-headed tops, and tumescent boles lean at defiant angles toward the tug of the earth like huge bonsai bowing to greet guests arriving for a ceremonial tea. Beneath the trees lies an expansive prairie-carpet filled with golden grasses and green ferns, stretching in all directions.

The music of the longleaf forest is equally direct in its appeal. The performance begins as wind moves unimpeded through the widely spaced trees and flows across the thousands of thin green instruments gathered in bunches at the ends of stout branches. The long, taut needles offer up silk-slim whispers on a slight breeze, the muffled, distant hissing of young owls. When stoked by strong gusts, those same long instruments ripple with a loud, slicing drone filled with resonance and overtones, a chorus of manatees inhaling-exhaling, inhaling-exhaling.

There is no other orchestra that makes such music, and in the case of this patch of old-growth longleaf pine, the Wade Tract, it's music crafted by one of the rarest forests in North America.

This facet of the forest, the question of rarity, is the most difficult to absorb. In the mid-1800s, the supply of longleaf pine seemed endless. Longleaf forests extended from Virginia to Florida to Texas and covered nearly 90 million acres. It was a forest that built a nation. The heartwood was especially coveted because wood-rotting fungi couldn't disfigure the light, cinnamon-yellow wood, and the tight, dense grain turned jaws of termites to jelly.

But longleaf forests today cover just 3 percent of their original range, and most are comparatively young forests that have been hacked and harvested at numerous points in their careers. An individual longleaf can live for over four hundred years, holding tightly to its patch of earth until struck by lightning or felled by a storm. A longleaf forest that has grown back in an area cut over a century ago contains only teenagers and young adults when compared to an old-growth tract.

One authority estimates that only five thousand acres of well-managed, old-growth tracts like the Wade Tract remain, and many of these ancient forests are found on private lands in the Red Hills region. Some of North America's most precious environmental jewels, or perhaps more appropriately, some of the continent's rarest natural artwork, lie between Tallahassee, Florida, and Thomasville, Georgia. Think of it as finding great paintings amid the roadside stands of the region; the bright colors of Van Gogh and Renoir serving as ornate backdrops to stacked jars of mayhaw jelly and pickled okra.

A simple question buzzes through my head like a pesky gnat: *Why were these ancient trees spared from the ax?*

Swaying near the branched arms of my two-hundred-year-old dance partner, I see and hear a complex answer to this question. An abandoned dirt road nearby is covered with brush and adolescent pines; the shoulders are steep and deeply etched, a scarp of rich red dirt cut by years of erosion. I hear a chorus of yelping hunting dogs on a neighboring property. The dogs have featureless kennels that collectively stretch the length of two tennis courts and are cleaned twice a day. Their bays are just as much a part of the landscape as the music in the trees. And then there is the dark, charred bark that covers the base of every tree, long smudgy socks that help when I forget a pencil. A sliver of blackened bark can be used just like a pencil to record woodpecker data in my field book.

The sights and sounds are part of a very strange stew, a cultural history peppered by fire-arm technology and fire ecology, slavery and slow transportation, tenant farms and industrial titans, and, most importantly, lots and lots and lots of sheer luck.

What the Ancient Trees Saw in Their Youth

A few of the oldest trees on the Wade Tract were slim saplings when Spanish anchors first dropped into Florida's waters. The Apalachee Nation called this area "old-fields," a phrase that suggests the land had been worked for many a good year. Populations of Native Americans never approached land-burdening levels, but they did clear land extensively well before European settlement. Early Spanish explorers described huge agricultural fields and extensive road networks among the villages, including a maize field stretching six miles. This may be an exaggeration or a faulty translation, but the population (which totaled about five thousand across the region) required mounds of maize and beans and squash, and towns and ceremonial centers moved frequently as soils of the ancient old-fields were exhausted.

The Red Hills's moist clay soils could sustain many crops in upland pine forests, but a simple need for potable water favored settlement near water bodies and away from the expanse of pinewoods. Apalachee villages included Ychutafun on the Apalachicola River, Uzela near the Aucilla, Bacica near the Wacissa, Ochete near the coast, and Inhaica nestled amid the lakes and streams of greater Tallahassee. The early inhabitants burned and hunted and probably enjoyed the music of the longleaf forests, but they turned soil and cleared land close to large sinkhole lakes and river traces.

A Bloody Road

The abandoned road I see may have been a footpath used by the Apalachee people, or the Seminoles who followed, but more recent technologies and great effort extracted this band of flat earth from the rolling hills. It was called Magnolia Road despite the fact that it runs here through an upland forest where longleaf pines, not magnolias, make up 95 percent of trees. For all its quietude and seeming comeliness, a scar on the landscape that has healed well, I know it to be a road built with misappropriate sweat and blood in a time when the concept of property was savagely applied to people with dark skin.

Like the theft of lands from Native Americans, slavery was a gruesome part of nation building. Thinking about this peculiar institution can cause the heart to twist and cringe, but slave-based agriculture played a strange role in preserving old-growth pine forests of the Red Hills region.

Cotton, tobacco, and other large-scale agriculture ventures were well established before the end of the Revolutionary War, but the new state of Georgia was a wild place that served largely to buffer South Carolina from Spain's colony in Florida. It took the Creek Wars of 1814 before enough land had been swiped to ease the way for settlement of Georgia's remote southwest corner, and even then a special land lottery was used to encourage settlement. In 1812, about two thousand people put their names in a hat in hopes of drawing 250–500 acres of Red Hills farm land.

Many newcomers first located on old-field lands near Tallahassee or the hammock lands surrounding the large lakes. Others secured lands north of Thomasville, but the soils found there were not suitable for cotton production, so much of this land developed as small farms while larger, less fragmented tracts enveloped the virgin pine forests surrounding the Wade Tract.

The modern history of the Wade Tract began when Thomas Wyche purchased 490 acres south of Thomasville and in the early 1840s settled with his extended family (including his parents, ten brothers and sisters, and six slaves). He purchased additional land quickly, but clearing for cotton production took great time given the primitive technology of the era. Although Wyche had amassed sixteen hundred acres at the time of his death around 1860, he'd managed to clear just a quarter of this acreage. Land clearing progressed with similar languor on other large tracts, and by 1860, nearly thirty years after settlements first arrive, Thomas County was covered by a mere 65,000 acres of improved farmland and a whopping 360,000 acres of unimproved forest land.

Given enough time and resources, settlers would have worked over the pine forests as surely as water created the Grand Canyon, but while soils of the Red Hills provided few obstacles to cotton production, getting the crop to market was another issue. Thomasville had no railroad until the 1860s, so early planters were forced to send the four-hundred-pound bales of "white gold" through Tallahassee to shipping ports along the St. Marks River. The abandoned stretch of Magnolia Road that I can see was built with slave labor to provide a more direct route to the shipping ports and avoid the usurious gatekeepers in Tallahassee. It linked up with Plank Road east of Tallahassee and headed south to the now-abandoned town of Magnolia along the St. Marks River.

Even this direct route was slow going when transportation was powered by mules. A prime six-mule team took a full week to carry a cotton shipment to port and return. About a third of the cash paid for the crop ended up going to insurance, lodging, storage, and *primage,* an antiquated term which, according to Webster, is "a small customary payment over and above the freight made to the master of the ship for his care and trouble."

With less money returning to the planters of southwest Georgia, fewer slaves could be purchased and less land could be cleared.

Screams for railroad transportation were not quieted until the Atlantic and Gulf Railroad linked Thomasville to Savannah in April 1861. Boom times were surely ahead with only a nuisance of tall pines to stand between landowners and the fertile red soils, but yet another wave from Lady Luck's wand interceded in the very month that the railroad arrived in Thomasville. At 4:00 a.m. on April 12, 1861, a single mortar was fired at Union soldiers stationed at Fort Sumter, South Carolina.

The Civil War cast long, dark clouds over the bright future the railroad seemed to bring to Thomasville. Cotton sales became unsteady, and the war siphoned off the yeomen and pouts who'd grown food for the South on their smaller farms. As food supplies diminished, the Confederate government encouraged plantations to grow corn, beans, and other foods needed to sustain the South. A truce held between advancing cotton fields and the longleaf forests of the Red Hills.

Big Chance. Fat Chance. Slim Chance: How Caprice Brought Us the Red Hills

245

On the eve of his march from Atlanta to the sea, Tecumseh Sherman told Lincoln "I can make the march and I can make Georgia howl. I propose to kill even the puppies, because puppies grow up to be Southern dogs."

The kenneled dogs I hear in the distance are not typical Southern dogs. They spring energetically as though immune to the heat, and they're a recognizable breed, not mutts. It's unlikely Sherman had a chance to threaten pure breeds such as these. Their sharp yelps didn't become commonplace until the close of the century.

Soon after Sherman's march, cotton plantations began crashing like severed chandeliers. Attempts to plant, cultivate, and harvest vast cotton crops using market forces, not slavery, failed miserably, and the large plantations split like loblollies in the mud. There were 611 farms in Thomas County in 1870, but this number increased exponentially to 1,600 by 1880, and then to 3,200 by the turn of the century. Many were the forty-acres-and-a-mule variety operated by black tenant farmers.

Fortunately for the pinewoods, the railroad that arrived in Thomasville in 1861 hit a roadblock that took decades to overpower. Original plans to build spurs westward to Bainbridge and south to Monticello to extend the Atlantic and Gulf Railroad from the Atlantic to the Gulf lagged in the dust of the post-war economy. For several decades, Thomasville remained the last stop on the line. As any Southern pup knows, being last in line can lead to deprivation, but when you're a hotel that sits at the end of a railroad line, you often have a captive audience.

Thomasville became a favored winter resort in the late 1800s because of warm winters, Southern charm, and the fact that the railroad went no farther. The city grew elegant hotels that included the Waverly House, Gulf House, and the 160-room Piney Woods Hotel, which some called the finest hotel in the South. The agriculture-based economy of the South was in deep freeze, but new industries of rail transportation, oil, shipping, and steel production plowed ahead with manifest destiny in Northern states, and these industries created a wealthy new society that sought refuge from the dreary winter weather of Cleveland, New York, and Philadelphia.

The arrival of high society and gilded dreams, coupled with technological advances on the firearms front, carried Red Hills forests through a period

Jim Cox

246

where other Southern forests fell at a rapacious rate. Winchester Rifle Company introduced its first repeating shotgun with choke boring in 1887. The new breech-loading system was grafted onto the old "fowling piece" and now made it as easy to hit a quickly flying bird as the broadside of a barn. Through careful fine-tuning, Winchester unveiled the first mass-market, pump-action shotgun in 1897; three to five shells could be fired in quick order, sending a spray of lead shot through the air.

Around 1890, J. Wyman Jones, a wealthy New Jersey businessman, purchased a wooded park near Thomasville and filled it with game birds that he hunted using the new weaponry. Before advances in gun technology, game bird hunting consisted of waiting long hours for quarry to fall into snares or fly into nets. The improved shotgun allowed active pursuit of game species amid the mild winters, and hunting parties traveled through tall pines and abandoned fields on horseback while a well-trained pack of English pointers scouted through brush for bobwhite quail.

What if golf had been the outdoor craze of late 1800s rather than crisp, cool air, the music of the pines, and the occasional report of newly designed shotguns?

Jones was soon followed by the Van Duzer family of New York, who purchased Greenwood Plantation; the Hanna family of Cleveland, who purchased Melrose and Pebble Hill Plantations; and then the family of Jeptha Wade, another Cleveland native, who purchased Millpond Plantation from surviving members of the Wyche family.

Wade was grandson of the founder of Western Union Telegraph and served as owner, president, or board member for a host of large corporations. Old pictures show a slim face and upward sloping eyes tucked beneath an extending brow. He rolled in money, as they say, but he was not a tightwad. He was called Cleveland's greatest philanthropist and made vast donations to Cleveland's art gallery, an orphanage, local schools, a university, and several other public ventures. He was equally generous in Thomasville and certainly has been immortalized in the arena of old-growth longleaf forests: any pinewoods biologist worth their salt knows of the Wade Tract.

Wade likely appreciated the music and beauty of longleaf forests. His interest in nature can be seen in the donations he made to the Cleveland Museum of Natural History. He was also interested in landscaping and created separate gardens on Millpond Plantation for roses, dogwoods, and tropical ferns and shrubs. His dwelling place on Millpond was a spectacular Spanish revival building with scores of rooms gathered around a large central courtyard. Wade consolidated land held by nearby tenant farms and eventually amassed nearly ten thousand acres before dying at Millpond Plantation in 1926.

The Prophet of Sherwood

Yankee money protected longleaf forests of the Red Hills. The hundreds of winter retreats organized from disparate old plantations and tenant farms totaled 3.6 million acres in the early 1900s, roughly the same acreage of longleaf forests that remains today.

The fortunes of forests in the Red Hills improved when Lady Luck brought a special eye to survey the half-million-or-so acres of plantation lands in the region. It was the eye of a special wildlife biologist who was as passionate about quail hunting as he was about recording rare bird sightings and enjoying the sights and sounds of an old-growth longleaf forest. He was a rare shaman of natural history and wild landscapes, if you will, and his sagacity led to the charred bark I see on these ancient trees.

Populations of bobwhite quail pitched into decline in the early 1900s. Quail need open pinewoods and agricultural lands where sun pours down to the ground, but the land once harrowed for cotton was growing thick with brush and young pines. A forest conservation program initiated in the 1920s sent federal agents across the region asking property owners to stop burning their forests. Soon afterward, the open prairie-carpet lying beneath the tall pines began to clog with hardwood brush and thickets. Hunters needed machetes as much as shotguns to pursue their quarry.

Plantation owners, who were keen financiers and corporate bosses when they weren't hunting quail, were not the types to sit back and idly watch quail declines bring a close to an era. Led by Col. Lewis Thompson, Harry Whitney, and Henry Beadel, several Red Hills owners banded together to provide about $46,000 in seed money to the U.S. Department of Agriculture to support a research project focusing on quail declines. A young biologist from Wisconsin named Herbert L. Stoddard headed up the Cooperative Quail Investigation beginning in 1924.

Stoddard had an eye that could fathom a forest as easily as it could follow quail at the end of a shotgun. Aldo Leopold, author of *A Sand County Almanac* and the father of wildlife management, once sent Stoddard a letter that summed up his peculiar genius:

> I am sending you by express a yew bow, which I have been making for you this winter. I have enjoyed it because it was a way to express my affection and regard for one of the few who understands what yew bows—and quail and mallards and wind and sunsets—are all about.

It was certainly Stoddard's understanding of wind and sunsets—the processes of the forest, not just the quail within—that was his greatest gift. He watched the booming lightning of summer storms rift asunder the aged longleaf of the Red Hills. The storms killed a few tall trees each year, and the gaps in the canopy poured sunlight onto the ground. Hundreds of seedling longleaf took hold in some of these sunny patches and began their slow ascent to the sky.

Stoddard heard the wind in the pines, as well as more distant sounds from the time of Native Americans and early plantation owners. It was the crackling of the fire that these people used to herd game and freshen their grasses. Fires pass through the pinewoods like a finger moving through the flame of a candle. It stays close to the ground, killing brush and oak thickets without touching the thin green needles on limbs high above the ground.

From these insights, Stoddard developed a method of selective timber harvest that removed a few trees periodically, not whole forests, much like lightning. He showed that fire was not only an integral part of Southern pine forests but also the cheapest and most effective way for landowners to control their brush and promote healthy quail populations. His recommendations for land stewardship could guarantee an annual yield of quail and timber, as well as a stable, healthy forest that contained all the elements and processes from the red-cockaded woodpeckers that need hundred-year-old pines to the ground-loving meadowlarks and gopher tortoises.

Stoddard published his recommendations and went back to Washington in 1931, but it soon became clear to Colonel Thompson and others that Stoddard's management techniques were not being widely applied in the Red Hills. In a bold move that only a well-heeled landowner could make, Thompson brought Stoddard back to the Red Hills and deeded one thousand

Big Chance. Fat Chance. Slim Chance: How Caprice Brought Us the Red Hills

249

acres of land to him on condition that Stoddard live there. Stoddard called the property Sherwood Plantation; he opened a forestry and wildlife consulting business in Thomasville; and for the next four decades, his hand carefully guided management of some of the most important ecological properties in North America, including the Wade Tract.

Stoddard could have made tons of money given the vast timber resources he controlled, but his eye was fixed squarely on maintaining the pieces of this complex puzzle using techniques that mimicked natural processes. When the new owner of the Wade Tract, Mr. Jeptha Wade III, asked Stoddard to harvest some of the timber in the patch of old-growth where I now stand, Stoddard reportedly said, "Let's get to that next year." Mr. Wade asked the same question again a year later, and the year after that, and both times the answer was "wait till next year." The following year, Mr. Wade reportedly asked, "We're never going to cut that patch, are we?"

The Future of the Legacy

Stephen J. Gould once described evolution as music produced by a special tape player. There are hundreds of billions of chance events the tape player has passed through to produce the sounds you hear at this moment, but if you try to rewind the tape and play it again, the music changes. The tape can never be played the same way twice.

You may rewind the serendipitous tape that stores the history of ancient forests of the Red Hills, but it's unlikely you would hear the same music I hear today. The Nature Conservancy describes the Red Hills as "One of the Last Great Places" on earth, but at each step there were other much-less-than-great possibilities. Native Americans clustered around sinkhole lakes that lay to the south; the plantations developed just in time to have their lifeblood drained by war; the railroad stopped at Thomasville; wealthy industrialists pursued quail using fancy new armament; a young biologist with phenomenal acumen lit a fire that still burns.

Jack of Diamonds, I cry!

Lady Luck has certainly smiled upon us. It could be she has an appreciation for all things living as well as an ear for great natural music. Perhaps she takes a literal interpretation of the story of Noah and includes forest ecosystems in the mix of things we are to preserve. Perhaps she simply loves old trees.

Jim Cox

It seems just as likely, though, that the destructive wand of "bad luck," was simply distracted at key moments. If the Wade Tract is a jewel spawned by sheer luck, the providence seems all the more impressive and precious. Caprice is an extremely dangerous bedfellow, even when it's the only warm body in the joint.

A slim chance is what we cling to in the Red Hills. Even as Tall Timbers Research Station and The Nature Conservancy attempt to conserve the ancient forests of the region, Tallahassee and Thomasville seem ever more intent on achieving a final kiss through their expanding neighborhoods and roads. There are also many new landowners sprinkled throughout the region, heirs of heirs of heirs in some cases, and some approach quail and timber management with an eye toward short-term benefits that rob the land of its natural diversity. As Stoddard noted, an attempt to increase a single component such as timber or quail often harms other components. New management techniques that focus narrowly on quail or timber also can be costly, very costly, and this can put a whole new perspective on the value of a two-hundred-year-old tree.

I arrive at another tree with more woodpeckers to band. Today's fieldwork has taken longer than it should, but I often stop and reflect in my line of work. Trouble is that, as I ascend my ladders and feel the tug of the wind in the tree, my mind wanders away from history and music and dance toward some darker questions: is it possible to conserve these exquisite ancient forests on these private lands, the last vestiges of a decimated landscape, or am I merely watching the final extinction of that landscape? Is it music through the pines that I hear, or the sound of a slowly advancing glacier, a devastating glacier powered by cash-floe? Will Lady Luck's wand continue to wave, or will it be a scythe called bad luck?

Jim Cox climbs trees for Tall Timbers Research Station. When he's not listening to the music in the pines, he crunches numbers and cranks out dry technical papers on the bird life of the Red Hills. One of his long-term goals is to see an endowed position created at Tall Timbers for the purpose of studying animals on the Wade Tract. Information on this endeavor and a virtual tour of the Wade Tract can be found at www.talltimbers.org.

Big Chance. Fat Chance. Slim Chance: How Caprice Brought Us the Red Hills

pale pink flowers

Gadsden County, 1956

Girl hanging tobacco leaves to dry

Havana

tobacco in bloom

Shade-grown tobacco fields, Quincy, Fla.

Hands on the Land in Havana, Florida

JUNE WIAZ

A curiously named town sits up in the northern Red Hills of Gadsden County, up on the western flank of the Ochlockonee River watershed. Havana, Florida, humbly bears its exotic name, the derivation of which is not readily apparent to the day-trippers who spend a few pleasant hours browsing the antique shops and dining in the handful of restaurants in its compact downtown. Only in the town's name can we find reference to an unlikely connection to the island nation across the Straits of Florida.

Façades of old buildings, many of them now quaint shops, point to times past in Havana, Florida—when the church was a dry goods store, and the feed store was truly the point of supply for livestock. An old building near city hall still has the *teja*, or Spanish-style roofs, found on those of the buildings of the town's Cuban namesake.

If you want to know what makes the little town of Havana, population 1,800, tick, you need to spend some time with Bill Spooner. Spooner is a former businessman, veteran, and historian with roots so deep in the sandy, clayey soil that even if he relocated, some other Spooner or facsimile thereof would grow from the same place.

Spooner literally grew up downtown, helping in the family store, which was near the ice plant and the slaughterhouse (now a collectibles shop named

"My Favorite Garden.") He used a horse to deliver groceries.

Uncle Sam wanted Spooner in 1950 for the Korean War, and after five years in the Navy he returned to his beloved Havana to run the family's clothing store, as his father and grandfather before him had done. All the while, Spooner was an amateur photographer. By 1977 he traded in dry goods for the wet recesses of a dark room as official photographer for the Florida House and Senate in Tallahassee, nearly twenty miles to the south. That lasted two years before Spooner became a stringer for the Associated Press. Spooner's extensive photographic collection includes shots of Jimmy Carter, governors, and sports figures, his true photographic passion.

Spooner, now retired, lives in a new golf-course subdivision just west of the railroad tracks. Bill Spooner is most passionate about that part of Havana's story that relates to a variety of tobacco now rarely grown in the United States—shade tobacco.

Shade tobacco was grown under shade, a process that rendered the leaves softer. Shade tobacco was used exclusively for cigar wrappers. It had to be handled with care, picked leaf by leaf from the bottom to the top (or "primed") on successive days, unlike sun-grown cigarette tobacco, which is harvested all at once. The shading kept the delicate crop from becoming sun-scorched and created the exact color and texture that made for the finest cigar wrappers.

Shade tobacco was a demanding crop. In midwinter, farmers would plant a seedbed. By February, sharecroppers helped erect the platforms to support wooden slats to shade the fast-growing tobacco that reached nine feet high at its zenith, a practice introduced at the turn of the century. It was said that on a quiet night you could hear the plants stretching skyward.

Around World War II, cheesecloth made the process somewhat less labor intensive, creating vast acreages of undulating fabric that from a distance appeared to be broad, white-capped lakes.

Nearby Quincy was also a major shade tobacco center. Some of the tobacco barns where the crops hung to dry and cure still stand in the region as a testament to what the hands on the land of the northern Red Hills have wrought.

Bill Spooner likes to share a fascinating part of the tobacco story. To reduce the labor demands of gingerly stringing the leaves together and handling them with great care, the cigar industry attempted a composite type

June Wiaz

254

of cigar wrapper made from homogenized tobacco leaf. What the innovators had not anticipated was the effect that the common practice of gnawing on the cigar might have. The composite wrapper crumbled apart in the cigar smoker's mouth, so growers were forced to return to painstaking tradition.

Tobacco farming in north Florida was incredibly lucrative. While the seeds might cost $750 for just a handful forty to fifty years ago, farmers could work relatively small acreage to get a handsome profit on a labor-intensive crop. Land could cost three thousand dollars per acre, so the local banker played a crucial role. The most prominent man of the lender trade in the early 1900s Red Hills was Pat Munroe, a man who became legendary in Gadsden County for his uncanny business practice of conferring loans only when the borrower also agreed to buy shares in the up-and-coming Coca-Cola Company. A friend of Munroe's was getting the company established and Munroe, perhaps to undergird his own investment in Coke, tied his loan approvals to a willingness of farmer borrowers to invest in the fledgling soft drink company. The families of those early investors from Havana and the larger and better-heeled town of Quincy made fortunes on their happenstance investment in soda pop.

When the railroad came to Havana in 1902, it bypassed the village of Salem (where a surprisingly old cemetery is the resting place for a revolutionary war soldier) and skirted two other villages that withered as the emerging town of Havana, consisting of little more than a school house, prospered. The iron rails were arteries oxygenating small towns with supplies and carrying off raw materials and locally produced goods such as sweet potatoes, lumber, sugar cane syrup, hog parts, and most of all, tobacco.

Until the early 1970s, tobacco was king. When child labor laws were implemented, production became prohibitively expensive. That hurt the white tobacco farmers, but also had unintended devastating impacts on the African-American tobacco farm workers as the tobacco acreage, according to historian Miles Womack, went from thousands to scarcely three hundred by 1976. With children under the age of sixteen no longer able to toil alongside their parents, family wages dropped. Local businesses, like the Spooner Department Store, suffered as well. American shade tobacco companies found cheaper land and labor in South America.

If the two-hundred-year-old live oaks that stand as sentries to the Havana Golf and Country Club could whisper stories through their veils of Spanish moss, they would tell of the harsh living conditions of the black tobacco "hands" and their families. Havana growers imported already indebted sharecroppers from Alabama whose borrowing grew as prolifically as the crops they tended. In slave-like conditions, these indentured servants lived in drafty one-room row houses on what is now the golf course. They often received gardening privileges as well as goods and services in lieu of payment.

Without the ability to accumulate money or land and pass it to the next generation, black Havanans were consigned to spin in the poverty cycle. White merchants such as Spooner would extend credit to needy black families at the beginning of the school year and at Christmas, sometimes knowing that they'd never be paid back, but these actions were but Band-Aids on gaping wounds of institutionalized racism.

After a time, the irrigated fields that sustained Havana's tobacco crop were used to support a number of highly water-intensive nurseries in the area, which supply mainly ornamental plants to retailers throughout the Southeast. Western Gadsden County, whose fertile soils produce mainly pesticide-laden tomatoes and mushrooms, is more dependent on migrant labor.

The tobacco culture that formed Havana has repercussions in the town today. The division of the economic classes during the days of shade tobacco remain apparent. While there is an overall good relationship between blacks and whites, there are some racial disparities that do not escape notice. The whole county, sadly, is a grant writer's fertile field, owing to the disproportionate social ills that afflict primarily the low-income African-American population—poverty, drug use, sexually transmitted diseases. The town of Havana is 53 percent black, but the public schools are almost entirely African American. Gadsden County's two "F-rated" high schools, one on the north side of Havana and the other near Quincy, are merging to form one new school in the hopes that newness itself will spark achievement. The poor education picture in Havana keeps many young families from relocating there. As a result, the largest influx of newcomers is retirees who want to settle on affordable land but don't fret about schools.

Drastically poor populations south and north of town drain municipal and county resources, and hardly any of the properties on Havana's outskirts would pay significant amounts of tax even if they were annexed. Police regularly seize drugs on the edges of Havana, mainly from transients. Havana at least is a "public power town," reinvesting into local projects the revenues from selling power to its residents. If the town's energy demands were met by an outside supplier, chances are that it would not have the resources to plow back into the community to support even a police department.

If you stop and observe the ebb and flow of this place, you discover daily routines, like the freight-train engineer and brakeman stopping their diesel-fueled beast on the tracks and hoofing it across Main Street for an early lunch. You discover a community that functions well. You see the mayor, Susan Frieden, jumping out of her car to prune a hedge that blocks a sign. "What's interesting here," Frieden says, "is that you never have a boring day."

Sleepy Havana grows less drowsy each year. City observers look forward to a growing tax base to make Havana the haven that day-trippers perceive it to be. The hands on the land of Havana may not have as much dirt under their nails as they did a few decades ago, but the memory of it is there.

June Wiaz has been a freelance writer since moving to Tallahassee from the Washington, D.C., area with her husband and two girls in 1996. Her academic background is in environmental journalism and science and technology policy, and before coming to Tallahassee she worked for the American Association for the Advancement of Science, the National Governor's Association, and the Environmental Protection Agency. Somewhere in there she and her husband also did a stint in Guatemala for the U.S. Peace Corps. June's work has appeared locally, as well as in The Book of the Everglades. *Earlier this year, she and co-author Kathryn Ziewitz witnessed the birth of* Green Empire, *the book about the St. Joe Company, after a four-year gestation period.*

Ochlockonee Woodpeckers

The river clasps a bank of rosy fog to its breast this sunrise. The warm Ochlockonee and the cold night air have created this soft mist body between them, and the sun-pink vapors now ride the river to the Gulf.

In the park's well-burned and wide-open flatwoods behind our tent, there's little flowering and few free-flying insects to chase or glean; we've had an early frost. Maybe that's why the birds I'm seeing this morning are lovers of what can be removed from the trunks of trees—mostly woodpeckers, at that.

First thing I spot a pair of small downy woodpeckers skirmishing high in a longleaf pine. Never more than a foot apart, they mirror an intense flattened posture to each other and oddly flutter their wings. They are bound together by their struggle, perhaps sparring over winter food territories.

A pileated woodpecker casts its rattling cry over the whole forest, stimulating responses from

red-bellied woodpeckers, nuthatches, and a single
beautiful yellow-bellied sapsucker. I searched out
the pileated, excavating a trademark longitudinal
cavity. It twists and cocks the flair of its crimson
head, pressing its ear to the trunk, listening,
chiseling, listening. Finally, a distinctive, wheezy
chirp signals the forest's signature bird—the red-
cockaded woodpecker. This one is working the
resin wells it has dug near
the entrance to its nest
cavity. It sets the sap
to streaming and the
old pine glistens like
an oversized, waxen
candle in the early
light.

    The woodpeckers are
to the pines, I think, as the rising
rosy fog is to the river: all one thing, condensed for
now into forms we think are separate, forms we
believe we can name.

drilled holes!

*yellow-bellied sapsucker
on red bay*

Apalachicola

Woodruff Dam

A Canon of Owls

O. VICTOR MILLER

I am a brother to dragons, and a companion to owls.
—Job 30:29

The weekend my stepdaughter leaves for college, her mother boxes up the Barbies and teddy bears and moves into her room. "You thrash," she explains.

"Thrash?"

"Flop around like a decapitated chicken, make funny noises." Her bejeweled hand flapjacks, more like a beached reef fish than a truncated fowl. "Also your breathing bothers me."

"My breathing?" I gulp.

"You go on for a while like anybody else. Then you stop for a really long time, until I think you've died. Finally you shudder, wheeze, and start back." She seems more annoyed by the continuation of my respiration than its cessation.

"That's it?"

"Sometimes, you smell funny." She wrinkles her pretty nose.

"Fishy? I fish a lot."

"No, just funny."

I give it some thought, concluding, "If I quit moving and breathing, I'll be dead, smelling *real* funny."

She shrugs. Her rest takes clear precedence over my mortality.

Well, fair enough, but the issue of personal odor is also a grave matter. Everybody has a unique redolence to scrub off or enhance with French perfumes. Biologists say we select our mates and locate our children by odor. Smelling funny won't get you invited to Kiwanis or fetch high scores in singles bars.

"What do you mean, funny?" I ask. Babies smell sweet because they haven't started to rot yet. Boys start going over around puberty. I'm half a century past puberty.

"You know. Funny. Not funny *ha-ha*, funny *strange*."

"Like chrysanthemums?"

"No, no, worse! Metallic, sort of."

"Metallic?" Kimchi smells metallic. In Cold War Korea we learned to sniff out economic opposition, Communist commandos. Koreans smelled like fermented cabbage. In the DMZ, smelling funny was some kind of serious shit. Shad. The insane. A new filling. And blood. Blood! God! What if my life's blood, thinned by heart medication, is fixing to weep out through my pores?

But I'm not worried that my personal odor will draw night fire, even in Georgia. My wife's objection to my respiration and subconscious kinetics strikes a deeper cord. Since a 1986 angiogram, I have come to equate breath and movement with life itself, not just the quality of it. Midway through a coronary catheterization, I died on the table and watched my demise televised on the vital signs monitor. A sperm-headed little catheter wiggled up riffles of my arteries then spit a cloud of dark milt into my aorta, transforming before my astonished eyes the headwater run of happy blips that leaped across the monitor into a monotonous flat line. The machines knew I was dead before I did.

The medical cadre knew, of course. I watched them with out-of-body objectivity. Resplendent nurses scrambled around a familiar corpse on a stainless table, punching it with hypodermics and cattle prods as I floated around with an aerial vantage with detached lucidity.

"We're losing him!" they announced. "He's going! Oh God, he's gone!"

"Hmmm," deduced the cardiologist. "An allergic reaction to the iodine dye is indicated."

I tried to move but couldn't. The tunnel of celestial light cascaded into a deep pool of palpable darkness, which occurred ironically when the doc jerked me back among the living with a squirt of adrenaline into my inert and insulted heart.

When I awoke in the temporal lights of the recovery room, I decided then and there that dying, though not altogether unpleasant, ought to be postponed. I vowed to do whatever I could to keep from doing it again for as long as I could, forever if possible.

"Why don't you go somewhere, take a trip. Air out a little," the wife says, picking up the remote and punching it to a sitcom with canned laughter. "It's unhealthy for middle-age men to hang around the house grunting over a laptop and making faces like someone demented. Take that Chattahoochee trip you're always talking about? You'll have time during spring break when I take Mary Catherine to Panama City beach."

"Air out!"

"A figure of speech." She extends her arm. A squealing housewife, jaws sandwiched between hands, wins a new washer and a Caribbean cruise. The MC, with slick hair and wolfish smile, jams a single rose at the ecstatic housewife, her face distorted by Gs of upward mobility. *Whee-uhl uh-of Fortunnne!*

"Well, she's wrong about one thing," I tell Clyde, my Boykin spaniel. "I may stink, breathe funny, and have bad dreams, but I ain't middle aged, not unless I hang in there to one-hundred-fourteen. Obsolete, maybe. An alienated bundle of hunter-gatherer instincts, over-civilized, an evolutionary retard in a high-tech age. "I grunt and sweat in sleep," I explain to the only other male in the family, "because there are no dragons to slay."

Clyde cocks his head in approximate agreement. Ordinarily I can't stand people who talk to dogs, but nobody else listens to me anymore. Not students, wives, children. Friends and students were interested to know what dying was like, and it's tempting to exaggerate, but I confess that even my death, when compared to recorded accounts of others, was both typical and unremarkable, except for a recurring dream that I'm lying on a preparation table. Over me is a dapper gent with a trocar and a wide grin. *This one ain't moving,* he remarks to his hunchback assistant in the tunnel of light. *Let's embalm his ass.*

"The Chattahoochee, Clyde. We'll put in at Fort Gaines and drift south with migrating eels to the Apalachicola River and the Gulf of Mexico. It's you and me, boy," I assure him. "You and me to the deep blue sea." Banality,

A CANON OF OWLS

263

another thing that chafes wives and students, doesn't bother Clyde. "The eels won't stop at the Gulf, though, like us," I explain. "They round the Cape of Florida for a sex-fest and family reunion in the Sargasso Sea, where they breed, die, and start smelling funny. All American and European eels are born and die in the Sargasso Sea."

Clyde cocks his ears. He understands as much English as he wants to. "We'll follow them as far as the Gulf," I add, "this time."

I score a case of MREs from a paranoid neighbor who keeps a stocked bunker under his lawn. I toss sleeping bag, jungle hammock, duct tape, and tin plates into a plastic washtub. I scoop the pinestraw out of the johnboat and knock the dirt daubers out of the Johnson 9.9. I find my fly rod in the attic, packed up with Christmas decorations. Clyde salivates and wags his nub, anticipating adventure.

Eric and Wendy Radke, newlyweds who own the wonderful shop where I buy Orvis seconds, agree to haul me to Lake Eufala, a dammed up section of the Chattahoochee. Clyde and I will be floating above migrating eels while wife and stepchild, along with every college student in the Southeast, migrate to the Florida coast for spring break and their own vernal spawn. There daughters cavort, murdering their childhoods, and mothers wearing gauze chaperone from seaside condos, reading paperbacks, watching sunsets, inhaling the bracing vapors of expiring youth.

I offer to subsidize the girls' trip if they drag my trailer down with them and pick me up in Apalachicola, Florida, at the end of spring break. Eric will hook up my trailer to Claire's car so she and Mary Catherine don't risk a nail. It's going to be great to get outdoors again, to answer the call of the wild, away from the stench of civilization. I'll cast the river rapids for smallmouth bass, pitch poppers to bluegills, the ravenous females stuffing their yellow bellies with protein for eggs. I'm bound for tide marsh and brackish swamp, where sweet-water marries brine, where warmouth, largemouth, weakfish, redfish, and snook meet coming and going, and an angler doesn't have the faintest idea what just sucked up his streamer and two feet of tippet before scatting to the sea.

"Where's your tent?" Eric inquires when we arrive at the landing beneath the power dam at Lake Eufala.

O. VICTOR MILLER

264

"No tent. I'll rough it like in the Army."

"When was that?" Wendy is a lot younger than Eric, who's a lot younger than I am. Eric's yuppie friends snubbed him for selling t-shirts from the trunk of his car to raise money for a Canadian lung transplant. I figure he needed a lung less than a new set of friends, but with two good lungs he was able to run down Wendy.

"I got out in '68," I tell them.

Wendy giggles. "That was ten years before I was even born." She stands on the bank in short-shorts, legs up to her earlobes. I decide Eric doesn't need a new set of friends or any friends at all. I love it when life deals aces.

Clyde bounces flat-footed into the boat and the 9.9 putts out into the roiling Chattahoochee. Perhaps because of the stable temperature in the river valley, pockets of wild plum and crabapple blossoms linger and are overlapped by jasmine, wild azaleas, dogwood. Wisteria blooms from crags and overhangs where steephead waterfalls gush from the walls of high cliffs and cascade down rocky ravines, splashing lace into the swift, green Chattahoochee. Unlike springs, steepheads are underground conduits of groundwater, veins opened by erosion. Clyde cocks his head to the hollow slap of our wake into the vertical banks of clay and stone.

Bald eagles and red-tailed hawks sail thermals, winding high, dipping into the river valley. Great blue herons stand haughty on fallen willows. Egrets and herons stalk the banks. Cruciform anhinga dry their wings. I lean back, propping up my feet, my arm over the Johnson, hugging the shoulders of an old friend. Too relaxed to fish seriously, I roll-cast indolently, dragging a popper with rubber legs behind the boat, picking up a few bream and tossing them back.

We round the inside of a wide bend to a sandbar where the biggest alligator I've ever seen lies like a corroded boiler studded with rusty rivets and sooty plates. Its tail curves behind it like a two-man crosscut saw. It's so big Clyde doesn't recognize it for what it is. The unrelated specifics he sees, buckteeth, tail, claws haven't yet assembled in his canine brain to conjure from reality the dim archetype of a primordial monster with a head like two ironing boards hinged by jaw muscles that bulge like cannon balls. "I need a picture of this one," I inform him. "He's a whopper."

Any change of pace energizes Clyde, who bounces to the bow and yaps as I idle in. *Pucka, pocka, pucka.* Finally Clyde's perception of parts crash together into a recognizable composite of danger. His eyes bulge and curly hair uncurls as he leaps into my lap and tries to scratch a hole to piss in.

The dragon rises on dewclaws, hissing off a head of steam. It charges for open water, plowing beneath us, splashing muddy water as his sawtooth tail grunts across the bottom of the bucking johnboat. The gator sinks into a suck hole of muddy water as man and man's best friend bond in quivering terror.

Author Bailey White has given me *Peterson's Field Guide to the Birds* and a pair of binoculars to urge me into bird watching. An avid wingshooter, I have advantages over other fledgling bird-watchers, having studied the fall flight patterns and feeding habits of many game species and, like Audubon before me, I have examined specimens up close and dead. I've engaged in gross anatomical dissection of individuals, culminating in the intimacy of gastronomic as well as intellectual digestion.

I'm doing better in the transition from hunter to bird-watcher than Clyde. When we jump a brace of resident wood ducks, he watches them splash into the air, trailing a rainbow of bright spray. He crouches, waiting for the bark of scattergun. I'm able to detach myself from a sportsman's bias because it's early spring and ducks are out of season, but he is unconditioned by legislation. When ducks rise above the cypress, he fixes me with castigating, amber eyes. For Clyde, bird watching lacks closure.

When two wild gobblers fly across the river, however, a blur of tarnished bronze and antique gold, I regress, snatching up my Colt Woodsman instead of the Nikon, blasting away. It's turkey season. Old instincts are hard to sublimate.

The gunshot lights up Clyde like Space Invaders. He bounces in place, his familiar world renewed. One turkey swoops to the Georgia bank, landing with an outraged gobble. Clyde thinks I hit the bird. I think it's possible, even with a .22 pistol. They flew by us like B-52s. "Clyde, catch him," I order as the flat bow touches the bank. He springs, ignoring Newtonian rules of propulsion and recoil, splashing into the water. He swims ashore, spinning his wheels up the high bank, yapping and disappearing into the thicket. Boykins are good turkey dogs, Clyde's breeder has assured me. Already I'm anticipating a change of diet from the MREs.

Following mayhem of canine and avian violence, a hysterical screech issues from Clyde followed by an angry gobble. If the turkey is hit, the wound

O. VICTOR MILLER

isn't mortal. Clyde skids howling down the bank. He scrambles into the boat, cowering from the victorious trumpeting of a gobbler who has hunkered down and royally whipped a dog's ass.

"You're both improving overall," Bailey White judges a few days later into a pay telephone receiver outside Boss's Oyster Bar in Apalachicola. "You just suffered a brief predatory relapse, a minor regression. Not to worry. At least you missed. If the truth were known, she continues, "you probably missed on purpose."

"Well . . . "

"Subliminally?"

"Well . . . "

At dusk we camp on the high Alabama bank, too sheer for alligators. I use my map to start a fire in the drizzling rain. The map of the lower Apalachicola, with its capillary creeks, oxbows, and rivulets, reminds me of my angiogram before an allergic reaction to catheter dye stopped my clock and I waltzed out-of-body with angelic nurses into a tunnel of pure light. I string the jungle hammock between blackjack saplings and tie Clyde to a sycamore. "Don't go near the river," I advise. Clyde shakes, flapping his ears.

My fire is for cheer, not cooking, since MREs have chemical heat packs activated by water. The three-course high caloric meals are an improvement over the C-rations I ate in Korea but still not tasty enough to tempt soldiers to stand around swapping recipes when they ought to be shooting folks. After spaghetti, applesauce, peanut butter, and pound cake, I ruminate on M&Ms and revisit Guard Post Barbara, where I watched a bayonet fight over an OD green can of fruit cocktail, the only item in a case of C-rations that tasted vaguely like food. I notice that MREs don't include cigarettes either. C-rats had a complimentary five-pack of stale Camels packaged in 1942 with the rest of the rations. Soldiers smoked dope in the foxholes because it was smoother than the Camels.

Sloshed on rice wine near a tank firing range, I tossed a case of C-rations off a tank to skinny Korean kids just to hear the crew bitch. They hated C-rations, but didn't want Koreans eating them. "They'll just black market them and buy rice," the gunner insisted as the kids zigzagged across the frozen stubble of a rice paddy.

"Free enterprise, so what?" My Cold-War effort against the Commies.

A CANON OF OWLS

The Alabama rain gets wetter, spitting out the fire. I ease into the jungle hammock, sitting in the sag, one foot steady on the ground. I recline, wobbling like a Model T with a broken tie rod. I lift my last leg into the hammock, which spins, slinging me out. After three tries I stay down. I duck under my tarpaulin, shielding my face from mosquitoes, rain, and Clyde's slobbery affection. The hissing downpour recalls the Korean monsoon when I bunched up into my poncho, snug in the rubbery smell—*just me, just me,* the cold rain whispers against the hood. Cozy too under the first wet spit of windy October snow *just-just* like a kid in the attic on a rainy day.

At first light I fumble up heart medication and arthritis pills, wash them down with cold coffee diluted by rainwater. Clyde turns up his nose at leftover pork and rice, finally eating it grudgingly. "The good life," I inform him. "Only 150 miles to go."

When songbirds start squawking for mates and real estate and a kingfisher shatters the glazed surface of the river, I cut the motor and reach for my fly rod. Before I can tie on a streamer, an obnoxious aroma bullies the air, a sweetish toasted cloy indicating a pulp mill. Clyde perks up, thinking I've opened another MRE. We round a dozen bends and there it is—sooty, gargantuan, and toxic like some Third World caricature of an Industrial Revolution made even more horrible by its pristine setting. Pewter smoke leaks into the dull air. No human life is visible behind the darkened panes, where a devilish glow pulses to the rumble of a giant engine. A bevy of great blue herons stands on the festering banks, wading into frothy black water to stab bloated fish. I break the Orvis down and put it back in its canvas-covered tube. "I hope that's not what's called a *funny* smell," I tell Clyde, who stretches out with head between paws.

I anticipate a rough crossing of Lake Seminole when whitecaps form on the river as we approach. Ominous furrows of smutty clouds brood over the west bank. The storm catches us a quarter of the way across. I speed up to keep the bow high so the waves don't swamp us, but the rainwater collecting in the boat slows us down. Clyde shivers in the rising bilge as the flat keel slaps crests and dives into troughs, gouging into the next wave.

I squint into the stinging rain as we buck and wallow through the whitecaps. "Hang on, boy!" I sputter, "we'll get there!" Clyde's toenails scratch for purchase. He loses his balance and falls into the ankle deep bilge. I yank out the drain plug at the base of the transom, the evacuating water barely keeping ahead of the rain. The plastic washtub of gear fills with rainwater, weighting us down. If we come off a plane, we'll swamp. Already the washtub is heavy enough to make us sluggish. I shoot holes into it with the Woodsman, counting on the water to stop the bullets. When the draining tub lightens, I tilt it and shoot three more holes through the bottom. Clyde looks at me like I've lost my mind. He staggers over to bite the lip of the tub and tries to shake it. Better than a turkey.

"You by yourself?" Against a backdrop of blue sky and sunshine, the black lock warden grins down to the fourteen-foot johnboat dancing in the chop, a chip in a lock the size of two football fields. "You ain't waiting on nobody else?"

"Just us!" I yell. "Can you run the locks for one boat?"

"Got to!" he yells. "It my job!" I tie off to the floating mooring. The gate closes and the lock groans us down as the warden releases the water. For the first time in many semesters I feel important, the great lock of a dynamic power plant lowering Clyde and me down the high wall of Lake Seminole to the Apalachicola River. It's like getting flushed slowly down a gargantuan hydraulic toilet. Gulls and terns circle, ducking behind the high walls into the lee, diving for minnows stunned by the whitewater explosion through the gates.

The lock opens and we break free, shooting the braided whitewater where the striped bass loiter, their primal inland spawn thwarted by a dam built in 1953 when rising waters flooded mounds of native Muskogee tribe who hunted and fished along the banks of the Chattahoochee, Flint, and Apalachicola a thousand years before.

I pull in to the dock of a riverside city park. A geezer in a blue jumpsuit and watch cap sits at a picnic table beneath the misty monolith watching the gates comb the river's white hair. He lowers binoculars and catches me with a watery blue eye. "Where you headed, son?"

"To the Gulf."

"You on the right river," he says. "Stay on sandbars well inside the channel and bank your fire to last the night. Keep one eye on that dog and the other'n on the gators."

I wait for something else. It comes. "I crewed the gang that built this sumbitch in '53 and ain't left since," he points a crooked finger at the colossus

A CANON OF OWLS

269

as though more than one of them hunkered dim and ghastly against a scud sky. "Reckon I'll die here."

"We better get moving," I say.

"The barges come up river at night. They bank the deep turns. Stay on the inside, high enough so the wake don't wash you and that dog off the bar else the Jim Woodroof Dam will be yore headstone too."

"Bank?"

"Ram the shore, son! To kick the bow around the curve! Who turned you loose out here in a johnboat?"

"My wife," I mutter.

The old seer hisses with laughter. Clyde looks his way, then stares up the bank toward the highway bridge. "Whoa, Clyde, load up." I crank the Johnson and putt out into the current, waving to the old man, who watches us through the binoculars until we round the first bend.

The river widens and the bright sun warms the air. I set our speed to neutralize tail wind with downstream speed. I duct-tape the throttle and move forward to steer by shifting my weight. I shuck my clothes. What are they good for anyway? Modesty? No fellow boatmen share the river and bright sunshine. No worries of odor, platitude, respiration, or kinetic slumber. I rip open an MRE, add river water to the chemical pouch. Acrid steam heats beef stew laced with enough preservative to embalm Cheops. I start fishing again, clear headed and serious now, with stiff wrist and elbow, punching the rod from the shoulder, tightening my backcast loop, thrilling when the forward cast straightens out perfectly and falls horizontal on the mirror of cypress and sycamore. Real and honest joy follows a sleepy mayfly, trailing a tippet fine as a spider web, dropping softly more or less into the spot I intended. Swishing cobwebs with the magic wand—snicker-snack, one two, one two. Breathing the sweet spring air, I don't care a damn about catching fish, but of course I catch them. I bring in longears, redbellies, a couple of crappy, and a two-pound shoal bass that fights like a brook trout on amphetamines.

The second storm of the day hits just before dusk. We beach on a sandbar inside the bend. I scramble around naked throwing together a lean-to of bamboo, tape, and palmettos. Catclaws, beargrass, cold rain, and poison ivy remind me that vanity isn't the sole function of clothing. Serrated palmetto stems slash sunburned hips; their blades cut and puncture buttocks. Spanish bayonets stab thighs. Whoa vines snag, catclaws scratch. Mosquitoes scent fresh blood and attack in squadrons. Howling, I dive into my makeshift shelter, thoughtfully constructed on a sharp incline for drainage. Studded with insect bites and etched with scratches, I wiggle, comprehensively sunburned, into my saturated sleeping bag, bucking for comfort like the last transitional throes of a great larval worm. The lean-to funnels water like a sewer, squirting me downhill into driving rain. I dig my fingers into the eroded embankment grasping bare roots, resting my face between two atrophied biceps. I can't toss and turn without wallowing in mud. Lightning flashes like artillery.

Clyde digs in shivering, his rasping breath depriving me of what moments of sleep I might otherwise snatch in brief respites from agony. Also he stinks. He wiggles in close, shakes and starts hunching the last dry corner of my sleeping bag. "Quit squirming, you son of a bitch." I can feel his stare in the dark. The truth hurts. "You smell like roadkill," I add, "and your breathing is driving me nuts." I turn the flashlight on him. His eyes glow red. He cocks his curly spaniel ears. He digs in deeper, kicking mud and wet leaves in my face.

The swamps and salt marshes don't surrender much high ground. Near the coast, we are eye level with the snakes and alligators. Two more nights adjusts me to the jungle hammock, which properly strung looks like a canvas coffin suspended between cypress and bay. Although precarious, it protects me from mosquitoes, Clyde, and rain. But I'm suspended in the crotch of a drawn slingshot. One wrong move will catapult me among snakes. I build a fire and bank it, tethering Clyde beneath the hammock, which I hang high in hopes that any alligator that eats Clyde won't be able to reach me for dessert. Funereal dreams are replaced by visions of reptiles.

The only humanoid in Tate's Hell Swamp, I've come to regard as luxury the absence of acute discomfort. Contentment is relative. Three days on a lonely river shifts perceptions. A plaintive owl calls from the far side of the river. "Owls have the knowledge of human death," I tell Clyde. The eels have noodled down Jim Woodruff dam and run the Gulf coast. They skirt the Florida cape, cross the Gulf Stream to Bermuda Triangle, convening in a soup of concupiscent and dying eels garnished with floating Sargasso weed. Terrestrial teenagers, anointed with pina colada suntan oil, bivouac along coastal breeding grounds, sniffing their labyrinthine way to beer, sex, death, and continuity of the species.

A brief rain spits into gray ashes of my campfire as distant thunder drums over the Gulf. The rain frogs, cicadas, crickets, and tremolo mosquitoes begin a chorus. Dripping water pings into a tin plate. Background music for bass bullfrogs and bull alligators, prelude to a canon of three owls calling from triangular corners of the night, incantations against lonely solitude—dirge, nocturne, and lullaby. The east owl begins; after three hoots the south owl joins in; then a westerly owl. The first cries double and triple to crescendo, fading and rising again, lonely solo to duet to trio, reminiscent of the haunting continuity of canons sung by children on camp busses.

> *Row, row, row your boat . . .*
> *gently down the. . .*
>> *Row, row, row your boat . . .*
>> *Stream. Merrily, merrily, merrily, merrily . . .*
>> *Row, row, row, your boat . . .*
>> *Life is but a . . .*
> *Who, who, who-who . . .*
> *Who, who, who-who . . .*
>> *Who, who, who, whoor . . .*
>> *Who, who, who, who-who . . .*
>> *Who, who, Wha, wha, wha . . .*
>> *Life is but a dream . . .*

I sleep peacefully as the owls sing a continuous and serial requiem around a nucleus of living night. I don't toss and turn, nor can I, bound snugly in a sag of jungle hammock. On his side, Clyde runs in his sleep, whimpering.

The wife is standing on a dock busy with fishermen when I round the last curve; she is tapping a Pappagallo sandal and bright toes, her Explorer and my rusty trailer in the Breakaway Fish Camp parking lot. "Why are you paddling?" she wants to know.

I push through clots of water hyacinth and tie up. "Out of gas," I lie. Clyde leaps out, lifting a leg on the first dry piling. I climb up wobbling for balance. She welcomes me with a perfunctory hug and a sniff. Mary Catherine has joined friends and migrated back to a cozy dorm. "How do I smell?"

"Different," she smiles, flaring her nostrils and wrinkling her nose.

"Good? Bad? Worse? Better?"

"Just different."

O. VICTOR MILLER

O.Victor Miller, *a native south Georgian, retired from teaching college English to live nomadically on a sailboat between a Kuna Indian village off the Caribbean coast of Panama and other areas of the planet that still support old-growth, clean rain, and healthy living things. Happy in his hammock between forestay and mast, he thrives like a fungus in jungle perfume under a lucid moon and stars.*

A Canon of Owls

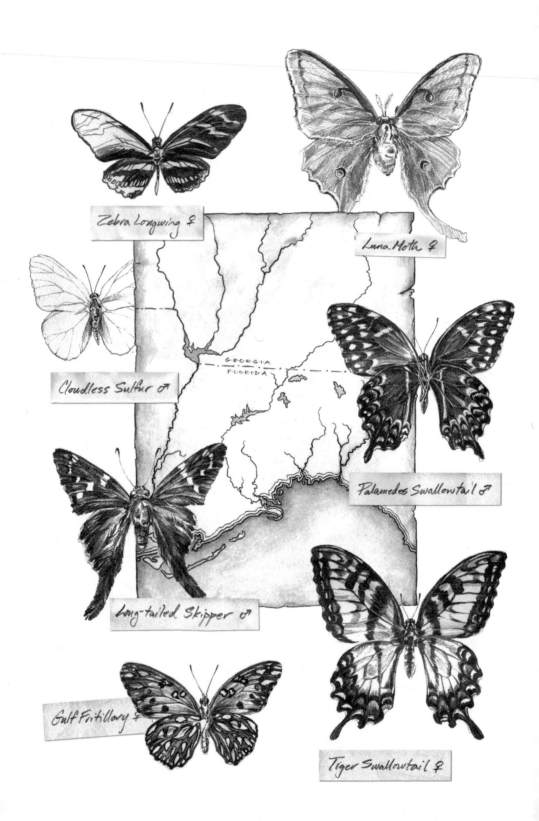

Zebra Longwing ♀

Luna Moth ♀

Cloudless Sulfur ♂

GEORGIA
FLORIDA

Palamedes Swallowtail ♂

Long-tailed Skipper ♂

Gulf Fritillary ♀

Tiger Swallowtail ♀

An Old Lepidopterist

BAILEY WHITE

One summer when I was a little girl, an old lepidopterist rented a cabin up the road from us. He moved down from Atlanta with his tiny, perfectly round wife, and a station wagon full of nets, spreading boards, and killing jars. He was finishing up his life's work, an exhaustive study of the butterflies of Georgia, and he was, we learned later, an eminently respected and renowned scientist in his field. But to the children in my neighborhood that summer, he was just a very kind old man with a lot of interesting stuff on his back porch, which he was happy to show off and explain to us.

His wife was a great homemaker and needleworker, and as soon as she had settled in and sent Mr. Harris off into the pine woods with his butterfly net and two pimento cheese sandwiches she began baking exquisite little cookies and knitting little pink sweaters for me and all my cousins.

In the late afternoons of that summer, when it began to cool off, Mr. Harris would come back with his jar full of buckeyes and checkerspots and hairstreaks, and the children from up and down the road would wander onto the Harrises' porch. Mrs. Harris would serve lemonade and cookies in the shapes of flowers and butterflies of no known species. Mr. Harris would sit in his chair and arrange his day's catch, and Mrs. Harris would teach my cousins and me to do needlework. We sat for hours, scowling with concentration, cross-stitching cute little scenes and heartfelt sayings on squares of linen. Mrs. Harris's knitting needles would go *click click click,* Mr. Harris would deftly pin butterfly after butterfly into the grooves on his cork spreading boards, and the ice would melt in our thin lemonade glasses.

Mrs. Harris finished our sweaters, but it turned out she had made them all in her shape and size—short and wide. My stringy arms and knobby wrists sticking out of the dainty little pink cable-stitched sleeves had a startling effect, like one of those clever tricks of mimicry butterflies use to frighten birds.

And after many weeks my sampler was finished. Through the snagged threads and bloodstains you could barely make out the words *HOME SWEET HOME.* Below, what was supposed to be a cute potbellied wood cook stove in a cozy country kitchen looked like a wrecked 1941 Ford in a scrap yard. My clever cousins moved on to crewel embroidery and petit point, but for my second project, Mrs. Harris tactfully started me on something called huck toweling, which turned out to be nothing but a dishrag on which I was to stitch a border of giant red Xs. After many rows I got tired of red and looked with longing at the shimmering pinks and dense purples of my cousins' satin-stitched Persian flowers. But Mrs. Harris said I must set a goal for myself. When my Xs reached a certain standard of consistency, then I could switch to green thread, "for a nice Christmasy effect," she said. By the time I got to green, my cousins were doing appliqué and cutwork, and something called tatting, which resulted in long bands of delicate lace.

In spite of the humiliating needlework, I kept going back again and again to the Harrises' porch that summer. I kept going back because on some afternoons Mr. Harris would tell about his adventures as a young lepidopterist. He would tell about his mentor and friend, Professor P. W. Fattig, and their entomological expeditions together. He told about the time an enormous beetle, unknown and undescribed in the scientific literature, flew by right in front of him and Professor Fattig and then disappeared in the swampy thickets.

Mr. Harris's voice fell to a husky whisper: "'Harris,' Professor Fattig said to me, 'did you see that?'"

"'Fattig,' I said to Professor Fattig, 'I did.'"

Mr. Harris was a wonderful storyteller, and as the afternoon wore on, my red and green Xs would begin to loop and tumble over each other, until finally, when Mr. Harris got to the story of Professor Fattig and the wasp with the inch-long stinger, I wove my needle into the huck toweling, folded my hands, and just listened.

The next summer Mr. Harris rescued me from the torment of needlework by inviting me to come with him to catch butterflies. He was very particular about his record keeping; after every capture he noted down the time of day, location, date, and any unusual circumstances. He showed me the yucca plant, host to the *Megathymus harrisi,* a skipper butterfly that had been named for Mr. Harris after his observations of it in its pupal stage proved it to be a distinct species from the similar-appearing *Megathymus cofaqui.* In the backyard of the Harrises' little cabin, we planted a butterfly garden—buddleia, pentas, and lantana for their nectar, and rabbit tobacco and passionflower, the food plants for the larvae of the gulf fritillary and painted lady. For the monarch, Mr. Harris brought down from Atlanta a special tall-growing variety of milkweed I had never seen before.

By the end of the summer, Mr. Harris' work on the butterflies of the coastal region was complete, and the Harrises gave up their little cabin. The next year his book, *Butterflies of Georgia,* was published. Not long after that Mr. Harris' mind began to wander. He didn't know me when I went to Atlanta to see him. Then he didn't know Mrs. Harris. She got too frail to take care of him at home, and he was put in a nursing home. By the end of this life he had forgotten everything he had ever known about butterflies.

Every year when school starts in September, I teach a special science unit to my first graders called Butterflies of Georgia. I try to teach them everything I learned from Mr. Harris in those summers of listening to his stories and holding his notebook and his killing jar while he dashed through the woods making wild swats with his big net.

The little house up the road that the Harrises rented for those summers is gone now, and wisteria has taken over the yard, but those milkweed plants Mr. Harris brought down from Atlanta reseed every year, and in August and September the woods and fields around the house site are transformed into a monarch butterfly paradise. The butterflies are everywhere, floating over the red and yellow flower clusters with their characteristic leisurely glide, looping and soaring and lighting and laying eggs. The plants are covered with monarch larvae of all sizes, fatly munching out neat half-moons from the edges of the leaves. The chrysalides hang like little jewels, changing color according to the light—lime green, emerald green, aqua green—with the golden spots and perfect golden stitching around the caps glinting and flashing.

I feel a kind of reverence in late summer when I visit that abandoned butterfly garden. I feel cheered and comforted, as if, somewhere up in heaven, with his tattered nets and stretching boards, an old lepidopterist is still looking after me.

BAILEY WHITE *lives in south Georgia. Her writing has appeared in many magazines and newspapers, and her best-selling book* Mama Makes Up Her Mind *was nominated for the Southern Book Award and the ABBY Award. She has also written* Sleeping at the Starlite Motel *and* Quite a Year for Plums. *She is a commentator on National Public Radio's* All Things Considered.

BAILEY WHITE

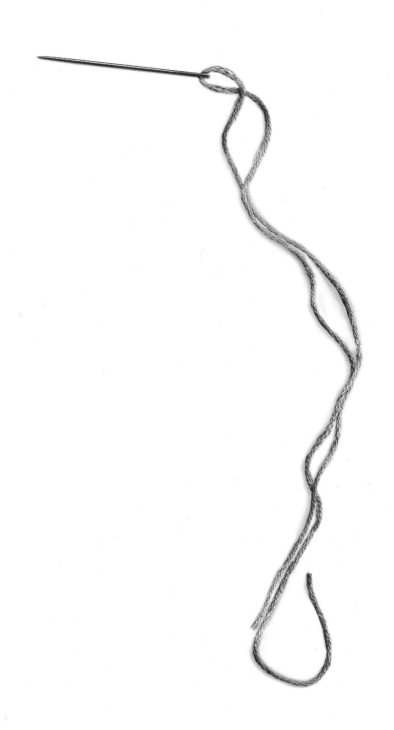

AN OLD LEPIDOPTERIST

Wintering Robins Early December

The stretch of Florida Trail we choose this cold Sunday morning scrambles west through pine flatwoods and a vast open sawgrass marsh. We push past the resist of palmetto and lowbush blueberry, over white sand, black mud, and tinder-yellow grasses; I feel as if we swim through the landscape. At gum swamp wetlands, we edge over buckled wooden bridges where raccoons have left markers of their meals: palmetto berry husks, crayfish bits and pieces, indistinguishable grassy lengths.

We count five slash pines and a cypress too big to encircle with our arms. Somehow they've drawn enough girth and weight from the ground to grow magnificent without anyone cutting them down. Wintering robins with their white eye rings and rusty red bellies are laid down in veils over these woodlands; I catch my breath when a big black pig explodes through the open pines.

Eventually, we break through a cabbage palm fringe and reach the open marsh. We strip off our fleece coats and rest, taking the bright sun into our skin. As we nestle into the marsh grasses, I think about how the birds use these coastal forests, and the butterflies, and bears, all so exquisitely timed. How the robins have reported from their northern breeding grounds to harvest our fall bounty: the tiny orange-red globes of yaupon holly, the iris-black gallberries, and the fleshy fruits of the gum trees. And how the ruby-crowned kinglets return, one to every wax myrtle, with their fierce crown-flashing defense of the berries they must have to live.

Most of us humans are so far from living in direct sustenance with our landscape. The fisher folk, the turkey hunters, the pecan pickers, the honey harvesters, the collard cultivators, they know these things, as the creatures do. How can I learn to live more and more in synchrony with this landscape that I love?

Moultrie

bright lemony green
pitcher plants

Havana Lumber Co.

Paradise Found Again

John M. Hall

The exceptional opportunity to grow up immersed in the woods of southwest Georgia during the 1950s sure didn't feel special at the time. In our local schools, we were taught only about historic, beautiful, and important faraway places with high mountains or ocean beaches. Fishing along the blackwater rivers or hunting the wiregrass hills was taken for granted as our unending right, but nothing remarkable.

My family story in southwest Georgia began about a hundred years ago. Although only a human lifetime ago, this area had few automobiles, and many farms were still maintained with mules. Most farmhouses had no electricity, but even the smallest household was very self-sufficient. Atlanta was a small city, a very long trip to the north.

For the residents of rural Colquitt County, a trip to downtown Moultrie was a visit to the center of the world. This county seat with its unpaved streets was designed and located to be a day's round-trip wagon ride for area farmers. Moultrie was a growing pioneer settlement fueled by pine trees and farmland. Just off the town square were lumber mills, tobacco warehouses, and railway stations to process and ship the county's products. Dirt lanes led off north, south, east, and west through unending miles of longleaf pine woods. Private property was unfenced and woodlands that could be seen from the courthouse were often open for public hunting and exploration.

Every Saturday Moultrie turned into a festival of mule auctions, street preachers, and farm supply buying. It seemed almost everyone in the county came to town on Saturday, arriving early and staying late.

In 1918, at the age of twenty-five, my grandfather, single and a recent veteran of World War I, made his way from north of Atlanta down dirt roads to prosperous Moultrie where the quail hunting was extraordinary. Later on, he raised my father, who grew up in increasingly progressive Moultrie. During my father's youth, the local schools were rated as the best in the entire country, and the small locally-owned farms received national recognition. He left as a teenager to serve in World War II, returning to Moultrie in 1953 with his bride and a university degree and started the county's first consulting forestry business.

In 1955, when I was five years old, my father moved our family to what was once a small farm at the edge of town near the headwaters of the Ochlockonee River. The river was an easy walk across a cow pasture. You never saw anyone at this part of the river. Here the river rose and fell through the year like a slow-moving tide. During winter floods it might be twenty feet deep, rushing high through the tree limbs—a dangerous torrent. In the summer you could find places to jump across the very same river. Every river-swamp expedition produced new adventures. It was common to find a fox with kits, see a low-flying barred owl or watch a giant pileated woodpecker tear apart an old dead snag. Even before reaching the river I'd find pitcher plants to open, or shiny black tadpoles by the thousands locked in shallows that I just had to inspect.

I sometimes took friends along to explore my secret world at the Ochlockonee's edge. Like Indiana Jones's lost tombs, at low water, the river swamp would reveal giant cathedral rooms with white sand floors and high ceilings formed by the green leaf canopy. As the water level continued to recede, you could walk from narrows and bends into more enormous rooms waiting for discovery. The room's massive ceiling seemed to be held high by straight columns of tulip poplar and loblolly pine. These great trees shot straight up more than sixty feet and were commonly more than forty inches in diameter. The highest part of the river's ceiling was always moving with birds and climbing animals. We enjoyed visiting a place we called "the center of the earth," a wild refuge completely hidden by thick, almost impenetrable walls of green poison ivy and cat claw thorns. Years later, in college, I read the accounts of great naturalists like Bartram, Thoreau, and Burroughs and felt a powerful and even spiritual connection to them, recalling my small river swamp ramblings. These were the beginnings of my quest for a life as a modern-day naturalist.

From my youthful, protected, and very simplified vantage point I also experienced a rural community of people that seemed divided into three separate worlds—town people, farm people, and black people. My father's land management business and my grandfather's downtown real estate office bridged all three and allowed me glances into the very different worlds comprising our small county. As I grew older, I noticed the growing stress between the human communities and also the natural communities. I became aware that the great river swamp was seen as having the lowest worth in the community; the sewage plant, the landfill, and meat processing centers were backed up to its edge to handle all of our human waste.

I left Moultrie when I was twenty-two, working my way into a career as a nature photographer and as a land conservationist for the world's largest conservation organization. For thirty years I had a wonderful opportunity to see and learn about many of the finest places in our country. I never expected to one day return home and find that I left what may be the best place of all. But that's what I've done, and I've discovered a paradise poised to change.

The world of the rural South feels so much smaller than it did in my youth, just when our increasing population needs more space. Economic dreams and plans set by the needs of our communities a hundred years ago did not address the way we live today. Speed has created a smaller world; country roads have been redesigned and paved, and are now good for sixty miles per hour in the turns. Helping the farmers get to town has also provided more help for town people to move out and live on farmland. Rivers once paddled or explored with small outboards are zoomed like racecourses with boats pushed by hundreds of horsepower. A day's worth of river exploration has been reduced to a ten-minute blur. Even many of our old farm trails have turned into all-terrain vehicle (ATV) racetracks traveled at thirty instead of three miles per hour. I've come to realize over the years that without finding ways to share special and important places their wonderful values will ultimately be destroyed.

And as we watch our Southern paradise lose its native vegetation, species,

PARADISE FOUND AGAIN

and culture at a quickening pace, we can't help but wonder if the diverse interests in our community can create a clear vision and develop broad support fast enough to really matter. Some people in rural areas like those found in the Ochlockonee River watershed may feel things are pretty good, especially compared to the Atlanta sprawl; there is no threat, so why act now? The answer is that now is the time with the greatest opportunity, before the pressure to change arrives. Millions of baby boomers are to retire soon and are very eager to move from an unpleasant quality of life to a real place where things still feel pretty good. The "creeping, then one day, gotcha" scenario has already begun locally, but it hasn't yet ruined the opportunity to save the best of this part of the world. We who love this area should use new "smart growth" tools to give this paradise a chance to be part of our children's and grandchildren's lives.

Some of its special attributes and sacred places are already gone, and some species and ways of life are at the brink. From the headwaters of the Ochlockonee River down to the marshy edge of the Gulf of Mexico we have damaged our paradise, but it is still a wonderful place. It's certainly not too late to preserve the integrity of this great watershed.

JOHN M. HALL *started his naturalist career working in the wilderness of Ossabaw Island, Georgia. His three decades of conservation work includes publishing thousands of photographs in national publications including* National Geographic, Smithsonian, *and* Natural History. *For eighteen years he was the director of The Nature Conservancy's first project to protect a large working ecosystem that in 1991 won the White House Award for Excellence in Community Conservation presented at a Rose Garden ceremony by President George H. W. Bush. He and his wife Karen have now returned to their south Georgia home to start a new conservation and photography initiative called National Landscapes.*

JOHN M. HALL

green tree frog

Paradise Found Again

longleaf
sapling

Singing the World Back

JANISSE RAY

My friend Cody is so passionate about longleaf pines that his wife, Linda, jokes about wishing she were a longleaf pine. "I'd get a lot more attention!" she says. Everybody laughs, but the joke rings true.

Five years ago, Cody, then sixty-four, began restoring the longleaf pine forests on two thousand acres of mesic rolling hills his family owns along Warrior Creek in south Georgia.

Before that, he had been—I hesitate to use the term—a tree farmer. "We had forestry consultants managing our place," he explained. "When they told me I needed to clear-cut a certain piece of land, I believed them. I agreed to whatever the consultant suggested. One day the consultants showed me a stand of mature longleaf pine on the place, complete with a wiregrass groundcover. They suggested that, for maximum production, the site should be clear-cut and replanted with a fast-growing variety. Right then, I knew that if we continued that kind of management, we wouldn't have anything left."

Not long after, Cody was invited to a landowner workshop at Ichauway, Robert Woodruff's quail-hunting preserve near Newton, Georgia. That day, he listened to scientists and ecologists from the Jones Ecological Research Center and the Longleaf Alliance talk about the pine flatwoods; on an open-topped wagon he rode through the wiregrass pinelands, past patches of blazing star that streaked earthward, hearing the calls of flickers and woodpeckers. Cody began to understand the ecology of his home.

"When I saw those beautiful forests at Ichauway, I said to myself, 'This is what I want.'"

Home again, Cody immediately took over management of his family's forests and set about to recreate them. He deeply regretted the bad advice he had received from forestry consultants. He wished he had been given alternatives (such as he had seen at Ichauway) to clear-cutting, bedding, herbiciding, replacement of native pines with "improved" slash, and other shortsighted forestry practices.

At sixty-four, Cody understood that he would not live to see his forest restored. Instead, he was driven by a belief that he was creating something longer-lasting than his own span of years, something bigger than his own desires, something built on faith. "I want to make up for my past sins of omission and lack of attention," he said. He had not a minute to lose.

That first winter, 1999, Cody bought ten thousand longleaf pine seedlings and began to plant them in openings that had been cleared for wildlife food plots.

Here is the question: can we reweave something that took 100 million years to weave? Once we have shaped, controlled, and simplified the world—once we depauperize the matrix—can we return places to the way they were?

Can we get a landscape back? And what exactly is "back"?

For some, "back" is the time before industrial logging came South; for others, it is the time before Europeans arrived, or even before the Creeks and the Chickasaws and the Seminoles began to set fires. "Back," once examined, may mean some static condition that never existed.

However we imagine "back" to look, likely we won't ever reclaim degraded places to their original conditions. But surely we can get them partway there.

You see, when we disrupt the course of evolution, it doesn't necessarily continue on its merry way once we replace the biological elements that were removed. We think all we need is the pieces. Science, so full of complexity and

JANISSE RAY

chaos, implying that quantity can be made equivalent to quality, misses the magic of a system.

The prefix "re" has two meanings: "new, again" or "back." Maybe restoration is not moving backward at all, but forward, to a different trajectory. So restoration may not be renewal, the attempt to revisit some mythical past or condition; more likely, restoration is the making of a new scenario, the creation of a new trajectory—not the original landscape, of course, but one more functional than a pine plantation, a field, a parking lot.

For Cody, "back" means *natural function*. "I want to replace enough of the longleaf pine ecosystem to be able to work with a functional landscape," he said.

The natural history of a longleaf pine ecosystem is well documented. A longleaf pine forest requires fire, especially in the growing season. Wiregrass and other groundcover plants must be present to carry the fire. The system needs a slew of beautifully adapted plants and animals, all tied to each other.

I met Cody about a year after he began restoring his piney woods, when at the invitation of our mutual friend, ecologist Alison McGee of The Nature Conservancy of Georgia (TNC), he flew to my home county and visited Moody Forest. The preserve was newly acquired by TNC and contained a beautiful stand of old-growth longleaf, even a few three-hundred-year-old trees. In the woods that day, walking, he and I discovered a deep and common affection for wild places.

Sometime later I heard from Cody that he had read the book I wrote about my love for longleaf forests and that he had been moved by it. The next time I saw him, something had changed. We weren't fellow naturalists, bent over wild indigo in the Moody woods, but friends: good friends. This thing that we both loved, that had no name, it joined us. It wasn't our knowledge of the woods. It wasn't common acquaintances. In the pine flatwoods, both of us were possessed with the same feeling of peace, as if our souls found a home there. A longleaf pine grove was sacred to both of us. We could see ourselves reweaving them.

We saw each other once or twice a year after that, once or twice at Ichauway and a few times in Atlanta, where Cody lived part of the year. Sometimes when we talked to each other tears came to our eyes.

Two years ago I was invited to a gathering on restoration in the Cascade

Mountains of Oregon. For philosophical reasons I did not want to participate: how could we afford to put effort into restoration when we continued to destroy thousands of acres of wild land a year? Wouldn't we be better served to put all funds available into protection of the last wild places? We should be buying land, I was thinking: mature and old-growth forests, habitat for imperiled species, remnants of rare ecosystems. Not restoring.

Then I thought about the Everglades, drained for agriculture, finally reclaiming some of its water and its life; and the Kissimmee River, channelized and straightened in the 1960s, being returned to a river of curves and floodplain, filling again with wading birds. I thought about groups of people, frontline forces, cutting invasive plants, from privet to Brazilian pepper, out of the woods. I thought about coho salmon, after a dam is removed, again able to attain spawning grounds.

We cannot protect a piece of earth and expect it to take care of itself, nor list a species as threatened and expect it to resurrect on its own. No. Our metaphorical human hand, which has laid its dark trail of loss and degradation onto all faces of the planet, must reach again to right our wrongs. Faced then as we are with the necessity of human action, we must breach and blow up and remove and replant. We must take charge of restoring the wild places.

Once Cody sent me a Gary Larson cartoon in which a group of the king's men are gathered at the bottom of a stone wall, around a very broken Humpty Dumpty. The tagline says, "OK, you guys have had your shot at it. Now it's the horse's turn."

"Once you take a natural system apart," Cody said, "it's really difficult to put together again."

But he's taking his turn.

In the summer of 2003, my husband and I visited Cody's forests near Albany. The day was achingly hot. We piled into the cab of Cody's truck, into the air-conditioning, and drove out into the woods. He showed us the whole place, the destruction, the preservation, the restoration.

He pointed out the first saplings he planted, now almost four years old and over head high, and the latest seedlings, only a few months in the ground.

Cody showed us where he had sown wiregrass seeds, ten pounds to the quarter acre, with a machine called a Grasslander. On the day we visited, he was waiting on a man who was planting wiregrass plugs for him. Cody had grown sixty thousand wiregrass sets under contract, using his own seed. He showed us where the planting had begun, little tufts studded at three-foot intervals.

"I'm obsessed with reestablishing wiregrass because it's such a keystone species," Cody said.

Later he took us to the part of his land that he had saved from industrial logging. The ground was heavy with ancient longleaf pines, soughing in the wind. Tall, dun-colored grasses made a lush carpet, interrupted by big gopher tortoise burrows and the narrow paths through the grass on which they traveled.

Most of our metaphors for restoration have been medical in nature. The forest is *healing*, it is *recovering*, it is *renewing* itself. This is our *prescription* for restoring forest *health*. Watch the *rebirth*.

But a cutover pine flatwoods is not sick.

Once, an ecologist I know asked a woman what she thought of a certain prescribed burn. She had worked in the burn unit of a hospital for years and years. "It just sickens me," she said.

Here's another bad metaphor: I don't know how to manage a forest but I can mow a lawn.

In that gathering in Oregon, writers and ecologists worked on new metaphors for restoration, because, as philosopher Kathleen Dean Moore says, "The people who control the language will control the world."

Was creation a tapestry, and we the re-weavers?

Was restoration more aptly re-creation, us assisting in the new Creation?

Was restoration a kind of orchestra, in concert? Or might it be a less structured arrangement, maybe a jazz ensemble or a sing-along, each animal filling a frequency? Could we, like the Australian aborigines, live among songlines; were we singing new places into being?

Could we liken restoration to courtship and marriage? Could we compare it to the making of a home?

I was in a small group that considered this idea. It made sense. Marriage has no end point in mind, but is a process. As is restoration. Home is a place of intimacy, sustenance, sanctuary, return. A home houses a *family* of beings embedded in each other. What a family shares is not so much words as

SINGING THE WORLD BACK

experiences. We would never presume simply to *manage* our family or home.

Our group came up with a vow: *Let's see what we can do to joyfully create an enduring home together for the rest of our lives and our childrens' lives.*

So far Cody has planted 200,000 longleaf seedlings on the land. This year he grew his own wiregrass sets and planted 120,000 of them.

He has reintroduced fire. He recently sent photos from this year's early-spring burn. He is standing, strong and healthy, in knee-high wiregrass grown from the plugs planted only two years ago, beside a line of blazing fire, drip-torch in his hand. The lovely fire is creeping through the woods.

He plans to keep bringing back the pieces of the system—other native plants, native animals. He's currently working with ecologist Kay Kirkman of the Jones Ecological Research Center on nursery plots for other longleaf endemics, including sensitive brier, pinebarren ticktrefoil, goat's rue, butterfly pea, rabbitbells, pineywoods dropseed.

Cody worries about the exotic species on the land, especially Bermuda grass that was spread by tractors plowing firebreaks and food plots. He worries that what he's doing is so expensive and so difficult that it will have no practical application. He knows, at sixty-nine, that he's going to run out of time. He hopes to "keep at it" for at least twenty more years. Someone once said to me that "instant gratification isn't fast enough for most Americans." Not Cody.

"I might see those trees get thirty years old," he says.

I once asked Cody a strange question. I asked him if he ever heard the land say thank you. He got tears in his eyes when I asked that, and instantly, so did I. "I hear it when I see the animals," he answered, "the gopher tortoises and the fox squirrels." He paused.

"Once I saw a fox squirrel," he said, "looking at me from around a stump. He was leaning around, looking, as if to say, *Where have you been?*"

My friend Cody is a re-weaver, a minor god in the work of re-creation, a walker of hymns, singing his family's forests into being, singing the world back into existence. He is a husbandman, a father, a homemaker, a man married to his ground.

To the fox squirrel, his answer: *I am here now. I am yours.*

Janisse Ray

Janisse Ray's *family has replanted one thousand longleaf pines on the small farm they own in Appling County, Georgia. She was the Grisham writer-in-residence at the University of Mississippi during the writing of this piece.*

Singing the World Back

Birdsong Solstice

The sun's attention is on the hidden, the buttress and base, the low to the ground. It's as if it inspects the roots of the forest, setting cold fire. Kathleen reminds us that it is the angle of the earth, backing our hemisphere away from the sun's body toward frigid space, that causes the slant of the light. It's winter solstice, the shortest day of the year.

We are gathered at Birdsong Nature Center, turned by the bitter air to the bonfire. As the sun dissolves into the Gin House Field to the west, dozens and dozens of wood duck whistle and skid through the tree line into the refuge of the swamp. Above us, the sturdy branches of the old pecans are cuffed with mistletoe circlets round as the moon. Venus is falling in triple slow-motion after the sun, but in the east, there is Orion, rising. The traditional solstice fire is lit, and it eats fast into a prepared tepee of oak logs, climbing so high and hot that it appears to break fireballs from its own body and hurl them against the black night. Once we've learned to gather and face each other like this, forced by the frigid night and this fire into the form of the circle, perhaps we will know better how to create circles of kinship and intention elsewhere. Not as escape, but as something to move toward, so that we may survive as a people among the natural communities and creatures we so love, on this element-driven Earth.

Orion

A Vision

WENDELL BERRY

If we will have the wisdom to survive,
To stand like slow growing trees
on a ruined place, renewing it, enriching it,
if we will make our seasons welcome here,
asking not too much of earth or heaven,
then a long time after we are dead
the lives our lives prepare will live
here, their houses strongly placed
upon the valley sides, fields and gardens
rich in the windows. The river will run
clear, like we will never know it,
and over it, birdsong, like a canopy.
On the levels of the hills will be
green meadows, stock bells in noon shade.
On the steeps, where greed and ignorance cut down
the old forest, an old forest will stand,
its rich leaf-fall drifting on its roots.
The veins of forgotten springs will have opened.
Families will be singing in the fields.
In their voices they will hear a music
risen out of the ground. They will take
nothing from the ground they will not return,
whatever the grief at parting. Memory
native to this valley, will spread over it
like a grove, and memory will grow
into legend, legend into song, song
into sacrament. The abundance of this place,
the songs of its peoples and its birds,
will be health and wisdom and indwelling
light. This is no paradisal dream.
Its hardship is its possibility.

Between Two Rivers:

Stories From the Red Hills to the Gulf

Acknowledgements

This book was conceived on a homebound trip from Athens, Georgia, in May 2003. Julie Hauserman, Norine Cardea, and I had been immersed for the previous three days in a Southern nature writer's conference sponsored by the University of Georgia, organized by Dorinda Dallmeyer. We were deeply excited by stories and workshops presented by Janisse Ray, Roger Pinckney, Rick Bass, and many others, and by our informal connections and conversations with lovers of landscape and culture from all over the South. We were particularly intrigued by our visionary colleagues Betsy Teter and John Lane from Spartanburg, South Carolina, and their Hub City Writers Project.

As we neared home, Norine chose an out-of-the-way route through Boston, Georgia, in the still-rural, pecan-grove-studded northern tip of the Red Hills bioregion. Outside the windows, we absorbed our homeland's beauty with fresh eyes. Inside the car, we began to sketch the bones of this book. We asked ourselves: what are the defining stories at the intersection of nature and human culture where we live? Julie recounted the obscure, metaphorically essential tragedies of the lost Cascades and the evicted Apalachee. We thought of the vast Red Hills plantations and the introduction of prescribed fire as a land management tool by Herb Stoddard and Roy and Betty Komarek. We began another list of the grand store of writers and naturalists in our region, lovers of the land all, who had never before been bound together in a purposeful chorus of love and outrage and wisdom.

We took our concept of a Red Hills Writers Project to the rest of the council of the Tallahassee-based environmental advocacy group, Heart of the Earth: Barry Fraser, Jeff Chanton, Lucy Ann Walker-Fraser, Mike Brezin, and Ed Oaksford. They embraced our idea, seeing its absolute relevance to our organization, in which we ask our members to pledge allegiance to this place where we have chosen to live—the Red Hills Bioregion—and to investigate what it means to become native to our place, in accordance with the ecological realities of the landscape. The Red Hills Writers Project is the council's project, and they have supported it throughout, along with newer council members Mary Beth McBride, Charles Hardee, Crystal Wakoa, Deborah Morningstar, and Melody Harris.

Early on, Janisse Ray (former longtime resident of this bioregion) and poet Laura Newton agreed to serve as literary co-editors of this book, even as they pursued lives already packed with teaching, editing, and writing. Janisse shoehorned a fundraiser into her schedule and was personally responsible for the participation of many of our investors. She also tutored our writers in the particulars of the personal nature essay and held out the highest standards of editorial excellence for this book. Laura's level head and encouraging editorial style offered a good balance to our team. It was an honor and a pleasure to work so closely with these good friends.

Not only did we need to locate and persuade the best of our area writers to join us, following the Hub City model, we needed to raise substantial start-up funding to cover our initial publication costs. Blessings to the generous old and new friends who believed enough in our endeavor to underwrite some of those expenses. Their names are listed on the following pages. Without their contributions, we could not have proceeded.

Early on, graphic designer and geographer extraordinaire, Lou Cross, joined the leadership team of the Red Hills Writers Project, and it is his vision that has made tangible the quality book you hold in your hands, as well as our logo, stationery, and website. Lou's creative genius is equaled by his commitment to our shared vision.

Nancy Meyer, fine artist and student of the secret geometries of the natural world, has donated an uncounted measure of time and talent and ingenuity to the look of Between Two Rivers. We are beholden to Nancy's keen artistry and enormously generous heart.

In the end, the Red Hills Writers Project has been almost entirely underwritten by local individuals and companies. We honor you, each and every one. The advice and assistance of Beth Kostka, Debbie Keller, Susan Kidd, Rex Boner, and Anne Nelson were also very, very helpful.

Thank you to Jim Wohlpart, Tony Stallins, Anthony Morgan, Doug Alderson, Ann Morrow, Beverly Dayton, and David Moynahan for all manner of brainstorming, technical support and expertise. Gratitude always to Velma Frye, David Canter, Patrick Chanton, Silas Raynes, Raven Burchard, and Sue, Garrett, and Erin Canter and the Heart of the Earth Council for help with the

Janisse Ray fundraiser. Competent copy editor Leeann Drabenstott Culbreath brought our language into line; we are so glad she has come to settle near us in the South.

Our writers entered into this project knowing that we'd ask the best of them, with very little recompense. They participated with grace and penned beautiful essays; they are warriors, all, on behalf of this marvelous place on the planet. Very sadly, one of our original writers, Wendy Bishop, never got a chance to complete her self-assigned essay. This gifted teacher and writer was unexpectedly diagnosed with cancer in the summer of 2003 and died three months later. We will miss her friendship, words and wisdom.

Jeff Chanton stands above all those who contributed to this book, offering the constancy of Red Hills clay and limestone bedrock to this daily effort of the last two years. He visited most of these places as the book was written, fact-checked some of the science, helped edit and proof nearly all the manuscripts, and supported our family in every way while I wove together the strands of this project. This is the truest of partnerships.

— SUSAN CERULEAN

Red Hills Writers Project
A Heart of the Earth Initiative

Investors

Without the generous contributions of the following individuals and organizations, we could not have completed this project.

Ochlockonee

Florida Wildlife Federation
Kent Spriggs

Wakulla

All Florida Mediaworks, Inc.
Native Nurseries
Delbert M. and Kathy Archibald
Dan Butler
Laurie and Kelly Dozier
Charles R. and Mary Jane Isleib
Cody Laird

Aucilla

Dale Allen
Loretta Armer
Loranne Ausley
W. Wilson Baker
Rex Boner
David Borland
Ledley and Oberley Brown
Robert and Sara Brunger
Bill and Rene Burnett
Norine Cardea
Suzanne Choppin and Mike Brezin
Rebecca Clemans
Andre Clewell
Rip and Kathy Coleen
Brandy and Ted Cowley-Gilbert
Jeremy and Tara Craft
Pam and Don Crosby
Deborah and Louis Cross Jr.
Susan Dickerson and Bob Roberts
Mike Donovan
Elinor Elfner
Kim and R. Todd Engstrom
Sharon Fairbanks
Grayal Farr
Susan Gage and Isabelle Potts
Adrienne Gautier
Sara Golinveaux
Ellen Gwynn
Nina Hatton and Roy Silverman
Tom and Kathy Herzog
Barbara and Eddie Hoffman
Milton Hopkins
Susie Howell

Roberta Isleib and John Brady

Linda Jamison

Gordon and Ruth Jerauld

Ivan and Margaret Johnson

Carolyn Kindell and Shaw Stiller

Donna Klein and Larry Krieger

Kate Konrad and Mark Griesbach

Peter, Candance, Chauncey and Sheriff Lakanen

Bill and Kathy Landing

Marion Lasley

Noreen Legare

Barbara MacDonald and Frank Varnadoe

Mary Beth McBride and Tom Anderson

Tom and Bonnie McCluskey

Rebecca Miles and Ward Broderson

Deb Morningstar and Sherrill Thompson

Joan Morris

Jennie C. Myers

Julie and Leon Neel

Kent Newton

Laura Newton and Terry Schneider

Ed and Linda Oaksford

Mollie and Bob Palmer

Howard and Carolyn Pardue

Stewart Parsons

Vickie Peace

Susan Peacock and Jay Boynton

Tom and Vivian Pelham

Joe Peresich

Kermit and Kathleen Rose

Mary Jane Ryals

Pam Ryan

Steven Seliger

Sarah and Terry Sherraden

Elise and Steve Smith

Susan Smith

Tony and Mary Perry Sturges
Susan Taylor and Mike Murphree
Mary Tebo
Larry and Sharyn Thompson
Walter and Vicki Tschinkel
D.J. and Gayle Underwood
Steve Urse
Anne Van Meter and Howard Kessler
Crystal Wakoa and David Moynahan
Gwendolyn Waldorf and Dana Bryan
Bob Walker
Lucy Ann Walker-Fraser and Barry Fraser
Tamara Weinstein
Andy Welch
Mrs. Doris Wiaz
June Wiaz and Barry Moline
Beatrice Wurtz

Sopchoppy

Jan Godown
Charlie McCoy
Lucia Maxwell

About the Editors

Writer and activist SUSAN CERULEAN lives with her family in Tallahassee, Florida. She loves to encourage new writers and pull together anthologies of personal essays; her previous collections include *The Book of the Everglades* (Milkweed Editions, 2002) and *The Wild Heart of Florida* (with Jeff Ripple, University Press of Florida, 1999).

Cerulean's latest book, a nature memoir entitled *Tracking Desire: A Journey after Swallow-tailed Kites*, is forthcoming from University of Georgia Press in 2005. Her essays have appeared in five anthologies and a variety of magazines and newspapers, including *Orion, Hope,* and *Defenders.*

JANISSE RAY is an award-winning writer and political activist whose home is her family farm in south Georgia. Her memoir *Ecology of a Cracker Childhood*, about growing up on a junkyard amid the vanishing longleaf pine forests of the South, was selected for All Georgia Reading the Same Book 2002. She has published in such magazines as *Body and Soul, Hope, Oprah, Natural History,* and *Sierra.* Her latest book, *Wild Card Quilt: Taking a Chance on Home* was released by Milkweed Editions in May 2003. She was the John and Renee Grisham writer-in-residence at the University of Mississippi in 2003–2004.

LAURA NEWTON is the editor of the *Apalachee Review.* Her poetry has been published recently in *The Potomac Review, Blue Mesa Review, Thirteenth Moon,* and *The National Wetlands Newsletter.* She completed her PhD in Poetry at Florida State University in the spring of 2004.

Further Resources

Here is a selection of the most active conservation groups in our bioregions. We hope you'll want to join their efforts to care for our landscape and community, if you aren't already so engaged.

APALACHEE AUDUBON SOCIETY, INC.
PO Box 1237
Tallahassee, Florida 32302-1237
http://www.apalachee.org/

THE CONSERVATION FUND
P.O. Box 1362
Tucker, Georgia 30085
(770) 414-0211
www.conservationfund.org

FLORIDA PUBLIC INTEREST RESEARCH GROUP
704 W. Madison St.
Tallahassee, Florida 32304
(850) 224-3321
http://www.floridapirg.org

FLORIDA WILDLIFE FEDERATION
PO Box 6870
Tallahassee, Florida 32314
http://www.flawildlife.org/

THE GEORGIA CONSERVANCY
Southwest Georgia Office
18 North Main Street
Moultrie, GA 31768
(229) 985-8117
http://www.georgiaconservancy.org

LAKE JACKSON ECOPASSAGE ALLIANCE, INC.
http://www.lakejacksonturtles.org/alliance.htm

LONGLEAF ALLIANCE
Solon Dixon Forestry Education Center
Rt. 7 Box 131
Andalusia, AL 36420
(334) 222-7779
http://www.longleafalliance.org/

THE NATURE CONSERVANCY OF GEORGIA
1330 West Peachtree Street, Suite 410
Atlanta, GA 30309-2904
(404) 873-6946
http://www.nature.org

THE NATURE CONSERVANCY, NORTH FLORIDA FIELD OFFICE
625 North Adams Street
Tallahassee, FL 32301
(850) 222-0199

THE TRUST FOR PUBLIC LAND
306 North Monroe Street
Tallahassee, FL 32301
(850) 222-7911
www.tpl.org

SIERRA CLUB: BIG BEND GROUP OF THE FLORIDA CHAPTER
319 E. Park Avenue
Tallahassee, FL 32301
(850) 915-0580
http://www.florida.sierraclub.org/bigbend/

SIERRA CLUB: GEORGIA CHAPTER
1401 Peachtree St NE Ste 345
Atlanta GA 30309-3023
(404) 607-1262, ext. 221
http://georgia.sierraclub.org

Red Hills Writers Project
A Heart of the Earth Initiative

We are a local group of writers and editors who believe in the power of nature-based anthologies, poetry and memoirs to move and inspire people, and deepen their understanding of and attachment to place. This project is an initiative of the Heart of the Earth.

In our first publication, *Between Two Rivers: Stories From the Red Hills to the Gulf,* we draw on our region's storytelling tradition, hoping to boost local commitment to the ecological and cultural heritage of the Red Hills and Coastal Lowlands bioregions through the literary arts.

For more information, visit our website:
www.redhillswritersproject.org

Heart *of the* **Earth**

Heart of the Earth is a movement fostering practical action to live more sustainable lifestyles within the context of the Red Hills and Gulf Coast Lowlands Bioregions, motivated and sustained by our spiritual connection to the Earth.

We encourage our members and friends to join us in personal pledges to reduce fossil fuel use by 30 percent within 36 months, and to investigate how to conduct our lives if we imagine ourselves truly native to this place. In support of these pledges, through memberships, community-building, educational workshops, discussion groups, newsletters and our web site, Heart of the Earth offers effective, science-based and doable solutions to the problem of global warming.

We enter into this work fired by the urgencies facing our planet, and our growing understanding of the impact of our human actions: that we, as North Americans, are only among 25 percent of the world's population, but consume more than 70 percent of the world's resources, and eat more than 60 percent of its food.

We believe that understanding the ecological gifts and constraints of our bioregion will allow us to develop effective and sustainable strategies so that all of us--human and nonhuman--may continue to live here.

Visit our website to join us, or learn more:
www.heartoftheearth.org

Happy Trails!

Book design by Louis Cross III
TSG Graphic Design
www.TSGGraphic.com
Illustrations by Nancy Meyer
Cover design by Louis Cross & Nancy Meyer
Typeset in Sabon 9.5/14
using Adobe InDesign CS
Produced by the Red Hills Writers Project
Printed on acid-free paper
60# Natures Natural (Recycled, 50% Post Consumer Waste)
by Thompson-Shore, Inc. Book Manufacturers
in Dexter, Michigan.